GETTING INTO FASHION

A CAREER GUIDE

GETTING INTO FASHION

A CAREER GUIDE

MELISSA SONES

BALLANTINE BOOKS · NEW YORK

All rights reserved under International and Pan-American Copyright
Conventions. Published in the United States by Ballantine Books, a
division of Random House, Inc., New York, and simultaneously in
Canada by Random House of Canada Limited, Toronto.
Illustration credits may be found on p. 237

Library of Congress Catalog Card Number: 83-91167

ISBN 0-345-30756-9

Designed by Michaelis/Carpelis Design Associates

Manufactured in the United States of America

First Edition: June 1984

10 9 8 7 6 5 4 3 2 1

This book is dedicated
to the memory of my father

CONTENTS

GETTING INTO FASHION

A CAREER GUIDE

CHAPTER 1

GETTING INTO FASHION

Fashion is glamorous business. Barbara Walters and Estée Lauder know it. They haven't missed a Blass show in years. Nancy Kissinger and Pat Buckley haven't missed a de la Renta either. "Fashion victims" is what *Women's Wear Daily* lovingly calls them. Listen to a bit from *WWD*, the newspaper which, as far as print goes, controls the industry:

"When Perry Ellis wants to visit his house on Fire Island, he doesn't worry about reserving a seaplane. He owns the seaplane. He knows it's a Cessna, but says he's not sure how much he paid for it. 'Six figures,' he says. 'Something like that.' What he is certain of is that the plane is khaki.

"Ralph Lauren also owns a plane. It's a Hawker Siddeley jet. Hawker Siddeleys cost about $6,500,000, but that doesn't mean they're perfect. [Hawker Siddeleys, it seems, are empty shells, so Lauren had to have the interior designed]

"Calvin Klein owns no planes. He charters them. When he feels like a weekend at his Key West house (one of four places he can call home) he hires a Learjet. That can come to almost $10,000, but it's good for a round trip."

Consider Michael Arceneaux, one of the country's foremost producers of fashion shows. He is credited with extravaganzas for Calvin Klein, Bill Blass, Issey Miyake, and Ferragamo in Italy. Says Arceneaux, "The problem with my getting into fashion was it didn't have enough show biz, so I brought show biz to fashion." Wouldn't it be terrific, after all, to hobnob in Paris, Milan, Hong Kong, or maybe Tokyo?

If you think so, stick around. You're hardly alone if glamour, money, and travel are among your reasons for aspiring to a fashion career. What else so easily explains the overwhelming popularity of design and buying jobs?

But design and buying are only two of a hundred opportunities in fashion, just as glamour is one of a hundred-plus reasons you're attracted to the business. Moreover, in the long run, your reasons for choosing fashion will matter little. You may be bored with a current job, fashion-related or not, reentering the work force, changing careers, or entering for the first time after raising children. What does matter is that you focus on the job or jobs that excite you, that you're super-determined to land them, and that you're willing to swallow your pride in the name of paying your dues.

Assume, like all successful people, you're not going to quit, whatever your goal. Not when you're feeling rejected and frustrated. Not when that glamour job means more stockroom than stagelights. Not when you're offered $10,000 to start. Not when someone else marches in with an MBA. Not when the boss is a bastard, the hours outrageous, and someone with far less creativity is winning out.

The best way to understand a business chock full of glamour, show biz, and dream jobs is with a healthy shot of reality—in this case a candid conversation with successful clothing designer Alexander Julian.

Indeed, the most powerful career advice often comes from first-person accounts. The rub is that you have to know how to interpret the account. In this case, look for evidence of the two success essentials: guts and goals. Julian defines his goals in the first paragraph of the conversation and acknowledges later that he's never abandoned them. For Julian, every major career advance involved guts. But to cement guts and goals you also need crucial career building blocks like solid work experience (Julian "worked every day after school"), education, extremely hard work, people skills, patience, and passion for the field. Read chapter 16 for more on success essentials, then, if you feel so inclined, return for a second shot at the Julian chat.

ALEXANDER JULIAN

Alexander Julian may not exactly be a household word, but he's well on his way. His company racked up sales of $44 million in 1981 and a whopping $88 million in 1982. His showcase store is Saks Fifth Avenue, which saw fit to stage a spectacular parade down Manhattan's Fifth Avenue in his honor. He is a four-time winner of the prestigious Coty Award, the Oscar of the fashion industry, and a one-time winner of the Cutty Sark Award for outstanding menswear design. His menswear is carried in the most sophisticated stores across the country, including Jerry Magnin in Los Angeles, Wilkes Bashford in San Francisco, and Perkins Shearer in Denver. Julian is thirty-five years old and married, with one daughter. He was born in Chapel Hill, North Carolina, lives in New York City, and maintains a summer home in Easthampton, Long Island, where his favorite pastime is sailing, and an apartment in Milan.

When did you become interested in the fashion business?

On my first trip to the market at six months old. My parents have a store in Chapel Hill, North Carolina. They also forbade me to go into the business. I designed my first shirts at twelve and my first jackets at sixteen. One reporter once wrote that "young Julian was raised with swatchbooks instead of fire engines." I worked every day after school. When I turned eighteen, I did an *assets and liabilities tally* and realized I already had eighteen years retail experience. But I started out pre-med at the University of North Carolina. After four Coty awards and a Cutty Sark Award, my father would still like me to go to medical school. Anyway, my father developed health problems and I was catapulted into running the store. One time when he was out of town—I was twenty-one—I used his money to open my own store. I was a fairly brazen kid.

How did you end up designing?

I remember it well. I was in New York designing sweaters for my store. A friend with a shop in West Hartford and I were walking down Madison Avenue and he said, "I really think designing is your forte. You should be doing it all the time because you're good at it." It was one of those incredibly frightening moments. I wanted to do it but there were so many things involved. Then another friend, who had sold himself to a clothing manufacturer as a creative talent even though he was really more of a salesperson, came to me for the creative end. So I did my first collection. There were no names on the clothes or anything, but I decided this was something I wanted to pursue full-time. I moved to New York and decided to give it three years. I figured if I didn't win a Coty Award before I was thirty I would quit. That was eight years ago. I got my first nomination after my second year in business and won my first Coty after three years. I think I was the youngest nominee.

What made you think you'd quit after three years?

I would have quit because I would have found out I wasn't as good as I thought I was.

What happened in New York?

I went to a very staid old company that wasn't involved with my kind of thing at all and sold them on the beneficial effects my designs would have on their company. It was a struggle. I almost went out of business at least ten times and almost hung it up another ten. You beat your head against that brick wall twenty times and the twenty-first time you make it. The amount of time it takes to get anyone in the fashion press to come over even once is unbelievable. One major fashion editor stood me up for at least ten appointments. She never even called. Finally she promised to see me on her way to work at 8:30 A.M. That morning I had everything organized: coffee, a little danish pastry. At ten-thirty I called her office. She had forgotten. I was so incensed I bagged up the best pieces from my collection, the cold coffee and stale danish, and splurged on a taxi. I barged into her office and said, "Here's your coffee, here's your danish, and here's my collection. You're going to take a look at it!"

Did you get publicity?
   Yes. I knew my clothes had validity. Getting someone's attention was what I needed.

How important is publicity?
   Very. We had one jacket featured in more magazines and newspapers than jackets we sold.

Has money ever been your goal?
   I didn't start out to see how much money I could make. I did it as a pure expression of what I thought was right.

   A group of high school seniors, when asked why they aspired to fashion careers, responded "money." What do you think of money as a goal in terms of potential success?
   It's fine. There are people like that in the industry, I'm sure.

What does it take to be successful?
   First, you have to decide to stick with it. Then there's a lot required besides talent. There's luck and being in the right place. I abide by the axiom "the harder I work the luckier I get."

How many hours a day do you work?
   Probably twelve.

Julian menswear

Dan Cahill/Ford Model Agency

Do you take vacations?

I do and I don't. I get away and I don't get away. It's interchangeable. The trick is feeling comfortable with the anxiety. This is a twenty-four-hour-a-day, seven-day-a-week business. One of my assistants told me she wakes up in the middle of the night thinking, Oh, God! What am I going to do with that shirt? I used to do that.

When did you hire your first employees?

First of all my wife works with me. With the time commitments and travel, if she didn't, I'd never see her. She does everything. Our first employee came after a couple of years. She was also an all-around person writing orders, calling the factory to see where orders went, everything. As of three years ago we had four including someone in clerical/production and a national sales manager.

Does everyone do a little of everything?

Yes. It's only now coming to the point where everybody doesn't have to do everything.

How many people work for you now?

Sixteen.

In what capacities?

Receptionist and secretary to bookkeeper, production and quality-control people, a sales manager, two others in sales, and an executive vice-president who kind of floats between the couture company and the licensees and works with merchandising. I also have a part-time knitwear expert in England and three others in the design studio here doing everything from channeling information to the licensees to working on design projects.

Do they actually design?

Yes.

Do you hire entry level?

Yes. I hired my first real design assistant right out of school. A Syracuse University professor, an old friend, called and said, "I've got this kid and she's perfect for you. She's my top student and I want you to put her on as a summer intern." At the end of the summer I hired her. She finished up in night school. Another person in sales who concentrates on stores came out of design school.

What do you look for in someone you hire?

The real core work I always do. I look for another pair of eyes and another set of sensibilities. There are concepts involved that I can teach.

Do you prefer design school graduates?

After my first Coty Award I was given an honorarium to teach a Creative Menswear course at Parsons School of Design in New York. My first lecture was entitled "How I Won a Coty Award with No Formal Design Training." Obviously, training is very, very helpful but the most important thing is having the right ideas. What I was trying to drive home is not to get totally bogged down in the technical to the exclusion of everything else.

Undoubtedly many people aspire to your success. What career strategy would you recommend?

One particular student approached me and said, "What do I do?" I said, "Take the retail route." Work your way up through retail. Get into buying, learn your way around, make contacts, and then try to establish a business. Obviously, I told him to do what I did. Another designer who went to design school told him the opposite. I still think retail experience is essential.

Your clothes are easy to spot. Do you think anyone can develop a style if it doesn't come naturally?

When I lecture, people always ask, "Where do you get good ideas?" The answer is "everywhere." Creativity is part of somebody's makeup but you can become more or less creative by your own particular involvements with the world.

What are major pitfalls to avoid?

This is the advice I put in *Who's Who*: To be successful in any endeavor, whether fashion or something else, an important element is to liken your endeavors to defensive driving. To reach your goal, you have to look out more for what others are doing wrong than for what you're doing right. So many things can go wrong.

Is there some way to learn other than by your own mistakes?

I'm afraid not.

Have you ever been tempted to get into another business?

Every new licensee is another business.

How many licensees do you have?

Ten. They account for a fair portion of sales.

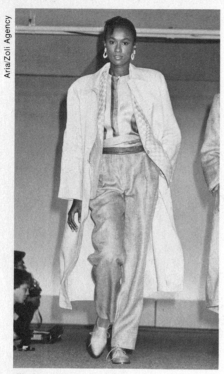

Aria/Zoli Agency

Womenswear for Spring '84

Do you design the clothes for the licensees?

We have total design and product control over every item produced with my name on it anywhere in the world. Everything starts here. We do it all. There are too many people that give licensing a bad name.

Do you have a personal career goal?

My goal is to singlehandedly change the definition of an idealist as a person in the loan line at the bank. We've just signed a major Seventh Avenue womenswear deal. It will be the first womenswear collection anywhere based entirely on in-house textiles.

CHAPTER 2

THE FASHION INDUSTRY

Fashion is big, big business. We buy a whopping ninety billion dollars worth of clothing every year. Check your closet. Even if you don't have enormous sums to spend on clothes, the dollar amount when every last item is totaled is far greater than you think. And that's just *your* wardrobe.

There are 5,500 apparel manufacturers in New York City alone, mostly on famed Seventh Avenue. Fashion is New York State's as well as New York City's largest business and certainly one of its major claims to fame, although apparel companies exist in every state of the union. The biggies are California, Texas, New Jersey, and the southern states. As for textiles, there are 6,000 companies nationwide, most with sales and marketing divisions in New York City and plants that do the weaving and knitting and research and development in the South. As for retail, there are over two million stores of various sizes with an estimated sixteen million people at work, making retail alone the largest job bank in the entire United States.

There are huge companies in the fashion business such as Burlington Industries in textiles, Levi Strauss in apparel, and Sears, Roebuck and Company in retail that individually gross over a billion dollars a year. There are top-ranking sales representatives who clear $200,000 a year doing little more than selling moderately priced men's suits. First-rate female models rack up $3,000 a day or more. Their male counterparts can pocket $2,500 a day. And there are infinitely more nonglamorous jobs that pay handsomely. A well-trained production manager in an apparel manufacturing plant may not visit Paris on business but may earn enough to vacation there. The same goes for a top-flight engineer or product development expert.

Most jobs, of course, pay far less, especially at the beginning. An assistant designer can expect to make between $10,000 and $15,000 a year, as can a production assistant, assistant patternmaker, or a textile stylist. An assistant buyer in a training program may earn between $15,000 and $20,000 depending on the program, and a sales trainee in textiles or apparel will probably land closer to $20,000.

TEAMWORK

Fashion is a team business. It is a group effort from the first ball of cotton picked or wool shorn to the hottest new boutique in Bloomingdale's, I. Magnin, or Filene's. That team effort is always spoken of in terms of its three major links: textiles, apparel, and retail. It is however, the job of fiber companies like Monsanto, Du Pont, and Celanese to start the ball rolling by shearing the wool, picking the cotton, and/or creating manmade fibers such as polyester, acrylic, and nylon from chemicals. Textile companies, mostly in the South, then buy this raw fiber, spin it into yarn, and weave or knit it into fabric. They're also responsible for dyeing either the yarn or the fabric.

The apparel companies or so-called manufacturers buy the fabric from the textile companies, design the clothing, manufacture it, then market and sell it to the stores. However unglamorous it may sound, Calvin Klein is a manufacturer. Finally, we spend that $90 billion at the retail level, in either a chain or department store, specialty store, or boutique. Sears, Roebuck is a chain store or mass merchandiser. Blooming-

dale's is a department store and Bonwit Teller a specialty store.

DIVERSITY

Fashion is a diverse business. You'd be hard-pressed to find an ethnic or social group without representation. Fashion is the largest employer of women and minorities and, as we said, there are people from virtually every state of the union working in fashion jobs. Sizes of companies range from Fortune 500 corporations to tiny "mom and pop" businesses. More important, fashion people are diverse in their individual talents and skills. They don't start out that way but fashion demands it. It is not unusual to find salespeople consulting and influencing designers, buyers nudging salespeople and designers, or the owner of a small store stepping behind the register during the holiday rush. No one in fashion survives without grasping a little of what everyone else is up to, a little of how fashion really works, and a lot about the bottom line—clothing must sell.

Most important for you as a jobseeker, diversity runs to the jobs themselves. Possibilities range from the artistic to the scientific, from the highly creative to the technical, from business to manufacturing, from journalism to jewelry design. The roster runs from tried-and-true favorites like clothing or fabric design, styling, buying, advertising, public relations, and sales to superb newcomers such as cable television, in-house video, and computer management. You can be a fashion coordinator for a store, advertising agency, magazine, or apparel manufacturer. Freelance positions are virtually endless, from the extremely popular option of starting your own company to being a model, makeup artist, hair stylist, or producer-director, and choreographer of fashion shows. So too, there's fashion illustration, photography, and styling. And there are freelance fashion consultants who assemble wardrobes for television newscasters and powerful public officials. They are among the freelancers who throw caution to the wind and create their own careers.

CREATIVITY

Fashion is an idea business. Take a typical apparel manager at Celanese, the large fiber company. Such a person was hard at work in November of 1982 conceptualizing what we will buy in the Spring of 1984. And he or she contemplated Spring 1984 at least a year before any designer and perhaps two before we see the clothing in the stores. He feels the heartbeat of the industry. He thinks about far more than fiber. He thinks about color, shape, silhouette, and style. He goes to the European shows. He thinks with the profitability of his company in mind, but he thinks just the same. He knows he's at the cutting edge.

So is June Roche, fashion director at Milliken and Company, a major textile concern. As much as a year before a designer sets out actually to design, a textile company's fashion director develops a so-called color story and considers what form the clothing of the future will take, what the trends will be. Will there be a Japanese influence? Will dresses be light, loose, and sporty? Is tight in or out? Will tailored business suits soar? A fashion director does presentations for garment manufacturers, for fiber folks, and for retailers.

We all know designers come up with ideas. Perhaps we don't know Oscar de la Renta's ideas come from the same place as those of people at fiber and textile companies and retail outlets. Everyone's ideas come from available fabrics, from what we're currently buying at the stores, from what we're really wearing on the streets, from the fashion shows in Europe, from American and European designers and companies well-known for taking risks and being two or three years ahead, from industry trade associations, from so-called color forecasters, from newspaper and magazine articles, from museum exhibits and cultural events, from the economy, politics, and from each other. The denim craze and punk look were originally inspired by street people. When Norma Kamali's sweatshirt fashion began to sell, apparel companies from coast to coast added fashionable activewear to their lines. When Yves St. Laurent revived the chemise for Fall '83, it was predicted that ready-to-wear companies would follow suit. As for economic influences on fashion, we may find ourselves sporting black dresses, as we did during the 1981–1982 recession, in part because black fabric can be reused season after season. As the treasures of Tutankhamun museum collection was successful for mass audiences so rich bronzes and metallics became popular in fashion. And as Marilyn Monroe is seen with renewed fascination and obsession worldwide, we will find more feminine, body-conscious clothing in the market. And don't forget that the effect of women in the workplace has been to inspire business suits galore. Fashion ideas come from an almost endless array of sources.

Ellin Saltzman, Vice-president and Fashion Director for Saks Fifth Avenue and a former *Glamour* editor, works with the identical idea sources to set trends for thirty-nine stores, to give an overall direction, look, and image. She does this six months or so before we see new styles and their corresponding themes in the store. Her job, backed by a range of assistants in the fashion office, includes coming up with a color and fabric direction, guiding buyers and display artists on the look of mannequins, even making films for branch store managers instructing them on display and promotion.

Ideas are the domain of fashion journalists, reporters, copywriters, broadcasters, and publicists as well. Members of the fashion press may even dictate ideas. As a rule, fashion editors and writers cover the shows, which take place about six months before we buy items in stores, and they "shop the market," picking and choosing from lines they see in showrooms. They scan for the best looks, some of which will appear in photos in the magazine or newspaper. These editors are involved in styling and accessorizing chosen outfits, and working with models and photographers.

The newest shapes for fashionable ideas, however, more often than not involve technology. One burgeoning field is cable television. Elsa Klensch is the reporter, writer, producer, and anchorwoman of a daily fashion feature and a weekly half-hour show on the Cable News Network. For her popular show, she gleans ideas from the same sources fiber, textile, apparel, and retail people do. She covers the top United States, European and Japanese collections, interviews the designers and beauty experts; and also travels to Japan and Brazil to report on fashion and living styles. Elsa Klensch began as a general reporter for a newspaper in her native Sydney, Australia. In this country, she worked as a fashion writer and editor for *Vogue, Women's Wear Daily, Harper's Bazaar* and the *New York Post*. She made her initial television appearances while representing *Vogue* and *Harper's Bazaar*.

PASSION

Fashion is an emotional business. It's often described as "high energy," "hectic," "fast paced," "urgent," "tense," "high pressure." "You must be able to think and move fast," says one career counselor with a fashion background. "This is a world for people who like ups and downs and adrenaline charges. It's very emotional," says another. One man feels fashion's emotionality justifies his preference for hiring family members, a relatively common practice. "Fashion's so emotional," he asserted. "You have to be on the same wavelength." The fast track, as responsible as it is for pressure, is also the root of fashion's thrill and excitement.

Any business that goes full cycle four or five times a year (most apparel manufacturers do four or five lines a year) is bound to be a bit crazed. One need only visit a Seventh Avenue apparel showroom during market week to see how hectic it really is.

One visit to the New York showroom of a California company was nothing short of mayhem. (Regardless of a company's location, it almost always has a showroom in New York.) The company's owner/designer brought in an elaborate spread from a local restaurant (careful to remember finicky eating habits of important buyers). Around the table, on couches and floor pillows, sat buyers from Bonwit Teller, Bergdorf Goodman, and Bloomingdale's. Between sips of champagne and wine, they checked their watches, called other showrooms to cancel and reschedule appointments. In flew a harried Saks buyer, "too nervous," she said, to eat. Then came the Neiman-Marcus buyer who had to see the line immediately or not at all. Then a fashion editor from *Glamour*, who, with myself and the Bloomingdale's buyer, was shown the line by one of the showroom assistants. Later on, when I met friends for dinner, buyers could be seen talking shop well into the night.

STAMINA

Fashion demands long hours. Not just long hours but the wrong hours are notorious in retail—Christmas, Thanksgiving, Sundays. One young associate publicist for an apparel company noted that typically in her job she takes editors to dinner at least two to three nights a week, on top of attending all the events she's put together, from intimate press dinners in the designer's apartment to elaborate cocktail parties preceding his fashion shows, details of which she also handles. This is in addition to accompanying the designer when he does trunk shows, the minishows designers and apparel companies present in department stores and elsewhere across the country to promote their current lines. "The only people I ever see in my spare time are very, very close friends," she said. "There just isn't time for anything else." Many fashion people claim membership in the "workaholic and loving it" club. Oscar de la Renta says he's always worked long hours, so it's second nature by now. This helps explain why so many insist you need a strong temperament and a limitless passion for fashion and its accompanying lifestyle.

INSTABILITY

Fashion is an unpredictable business. Some prefer "unstable" or "constantly changing." By any name, unpredictability is fashion's charm as well as its poison. Bubbling creativity and a frantic search for newness (four or five times a year) have appeal and are also what fashion shares with other glamour businesses such as film, television, and publishing. In fact, unpredictability may be what glamour careers are all about. It's poison in that, well, you just never really know what's next. When people in fashion jobs from textiles to retail were urged to describe a typical day on the job, most chuckled to themselves, adding, "What's that?" Unpredictability makes fashion addictive to those who are easily excited, stimulated, and challenged by constant change and nonstop ups and downs.

ADDICTIVENESS

Fashion is addictive. Indeed, some of those stimulated and excited by retailing have called themselves "retail junkies." Career counselors count fashion among the industries to which people develop an across-the-board attraction, as opposed to their becoming attached to a special skill. For instance, a salesperson dissatisfied with his or her job would rather switch to another fashion job than move into sales in another industry.

CAMARADERIE

Fashion is a people business. In job-hunting lingo: "It's who you know, not what you know." Moreover, there are a lot of close-knit family-owned companies. For good reason, insiders call fashion a "word-of-mouth" industry. Colombe Nicholas, President of Christian Dior New York, says, "Something to consider, no matter what level you are, is that you meet the same people over and over again. Even if you leave a company, you should leave on a friendly note. I've tried to do that, so as a result I have close ties with many people I've worked with." On what she looks for most when she's doing the hiring: "I look for someone with a very gregarious, outgoing personality. We are in a people business. A service business." Finally, on *the* premiere key to success: "Be pleasant. No one likes a bitchy person. No matter how much your feet are killing you, no matter how many towels you have folded, no one likes a complainer. Walk in in the morning and be 'up.' People like 'up' people, so you'll be recognized."

Once you're in the business, people can be an enormous asset. Many fashion people credit a first boss or someone in the industry with being a lifelong mentor. People move on because someone they met lent a hand. And when a group of people in textile jobs—from coloring, styling, designing, and sales to raw materials purchasing, merchandising, and production—were asked to name the overwhelming virtue of their jobs, they said, "The friends I've made in the industry." On the negative side, word of mouth can hurt.

PERSPIRATION

Fashion is a seat-of-the-pants business. It is a hands-on, pay-your-dues business, a foot-in-the-door industry. It is a world where a textile company personnel director insists he'd rather see candidates who had at least "slung hash" in high school than those with lots of fancy degrees and no work experience. Because this is largely an industry of small companies, of entrepreneurs, ofttimes of immigrants who "paid their dues," they expect the same from you. There is little tolerance for theories or dreamers and immense reverence for action. This is an industry that considers a liberal arts program, or even a graduate degree, fine and dandy, but knows that real learning takes place on the job.

MYTHS AND MYTH MAKERS

THE MYTHS

A tiny percentage of industry elite will tell you that the following myths aren't myths at all. Glamour and money, they'll tell you, came with the job. The myth makers, and the media in particular, will be more than happy to help you believe that this tiny fraction of the industry for whom myth is reality, represent not the exception but the rule.

The danger for the newcomer isn't so much in establishing fame or fortune as a goal. The danger is that your own beliefs, reinforced by the myth makers, may cause you to shortchange or undercut yourself. On more than a few occasions, false expectations have stood between some of us and hard work. Indeed, there's a fine line between false expectations and a healthy sense of possibility, a career essential.

Overnight Success

"How long did it take you?"

I was asked the question by a high school senior wanting to become a self-supporting writer. When I answered "eight years," she gulped. "Oh God! I don't want to wait that long!" Another, whose dream job is to have her own design company, says if she doesn't "make her mark" by twenty-four, she'll quit and go into computers.

You are not going to be an overnight sensation. This isn't Hollywood. Overnight success takes years to create . . . except for maybe a model or two. If you're skeptical, take it from those most often accused of early success.

Jane Evans

"Am I an overnight success? No! Far from it!" says designer Jhane Barnes, who, at twenty-nine, runs her own company with a sales volume in the United States of about $3 million and an additional $5 to $10 million in licensing agreements abroad. She has already won both the prestigious Coty and Cutty Sark awards. Barnes went into business for herself with a $5,000 investment from a fashion school professor at age twenty-one and is frequently cited as an example of early success. She has, however, been in the business eight years and feels she has many to go.

Quips Tom Fallon, long-time promotion director of Bill Blass: "Bill's not an overnight success. Absolutely not! The man's been in the business twenty-five years! He's often said success didn't come fast. He also often said it's good because he built a solid base, both work-wise and emotionally, so he was able to handle the money and fame."

Jane Evans is often touted for her early-won success. As executive vice-president of General Mills's Fashion Group, which, as of May 1982, took in $657.3 million in revenues, she is the top-ranking woman in the apparel industry. Jane Evans is thirty-nine.

Now to the man everyone wants to emulate. Calvin Klein grew up in the Bronx in New York City. His father was in the grocery store business. Calvin Klein claims he wanted to design clothes and open his own business from age five. After fashion school, he took a job as an apprentice in a coat and suit house, working nights and weekends. In 1968, he and his best friend and current company president, Barry Schwartz, began their own business designing and manufacturing coats. The rest is history. In 1982, Calvin Klein turned forty.

So, if all goes well, you can expect to be an overnight success at forty. That is, of course, if you are one of the chosen few. Alexander Julian is one of the few: He gave himself a five-year plan aimed at winning a prestigious award by age thirty, and he did. Just as many others hate the idea of five-year plans. What everyone agrees on is that overnight success never feels like overnight success, no matter what it looks like to everyone else. It feels like hard work and long hours, and a great deal of patience.

A Four-Star General or Nothing

One sorry aspect of aspiring to your own company, as many people do, is not exploring options which may be more suitable to your personality, lifestyle, and skills, and most important, guarantee you satisfaction, fulfillment, and happiness. As Tom Fallon of Bill Blass aptly put it, "Saddest of all is that people looking into fashion too often only think of design jobs." The thinking goes something like this: In any other job the outside world won't notice me, so why choose that job? Behind the scenes, however, you can easily become important to the company, even indispensable to its president. Listen to Oscar de la Renta:

"In the sample room we have mostly old-timers. That is the area where I think we are going to have the biggest problems in the future if this industry is going to remain healthy. Most of the people in the sample room are old. They've been in the business a long time. Most were not born in this country. They're French, Italian, Greek, Spanish. We actually have two young Russian girls. They're the youngest in many, many years to look for work here. It is very strange that no one wants to be a seamstress, you know? A tailor . . . it's a wonderful profession! It pays well and you can learn fast. But whenever we need someone for the sample room, they're always very difficult to find. It's not glamorous enough. No one wants to be part of an army. Everyone wants to be the general. Everyone wants a title."

Job interviewers report being put off by otherwise qualified candidates because they perceive too much ambition too soon. Have you put the cart before the horse? Interviewers want to know whether you will "pay your dues." Are you a team player? Will you stay with the company? Can the employer count on your loyalty?

In extreme cases, employers report hiring assistants and letting them go because they felt these assistants, after months on the job, were not loyal to them, the company, or the product. They were, they suspected, picking up the ins and outs of the employer's business in order to quit and establish their own. What irked these company presidents was not their employees' career goals. After all, they have the same goals. What these employers complained of was the flexing of such goals in beginners, in those they feel need solid track records and who should be willing to pay their dues by learning on the job.

Glamour and Money

"Is your job glamorous?" I asked one department store vice-president and fashion director.

"Yes," she admits. "I travel around the world. I mingle with other creative people. But a lot of it is surface. I have a glamorous job with hard work—carrying shopping bags full of accessories, dragging rolling rods around. . . ."

"I go to glamorous places and work with glamorous people," says Michael Arceneaux, the freelance fashion show producer. "I also have a beer when I get home and watch the six o'clock news." What about money? "I make good money, very good money," he ventures. "I can't say exactly how much, but you must remember my job isn't secure. Most people are looking for security."

A word from a vice-president and corporate training director at a major department store. He is responsible for selecting people for executive training programs, who will eventually join the staff as buyers. He estimates he receives up to 15,000 job requests a year, including phone, mail, and/or in-person requests. "Most people tend to glamorize this business," he explains. "They mean Paris, not Staten Island. That's not the [reality of the] business or its motivation. You're better off being a tour guide for a travel agency. The problem is people see it as a fashion business—as being a clotheshorse full-time. There is reward in that, but it's a business first."

If you accept the glamour myth, you accept the possibility of not exploring job options suitable to your private world in favor of those suitable to the public world. One high school senior confided that deep down she wanted to be an illustrator because nothing made her happier than sitting quietly at the drawing table doing her best. But she felt pressure to choose fashion design, something she admitted she didn't particularly enjoy.

There are few glamorous jobs, if any. Even Seventh Avenue isn't glamorous. In fact, jobseekers from other parts of the country who visit the fashion capital for the first time are ofttimes startled by its rather dingy façades, worn elevators, unfashionable shops, and nonstop traffic tie-ups caused by armies of clothes racks and trucks jamming the streets.

Is there a quick cure for starry eyes? "Your first day at work," says the fashion director.

THE MYTH MAKERS

The Media

It's always a good idea to take glitzy films, television programs, magazine stories and books with a grain of salt. The *Women's Wear Daily* quote on the first page of this book makes great reading but is hardly the stuff intelligent job choices are made of.

Take *Vogue*. Its fashion spreads are excellent because its editors use the best fashion photographers in the world. They use those whose work is as much at home in galleries or museums as in magazines. Names like Irving Penn, Richard Avedon, Francesco Scavullo. These photographers excel at injecting an element of art . . . and fantasy. They work with the world's most stunning models, the foremost stylists, lighting and set designers, to create just the right sense of drama. *Vogue* is all the more tantalizing because the contents of its pages are accessible . . . at a price. The charmed life implied in these photographs isn't easily obtained, however.

Fashion magazines or newspapers should be part of an ongoing and rigorous "research" program (see chapter 16) through which you become familiar with industry lingo, with style, with trends, with ideas, and most important, with how this relates to everything else you see and do. These publications are a barometer of what's happening. As one industry leader said, "*Women's Wear Daily* is more important than any textbook."

Teachers and Counselors

The fashion school professors know all too well that disappointment can lurk for "unrealistic" jobseekers. So, they arrange "reality-based" programs—work studies, internships, visits to retail, textile, and apparel firms and from industry leaders—to offset misconceptions.

But it doesn't always work. As one design major who switched to patternmaking said, "They [the professors] make everything seem glamorous." Remarked one starstruck New York high school student of her favorite teacher, "She knows *everyone*.

I mean *everyone*." A fashion school admissions officer confided he thinks that schools, New York ones in particular, encourage unrealistic hopes by the mere act of inviting name designers to critique students' work. The unconscious message, he says, is that you will be a celebrity, and overnight at that.

Concludes one design graduate aptly, "Teachers tell you the realities till they're blue in the face, how much harder it is out there, but you just don't believe it. I didn't know till I was laid off. I thought it could never happen to me."

Parents

Parents aren't exactly myth makers in the conventional sense of concocting an imaginary world. But they may discourage and inadvertently convince you to short-

Jhane Barnes

change yourself. Alexander Julian's parents forbade him to go into the business. "They still wish I was a doctor," he jokes. Among entrepreneurs in creative businesses, it's surprising how often this is the case. Geoffrey Beene's family also wanted him to pursue medicine. Liz Claiborne's parents wanted her to go to art school. Jhane Barnes, the men's clothing designer, says her folks are still concerned, even after Coty and Cutty Sark awards, that she didn't get a liberal arts degree. Others, of course, think it's marvelous. But why shouldn't parents be concerned when children want to enter potentially high-risk, unstable industries with high turnover and heavy competition? If you are creative and derive satisfaction from it, go for it. Parents usually come around.

Friends

It was a friend who first encouraged Julian to enter the business. Calvin Klein has often said there'd be no Calvin Klein without best friend and business partner, Barry Schwartz. Friends often are our best and most supportive contacts throughout our careers.

The flip side of the coin, when we're in school, can be peer pressure. Like parents, your peers aren't conventional examples of myth makers. But a little objectivity—and respect for your own heartfelt goals—never hurts. Remember the young woman who

ACKNOWLEDGMENTS

Thanks again to everyone whose contributions are obvious within. Equal thanks, however, and sincere appreciation to: Bill Ditfort, Ron Chereskin, Dianne Benson, Barry Kieselstein-Cord, Kenneth Jay Lane, Jackie Rogers, Eleanor Lambert, Mary McFadden, Jean Louis, A'lone Alakazia, Carol Klinger, Maddy LeMel, Richard Fromberg, Patti Cappalli, Bijan Pakzad, Anne Sica, Sandy Elias, Lee Bright, Nina Santisi, Debbie Moses, Patricia Lennox, Chip Tolbert, Mark Kaufman, Linda Gaunt, Joan Cuomo, Stephanie Pulver, Nancy Walter, Ken Mildred, Marian Thunberg, Anne Keagy, Irwin Kahn, Bernard Zamcoff, Newton Godnick, Arthur Price, Brenda Racoosin, Sharon Levy, Stanley Mont, Christopher Ryan, Emil Beland, Al Metayer, Gloria Veeder, Michael Weingarten, Michael Harder, Alexis Kirk, Linda Lee, Ron Devine, Lois Rowe, Herman Bott, Liz Mazurski, Janet Mason, Debbie Rahn, Bob Klein, Ellen Verini, Margaret Muldoon, Ellen Bezahler, Mike D'Angelo, Larry and Lois Nipon.

Also to: Carol Elliott, Erica, Liz Royte, Hadassah Gold, Louis Slesin, Lesli Rice, Michelle Rapkin.

simply wanted to be an illustrator but felt her friends allowed more prestige for aspiring designers? Who wants to be unpopular? Some students report that even though professors stressed advantages of careers in patternmaking, production management, and textile technology, they opted for popular jobs instead. It's up to you. But remember: In the business, respect abounds for a wide range of jobs, and in many cases, they're not the jobs you think.

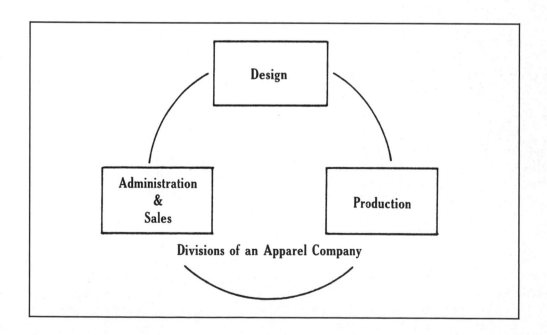

Divisions of an Apparel Company

APPAREL DESIGN

DESIGN

Designing clothes involves a surprisingly small and ofttimes close-knit coterie of creative people. A typical group includes a head designer, design assistants, and samplemakers. There may also be crucial interaction with a fashion coordinator/stylist and a fabric buyer.

The design process usually begins a year or so before we see the garments in the stores. Basically, a head designer begins by conceptualizing the line. Ideas come to mind based on anything from the economy, cultural events, and politics to what's being worn on the streets and what sold well the season before. He or she may go to the European shows. The first step is coming up with the colors, then shopping the fabric market, and finally sketching out the clothing itself. Then the designer or an assistant makes a first pattern and the samples are cut and sewn by samplemakers. Another set of samples, the duplicates, is often made by the same or another set of samplemakers for salespeople so buyers have an idea what the clothes will look like on the hanger. At various junctures, items may be tried on a fitting model, adjusted, and readjusted. At other junctures there are merchandising meetings, often attended by the company president and the designer, to pare down the line during two to three months of heavyduty, all-out labor to meet the line's deadline. When the line opens, about six months before we see the clothing, buyers come to check it out. There may be a show for the press, buyers, solid customers, and celebrities and socialites. This happens, though, in only a fraction of the industry. That's design in a nutshell.

But if there are hard and fast rules about designing, no one knows what they are. There are no typical days. No job title means exactly the same thing at different companies. Salaries vary considerably. The numbers of fashion people who do a little bit of everything, whatever their titles, stagger the imagination. No two companies, no two design staffs, and no two head designers work in exactly the same way. For

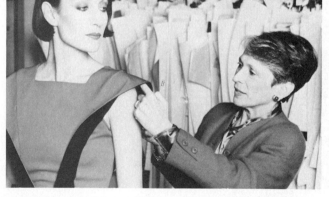

example, at Albert Nipon, Inc., the well-known womenswear company we'll cite throughout this chapter, Pearl Nipon is director of design. In her part of the operation, six head designers work under her, each with a staff of two assistants and four sample ladies. Each of the six design groups works on two of the company's five lines (divisions). Her design studios happen to be at the factory in Philadelphia.

But that's only one company. Other designers work out of a main office in close proximity to the showroom, and administrative and salespeople. The factory or contractor is elsewhere. Some designers do elaborate sketches, some doodle, some drape, some rely on assistants or design services. Others don't draw at all. Some prefer weekend hours; others opt for office time. Midnight sketchers abound. There are assistant designers who do little more than fetch coffee, field phone calls, and shop trims; others are lucky enough to be involved in designing clothing, perhaps because the head designer is off doing personal appearances, promotions, talking to the press, handling licensing arrangements and other crucial business matters. In some companies, there is no designer at all. The owner and salespeople along with a production patternmaker come up with the styles.

An important design consideration is the number of lines a staff produces each year. Four or five lines a year—Fall, Spring, Summer, Holiday/Resort, and possibly Fall I (basically early delivery of Fall)—is the norm. For his couture collection Bill Blass does two, Fall and Spring, as well as a Holiday line he says is really early delivery of Spring. There are menswear companies of the classic, less fashion-forward ilk that also serve up three lines each year, Fall/Winter, Spring/Summer, and Holiday/Resort. The design staff of one lingerie company delivers two lines a year. A tie designer is less bound even than a lingerie designer by the constrictions of climate and season and can add to a line year-round. A California company concentrating on upbeat activewear for a casual warm weather market won't be big on cold weather clothes and Fall/Winter collections, as might an outerwear firm that sells heavily in the east.

Naturally, one design staff consideration is the number of lines to be done each year. Staffs producing the most lines, however, don't automatically have more hectic schedules. Another consideration is just what you're designing. Companies exist for everything from dresses to sportswear, coats, suits, rainwear, knitwear and sweaters, men's clothing, kid's clothes, bridal gowns, theatrical costumes, on and on. There is clothing referred to as "fashion," and there's what some call "apparel," like uniforms for junk food restaurants.

A third design consideration is just how much "newness" you're injecting into each new line. The so-called couture or collection designers like Bill Blass, Oscar de la Renta, Geoffrey Beene, and Mary McFadden, must deliver a new line every season. This means shopping new fabrics and trims, sketching new designs, and displaying them in a new show. Then multiply that by two to four collections a year. Change is less important in, say, moderate to budget menswear, where a line will probably continue to feature navy blazers, grey flannel suits, and tweed sportcoats. Then again, in a few pages, we'll meet a lingerie designer who insists lingerie is a far greater challenge than ready-to-wear or sportswear because newness itself is an insurmountable challenge.

Head Designer

No single job attracts more public attention and none is more popular with job-seekers save, possibly, buying. Rumor has it that on the average up to 5,000 people apply for every one design job. Name designers are flooded with résumés. But it wasn't always that way.

Twenty or so years ago, most designers were hired by apparel manufacturers just as any other employee. They did their jobs and went home without hype. We rarely knew who designed our clothes and we rarely cared. A similar situation exists for today's textile stylists, who are personally thrilled to see their designs on home furnishings or as seat covers on major airlines, while we couldn't care in the least.

Today, many designers own their own businesses and have their names on the label. These designers often hold down two jobs. They are designers as well as presidents of apparel manufacturers. They undoubtedly have or look forward to lucrative licensing agreements with companies outside their immediate areas of concentration. So we see designer sheets, home furnishings, luggage, jewelry, keychains, eyeglasses, table settings, cosmetics, cars, and chocolates. Pierre Cardin tops out with 540 licensees.

There are also designer/president/retailer combinations. Betsey Johnson, from whom we'll hear later, owns boutiques devoted to her styles as well as a design company that distributes commercially. Europeans—Giorgio Armani, Emanuel Ungaro, and Yves Saint Laurent to name just a few—have gone the boutique route for years. The Japanese—Mitsuhiro Matsuda was the first in New York—have caught on too.

But there are plenty of positions for designers in the old sense: those who work diligently for an apparel manufacturer. Indeed, a serious stint with an apparel company, as a designer or a design assistant, is prime training if your own company's a goal. Salaries for designers range from about $300 a week or $15,600 a year at the low end to $75,000 a year at the upper end. There is absolutely no norm or average salary. Your pay depends on your skill, experience, company, and what you want. Let's begin with a look at one of these positions.

Heidi Thorner is a twenty-eight-year-old designer-director with a $66 million better-budget lingerie company that caters to a volume market. It sells to stores like Sears and J. C. Penney. Heidi has a four-year degree in textile chemistry from the University of Vermont and a one-year associate degree in design from FIT. Of her first job, for another lingerie company at $150 a week, she comments "They put me in a room and said 'make nightgowns,' and I did." Heidi doubled the company's volume and in 1979, her current employer made an offer she couldn't refuse. Heidi says she prefers her current job because "I have total control of my product, creativity and time." She adds, "This is a good way to break in if you want to build a reputation in the industry where you're respected and people know who you are. If you work for someone like Bill Blass, everyone knows Bill Blass. They may never know you."

Heidi does two collections a year. She's typical of designers in her feeling that actual designing is by far the easiest part of the job, offers the most pleasure, and takes the least amount of time. Her final line contains 80–100 pieces for which she initially designs 400.

Heidi's first step is the color story, which she begins about six months ahead of ready-to-wear designers or a year and a half before we see her nightgowns in stores. Heidi's color ideas come primarily from what she feels. She also collects color ideas from the major fiber (yarn) companies like Celanese and Du Pont, and she always takes her market into account. For instance, she's careful with yellows and greens. "They just don't sell because they are difficult to wear. I have no idea why. But you have to be right because the chain stores like Sears and J. C. Penney do their own color presentations as well, so they know what's going on. Competition's fierce."

Next, she puts the colors together using yarn she tapes on paper. At this stage, she has a decent idea what her fabrics will be because she started ordering the solid-color standbys that make up the bulk of the line a little while before. But she continues looking at and ordering new ones. "Something might be hot," she says. Heidi has no definite budget, although her fabric bill tops the million dollar mark. She divides the fabrics into groups—cottons, stretch terrycloth, etc. Fabrics and yarns are taped down on paper if she has to do a presentation. Otherwise, she says, she simply keeps the colors and fabrics in her head.

After color and fabric come trims, especially laces, ribbons, and embroideries. "I draw my own embroideries and appliqués because it's a very competitive market and we're better off if ours are exclusive," she explains. "Trim companies usually call me and sometimes I call them but either way I see just about everyone's line. You could spend all day doing that, but I probably see at least twenty-five lines a season. The price of trimmings is very important at this stage."

The color/fabric/trim stage takes about two weeks, then the two-month clothing design and samplemaking business begins in earnest. It also coincides with arrival of the piece goods (fabric). Heidi does her actual designing at home, usually in the course of two complete weekends. "I organize everything into folders, say, one for long robes, another for beachwear, and another for dusters." In the folders she puts thumbnail sketches she does on the sheets of paper sprawled across her apartment. At the office she gives sketches, one by one, to her one assistant designer, who makes the patterns and cuts the fabric. Her five samplehands sew the garments.

Try to imagine the harried day-to-day cranking out of 400 pieces in just two to three months. Although this isn't the case with Heidi, you can also picture what happens when a line is late. Sewers stitch around the clock. Designers sleep at their desks. In the case of expensive houses, dresses are completed minutes before being paraded down the runway—perfectly chic, of course.

Heidi puts her garments in groups of twenty to thirty, and as each is finished they're discussed and whittled down at weekly merchandising meetings attended by the company chairman of the board, the sales manager, other executives and herself. "We base our decisions on past experience, on price points, on who we want to reach, on what did and didn't do well, and we keep going week after week until the line is finished. I have to totally separate myself from what I've done and tell myself that our decisions have nothing to do with me and the clothing just has to sell. There's no room for a big ego or taking decisions personally. That's what separates the real designers from the kids who think they're designers."

What happens when the line's done? "A vacation," says Heidi.

Actually, a head designer does a good deal more than complete collections. First of all, while he or she is in the throes of a line, there is always a finishing touch or two to be put on the previous line or preliminary work to be done on the one to come. Heidi is responsible for sample garments that are continually ordered for special customers. "That's a lot of work!" she adds. "I'm always thinking about the next line because there's never time to just sit and think. I make sure the staff is happy and all the work's done."

Echoing the sentiments of most designers, Heidi advises potential designers to go to a good technical school. "It's real important to know how to do the technical stuff. It's also helpful to take business courses." Add a retail sales stint for good measure.

Couture or collection designers follow the same general process, with some differences. For one, couture accounts for a minuscule portion of the overall market. For another, such designers are company presidents as well, something we'll see at close range in chapter 10. Third, they sometimes do more than two lines a year. As we mentioned, Blass does two to three for his couture line. Blassport, his sportswear line, and Blass III, his moderate-priced line, have Summer lines as well.

As far as actual designing goes, looking at what Blass does is useful because it underscores differences generated by personal approach. Blass is a diehard advocate of serious sketching ability. Says Blass, "Sketching is the language of designers, and the most important thing any designer can do is learn to sketch. There's very little time in the workday for designing, so it's essential that the ability be second nature." Says a coworker, "He's across from me on the phone and he's sketching. He gets up in the middle of the night and sketches. He sketches on a plane, waiting for a streetlight to change, anytime something catches his eye. I've seen sketches he did as a boy in Fort Wayne, Indiana. He was raised in the Depression in the Midwest. He drew ladies in evening gowns in the nightclubs. It was just something in him from early on."

SKETCHES BY HEIDI THORNER

Blass won a drawing award from the *Chicago Tribune* at 16, which prompted his selling sketches to New York firms. New York job offers followed, beginning in 1940. He worked his way up from sketcher to one of a stable of designers to head designer. In 1970, he bought his partners out and changed the company name to Bill Blass, Ltd. It is now a $200 million business, with eighty-five people in the New York office and thirty-two licensees, including a big Japanese licensee, cars, chocolates, furs, swimwear, sheets, and towels. He dresses the First Lady, actresses, and socialites.

Because he doesn't pattern draft, cut, or sew, it's important to Blass to hire highly qualified people. He has six assistants and fourteen samplehands. Only one assistant is for the Bill Blass couture collection that is presented in his glamorous show (see chapter 9). The other five assistants are in his Blassport sportswear and Blass III moderate-priced divisions. Like other company presidents, he runs regular merchandising meetings. In fine tuning a line, there's one important difference here from Heidi Thorner's approach. There's far less second guessing because Blass knows many of his customers personally. He knows their lifestyles because he attends their charity functions in Houston. He's in their homes, so he knows the sheets and towels they want. He knows he should eliminate wool coats because, at his price range, women have a wardrobe of furs instead.

Blass's initial ideas for a line come from fabric. He runs the fabric department and travels to Switzerland, Italy, and France for inspiration. He will spend upwards of $1½ million on fabric.

Fabric buying goes hand in hand with the job of costing. Explains the coworker, "At this price range, if you have a bright red floral print fabric that can't be used again, you have to compensate. If we buy ten thousand yards of wool jersey, we can keep it for ten years and have five thousand yards at a lesser price later on, or we can dye a bright red crepe de chine black, so we'll have seven thousand yards of black. Then the fabric buyer, who runs the department, will say, 'Do you realize you spent one and a half million dollars and we have ten more fabric lines to see?'" The trimmings department keeps track of how many buttons, ribbons, or roses will be bought for upcoming lines.

When Blass makes a sketch, he gives it to an assistant, who makes up a basted fitting which goes on the house model. At this point he may reevaluate the design, going so far as to scrap it entirely. There may be a long series of fittings on a fitting model (size 8) used primarily to test design and eventually show samples. Then once an item is approved, a finished original sample is made. It goes from the sample room to the duplicate sample room. For the process he hires a duplicate model meant to approximate his ideal customer's size (in Blass's case a size 10) and be a test for the real pattern. The duplicate is then shown to Blass for his comments. Maybe the ruffle doesn't fall right because the model is too short-waisted or it just doesn't capture the right expression. Back it goes for adjustments. Once Blass approves, a paper pattern is made and it's sent to the factory.

Obviously enough, Blass has other responsibilities. He travels for personal appearances and does quasi-custom work. For instance, he'll fly to Tulsa for a charity ball. There are women there who buy as many as twenty of his styles in a season. "One of these regular clients says to Bill, 'It's too bare up here—couldn't you do something? You know, I wouldn't mind a ruffle,'" says the coworker. "A lot is quasi-custom work and sometimes Blass is right there making the adjustments."

Blass on getting into fashion: "As far as young people go it is very important for them to get a broad education—liberal arts with a background in business and in language because being a designer is also being a businessperson, and the business is more and more international in nature. Then specialize in design training for however long. Of course, the best education is going to work in the industry. Get a foot in the industry however you can and not necessarily as an assistant—as a model, salesperson, marketing person, anything."

Carol Horn, a women's clothing designer, recommends a similar strategy. First she strongly agrees on business courses. "You have to learn what price range you're in, who your customer is, what price quote your fabrics should be. The nice thing is just sitting there and thinking of ideas and making pretty pictures, but reality is that it must come out to the right price. There are a lot of intricacies, particularly in the fabric market." She also recommends the foot-in-the-door route. "Start out as a cutter. Take any job to get your foot in the door whether it's a receptionist or working at the back end. A receptionist is now learning to enter orders in the production area. The girl in back who is my draper was a student of mine at FIT. My assistant I hired right out of design school."

Pinky & Dianne, the two talented designers from Indiana, whose company prides itself on its sleek, sophisticated yet sporty creations, confess that their operation is too sophisticated to hire beginners or those right out of fashion school. Now that their company manufactures in Hong Kong, Pinky Wolman and Dianne Beaudry feel that traveling alone and dealing with patternmakers in a foreign country takes experience. On the other hand, a receptionist worked her way up and Pinky herself started as a seamstress.

Pearl Nipon of Albert Nipon hires entry level, often from local design schools, and she also takes on students as interns. "I have taken people from our six-month training program and given them permanent jobs." Lola, whom we'll read about in the "Assistant Designer" section, is one example. Like all employers Pearl Nipon requires a portfolio for design jobs. She also wants to see experience in all aspects of design. "I feel a good designer knows everything about a garment. He or she knows how to sew, how to make that first pattern, how to sketch it, how to drape it. If they don't know how to sew the garment, how are they going to direct the samplemaker? It's very important." And a final word of caution. "When a person comes to me and has been three months here and six months there they'll never get a job, because I see a person who doesn't have the tenacity to stick with something. There is a feeling that being temperamental is artistic. In an employment situation with a lot of people, that kind of temperament upsets things," Nipon concludes.

GEOFFREY BEENE

Geoffrey Beene was born in Haynesville, Louisiana, in 1927. At the age of sixteen, medicine was the career his parents had chosen for him. After three pre-med years and one year of medicine at Tulane University, he realized he did not have the proper dedication to be a doctor, dropped out—and while waiting to enroll in the University of Southern California he became fascinated with I. Magnin's windows, applied for and won a job in display. This lead to his meeting many notable persons who encouraged him to go to Paris to study. He studied there for two years and went from Paris to Seventh Avenue as an apprentice in several houses before inaugurating his own house twenty years ago.

Among his many career achievements, Beene is particularly proud of his role in awakening Europe to American fashion and the fact that we could make more than "blue jeans." His show in Milan in 1976 was a major breakthrough. Beene has twenty-three licensees, is well-known for his sense of privacy, rebellious nature, his Southern manner and accent, his trademark wardrobe of loose-fitting, soft sweatery clothing, his love of flowers and travel, and his constant fascination with the neutral color of grey.

What do you consider your hallmark?

My hallmark is identified by a certain movement in my clothes which comes from the cut and fabrication. I can often recognize my clothes from far away simply by their movement. The premise of every collection is comfort, and modernity is the concept. They are designed for a mobile society.

Many consider you more original and less constrained than other couture designers. Do you agree?

Perhaps, but the process of simplicity is a very complex one. I have tried for years and years through trial and error to arrive at seeming simplicity of style. Fabrics are the dictate of what a collection will be. Coloring, textures, and cuts simply define what they command. A constant awareness of the body is evident in my designs. I think the study of medicine, gross anatomy, and life drawing have been enormously helpful in my concept of clothing. Without this awareness, clothing is flat.

Is that where you see young people going wrong most?

Yes, no clothes have any true meaning unless they work with the body. I often encourage assistants, apprenticing in the studio, to take life drawing at night. A woman's body is round and voluptous. I require that my models try everything except handsprings to insure the clothes can move without any restriction.

What do you think is responsible for the flat approach? The schools?

Yes, the students are taught to design for mass markets, or they're reading "get-rich-quick" trade papers. I don't think individual creativity and expression is encouraged enough—too much sameness!

Is thinking differently from everyone else necessary for greatness in the field?

For a time, one can go along with the crowd during the learning process, but in the end, no one can achieve thinking like everyone else.

Has your view of fashion changed at all over the years?

Yes, I changed from constricted to soft clothing in 1973. On my first job, which I had for a few years, I designed what was demanded of me—little uptight dresses! I was fired when I started to express the freedom of my own style.

I doubt you have a typical day, but I'd like some idea what you do day-to-day in your job.

I'm a Virgo and fairly orderly and organized. I awaken at 5:30 each morning—which usually draws gasps from New Yorkers! If I don't get up early before I go to the office I have no time to think creatively. Once I arrive at business and the telephones start, my creative thinking is interrupted. The early morning, when I have time and privacy with my dachsunds, are the moments I cherish the most. I very often go to the flower market before arriving at work simply because I love flowers and I'm inspired by their coloration, symmetry and fragility. I arrive at work around eight o'clock and leave for lunch at noon. I don't indulge in business lunches; I don't think they aid digestion. Instead, I change my working environment. I have a car and driver—and usually escape to The Village or Soho or Yorkville. I have a light lunch, in the evening I dine well, usually out. By midnight, I'm in bed. I need very little sleep.

You do most of your actual conceptualizing of the line in the morning, then?

Yes. This last collection took almost five months from the design of fabrics to the completion of the collection. I design most of my own fabrics. I go to Europe to work with the mills in Italy and Lyons, Zurich, and London.

While you're working on fabrications, do you have a solid idea what shape the actual clothing will take?

Only vaguely. The fabric is the dictate.

Do you sketch?

Not well and I don't drape well either. If one has an idea and can verbalize, the draping and sketching can be delegated. People who feel strongly about ideas—idea people—should not have to go through a tedious four-year program of textbooks.

Back to the trial and error design process, you work closely with models?

Yes, they inspire! I have two assistants and one fitting model with whom I work very closely. There are roundtable discussions of directions and moods. It's a marvelous experience to bounce ideas off other creative people. The momentum is on the success of each design being good or bad. When it's good that energy goes into doing the next one. When it's bad, one sort of withdraws and gains one's confidence all over again. It's a day-to-day routine that takes about three months to complete.

What is your interaction with the licensees?

Maintaining quality and trying to take things a bit further than they would normally desire. It's a major job. I have two people in charge of the licensing operation. All the licensees need the input of fabrication. After that, we conceptualize. Some have their own design teams. Some don't.

What about licensing telephones? Have you designed them?

I did. I'm very involved in the visuals. It takes a long time to make molds and it's very costly. The new telephones arrive early 1984. The licensor brought in their technical designer and I worked with him a couple of months off and on. The instruments look handsome. My idea was that the telephone should be "at home" in its own environment—wood finished in the kitchen, malachite in the study, tortoise in the office, etc. Textures and colors of my ready-to-wear are prevalent in my telephones.

Are there any items that you'd like to license, you don't already have?

Maybe food. I have a certain knowledge and love of food that I could easily impart. I have over 450 cookbooks. The most logical food would have to be beans . . . GEOFFREY BEANS! No?

NORMA KAMALI

Quiet Success

Seductive, outlandish, daring, conspicuous, dramatic, theatrical, entrance-making, humorous. Apt adjectives for Norma Kamali's clothes. Coy, shy, quiet, retiscent, straight, business-minded. Adjectives for their creator, Norma Kamali.

Celebrities have been onto Kamali's outrageous couture gowns and bare cutout swimsuits since the mid-seventies. Diana Ross, Donna Summer, Raquel Welch in *Woman of the Year*, Yoko Ono at the Grammy Awards, Carly Simon on an album cover. Moreover, Kamali is credited with introducing hotpants in 1968.

Most of us, however, didn't pick up on Kamali until 1981 when she brought us "sweats," thirty-five bold items from skirts to jumpsuits and dresses fashioned from sweatshirt fabric. Sweats brought in $10 million that first year. Kamali's enormous success with sweats was due in part to the affordability of the garments, the result of a savvy 1980 licensing arrangement with the Jones Apparel Group. Since 1981, Kamali has signed agreements for children's sportswear, socks and tights, shoes, sneakers, and hats.

As her public knows, there is more to creative Kamali than sweats. She is also known for her sleeping-bag coats, her jumpsuits of parachute nylon, her short rah-rah skirts, her trademark 1940s shoulder pads, and her sense of humor. Devotees know Ethel Mertz, the wrap dress, and Fred Mertz, the baggy trousers with the shoulder straps. They know that when it comes to inventing new shapes for tired fabric, Kamali's king. Her "lane" pumps for Spring 1984 are black denim.

Norma Kamali won Coty Awards from the nation's fashion critics in 1981 and 1982, the Council of Fashion Designer's award for outstanding fashion design in women's wear in 1983, and was inducted, along with Ralph Lauren and Calvin Klein, into the Coty Hall of Fame the same year, a year in which her operation grossed $25 million, double 1982. In spring of 1984, Speigel, the powerful Chicago mail-order house, devoted an entire catalogue to the clothes of Norma Kamali.

For a successful designer, Kamali is markedly anti-establishment. Her showroom isn't on Seventh Avenue. She doesn't give fashion shows. She adds to couture collections at will, not at a season's whim. She decries fame as muddying the heretofore honest reactions of customers. She counts her store, where she still occasionally waits on customers and cares for a devoted, mostly female staff, the core of her business.

Norma Kamali was born Norma Arraez, is of Basque-Lebanese descent, and grew up on the Upper East Side of Manhattan, where her father ran a candy store. Kamali credits her mother, a housewife who made kicky costumes for the many neighborhood plays in which Norma participated, with inspiring her love of homemade clothes and of dressing up. In one scenario, Norma-the-schoolgirl is seen squeezing between desks wearing eight skirts, layered atop one another.

Norma Kamali wanted to be an artist, went to the Fashion Institute of Technology in illustration, graduated in 1964, and reluctantly took a reservation clerk's post at Northwest Orient Airlines. At 19, she married Eddie Kamali, an Iranian student. She also managed weekend jaunts to London, a job perk, where from 1964 to 1968 she fell passionately for the creative verve of the youth revolution, the Beatles, the Rolling Stones, King's Road and Carnaby Street. The crazy clothes she bought in London ended up filling the basement boutique on East 53rd Street that Norma and her husband opened in 1968. In 1974, they moved to splashier quarters on Madison Avenue. When 1978 rolled around, Norma and Eddie Kamali were divorced and Norma Kamali inaugurated her West 56th Street store, christened OMO for "On My Own." In December 1983, Kamali reached another plateau with the introduction of a fabulous new tri-level store, across the street on west 56th Street, where we're now chatting, early in 1984, in the store's angular concrete shoe department.

When did you become interested in design, in having your own style?

I had no idea this was something I would do when I grew up. I needed to fill my first store with clothes and I enjoyed making clothes and it just evolved from there. I think it evolved and grew because somebody actually bought something. My inspiration really came from a retail environment rather than design school or years of study under a famous designer in Paris.

Do you think, as many do, that retail experience is necessary?

I can only speak for myself. It's my way: understanding what people want, what the street is about, what's going on outside my little room. It really comes from out there and from people coming in and buying something or not buying something. That's how you find out everything about what you're doing. I don't think I could design without a retail store.

So, the street is your inspiration?

Absolutely. Everything that has to do with what's happening today: the politics, the economy, the people in your environment, what people are talking about and thinking about. If the economy is feeling tight its rude and offensive to give flamboyant clothes to the customer. I decided to do an affordable collection because sweatshirting felt more appealing to me than beaded gowns.

Diana Vreeland said you have a great deal of integrity and honesty. Do you know what she means?

I do. It's a great compliment because it's really something I believe is absolutely true. I think it's what makes me be me. There are times when I've made terrible mistakes, done horrible things I thought were great. They may be horrible but they're me and that makes them not so terrible. For me to do another designer's dress, that would be disgusting.

Does that also apply to young designers who walk in with portfolios that imitate the work of the designer they're approaching? Many designers say they're put off by it. Do you agree?

Yes. I used to think it was a terrible thing to do. People always send me work that looks exactly like something I did the season before and I think, Why is this person sending me this? But now I realize there is a stage a young designer has to go through and maybe its not so terrible to learn through someone else's experience as long as you don't claim it as your own. You don't have an identity yet but you know what you like and don't like. It's okay if you learn about cut and draping and merchandising and presentation through someone else. I didn't do it that way. I have this stubborn streak that wants to do it my way.

You talk about making mistakes. Can you give a specific example?

For every good thing you do, you make a couple mistakes before you really start evolving. I definitely had a strong feeling for brown a couple seasons ago. We sold brown in a smaller way to a select customer but I was jamming it down lots of people's throats and it was wrong. It's obviously going to be the thing next season.

Why did you go wrong with brown?

First of all, this business has to do with emotion, not with guns and killing people, but with making people happy. I feel it here. I feel it about people. I feel that way about everything. I feel what happened previously, what colors everyone's wearing, what direction will be next. And I felt brown.

Do you have assistants?

I have a lot of assistants but none of them are designers because that's what I want to do.

Do you hire from design schools?

This probably isn't very good for your book but I purposely hire people who aren't fashion people. Everybody here has a personal style but they're not fashiony. They're not in awe of me or fashion or this business.

How do you design?

Sometimes I drape, sometimes I sketch, sometimes I write words. As far as time put into it, it's hard to say because its seven things happening at once. I'll fit a top while I'm planning strategy for my swimwear and working on the store. It's everything at once.

Do your licensees have design teams?

I'm different because I design all the lines and I don't have an assistant doing that for me. The licensees have somebody who works with me. I'll give them all the things I want to make it happen, the sketches and all the specifications. I'll give them colors and I'll give them drawings or I'll find certain fabrics I want them to copy. For instance, with the shoes, I do all the drawings. If there's a certain stitching I saw in an old shoe and I want that stitching, I'll give them a sample of the stitching.

How many hours do you work in a day?

Last night I woke up in the middle of the night and I couldn't sleep and I started thinking about doing a shoe that would be really great. It's not that I wake up all the time like that but it's just a part of you. You don't say I'm going to work from this time to this time.

You have licensees, you have a couture collection, you have a store, and you manufacture and distribute your swimwear. Those are distinctly different businesses, aren't they?

Ummmhuh. They're very different, especially retail and manufacturing.

Well, I love the way your clothes are grouped here.

That's part of what retail is about. It's constantly re-merchandising stock and displaying it in as many ways as you can so people understand it from all points of view. When people are hired to work here they don't come unless they really want a career at it because you can't just stand and sell something. It has to do with the way you hang something. Even how far apart the hangers are. There are so many little subtleties.

Do you have these subtleties in mind when you're designing?

It's not up here but it's back here. There are certain things you design that are horrible on the hanger and they're wonderful on the body, so you have to try to use a different medium in showing the customer. How can the customer see how this really looks?

And who is this customer you're picturing? Are you picturing yourself?

I am.

It must make you feel good that who you are is somehow at the heart of so many people, no matter how shy or private you are otherwise.

I think I'm the average American woman. There are parts of me that relate to every woman around. I'm not a designer who's distant or away or looking at their women that they design for. There are a lot of movie star designers. I mean I think Calvin Klein is a movie star. He really has that appeal. Bill Blass, too. He's like Clark Gable. You know what I mean? There's a personality about them. And I'm not that way at all. I'm just one of everyone else which makes me comfortable.

So what gives you pleasure besides designing?

Oh, I have a lot of interests. In getting involved in doing this building I developed an incredible interest in architecture. I have a passion now for architecture. I've learned so much and I think there's a reason you learn a lot. I always have to use everything I learn and I know I want to use this and I want to do something with it and I don't know what but I can't stop buying architecture books. I'm starting something.

What about future plans? More retail stores? More licensees?

Doing lots of products isn't what my future is about. I'd love to do cosmetics. I have a feeling about what I want to do with that and I want to put a lot of energy in that in the future. And I think that retailing is so much a part of me. I'm not sure that it's more stores. It could be catalogues. It could be a new approach to retailing. Anything that gives me independence I love. Reaching the consumer independently, not through someone else's interpretation. Those are immediate goals.

BETSY JOHNSON

A DESIGNING MIND

"I don't care about clothes, I care about making clothes. Your designs should reek of you on the hanger whether or not your name is on the label. The only way to find out if you really have it as a designer is to make clothes for yourself and your friends and see how it feels to wear them. I would never work with anyone who didn't know how to make clothes.

"You have to know how to translate your ideas with your hands and with your mouth, not just with pen to paper. I've worked whole collections out in countries where I couldn't speak the language. The way my patternmaker and I see something are two different things. Go to the factories where they sew the clothes and really get to know production. For the sweater design work, my forte in the early seventies, I learned how those machines worked first. Success takes a willingness to work with anybody on any level. Twenty years later you're using the same button man. I still work with some of the same fabric houses and get fabric from the same places I got it from in high school.

"Since I was three my mother made my dancing costumes for me. I liked living in satin and sequins and fringe and feathers. In high school, I liked cheerleading costumes the best. So in 1964, while working at *Mademoiselle* magazine as a coffee girl/gal Friday with a sixty-two dollar take-home pay, I started making what I liked to wear: high-armholed, leotarded, funny little T-shirt kinds of stuff. Dancing clothes are history now but the whole glittery, rock and roll, oppy-boppy, dancing thing was just starting. There weren't any true blue comfortable clothes. I like wrinkled-up, worn, lived-in kinds of clothes. This is my favorite skirt. It's four years old.

"And your work totally depends on the type of life you lead. I try to keep a pretty healthy life going but it definitely has its ups and downs. Actual designing I do three

Hi-Low Dress
#62

nights a week. I have a drink, stay up all night, just wonder, and go crazy thinking. Just thinking till it gels. Today I happen to be working all day and all night because I'm just about to take my first vacation since my honeymoon two years ago."

BONNIE STRAUS

THE DESIGNING LIFE—CALIFORNIA-STYLE

"There's opportunity here in design, in production, in patternmaking. A lot of people who are tired of New York send résumés to me. But if I'm not sure someone really wants to stay with me, I won't ask them to move here.

"Creativity-wise it's wonderful. You have lots of designer-owned companies where people do everything. I started six years ago in California. I moved to California at nineteen after graduating Pratt in New York and ended up buying for Bullock's. Retail is the greatest experience for a designer. My husband and I opened up two smaller businesses first and finally this.

"I have eighteen employees ranging from a patternmaker, who interprets the garment from sketches, and a production patternmaker, to cutters who cut samples and those who cut for production. There are people in reception, sales, the showroom in New York, the showroom at the mart here, a representative in Texas, and a road person. Of course, we have a shipper, a packer, customer service. Entry level, I work with a local college to introduce students into the cutting area.

"Lifestyle for lifestyle, I wouldn't give up California. The industry's not as big as it is in New York, and it's wonderful for the person who wants to enjoy home and sun and people and doesn't need the craziness. Just try to find a salesman out here on a Friday during the summer, or after five. You have potential to make money, although my money would triple in New York because buyers come and go all the time, many more fabric lines are shown, you can wheel and deal more, and people always seem to have someone behind them—a business entity of some kind like Calvin Klein has Barry Schwartz. But I love California."

Assistant Designer

Like designers, assistant designers vary in approaches to their work, in responsibilities on the job, and in paths pursued into the industry. Salaries vary, too, although beginning assistants right out of school usually get from $225 to $300 a week and, after a year's experience, $275 to $400. Overall, an assistant designer is at the beck and call of a head designer. It is choice experience for those interested in working up to head designer or in starting a company. As for preparation, design school is your safest bet.

Carol Elliott is as typical an example as you'll find. For the past nine months she has been assistant designer for the year-old sportswear division of a well-respected and unusually large moderate-priced womenswear company with an annual volume of over $80 million. She landed the job after hearing about it from the chairperson of the fashion department at Parsons School of Design, from which she had graduated three months earlier.

She assists with four lines a year: Fall, Holiday, Spring, and Summer. Although the firm is on Seventh Avenue, items sell best in California, Florida, and Dallas. "Our

clothing is very American but not urban," says Elliott. "I know more people in Portland, Oregon, where I'm from, who know of the clothes than here. But in the market it's very respected. They know there's volume. And that's really good for an assistant designer."

It is Spring now and Elliott is working on next Spring. "My boss went to Europe and the Orient two to three months ago for two weeks to get ideas. She sets the colors but we do the research work. We contact color forecasting services like The Color Box and Color, Incorporated. We do a lot of legwork like finding garments on the market, going to color forecasters to see their presentations, and going to stores."

Every week there's a merchandising meeting where the line is presented as it progresses. As in other firms, the line is done in groups organized by fabric. Successful standard items such as T-shirts and jogging pants automatically carry over from the previous season. Elliott is included in the meetings, also attended by the president of the division, the president of the company, the head of production, the head designer, an illustrator (sketcher) who works on the presentation boards and showroom drawings, and a woman specializing in plaids and stripes for various fabrics. At twenty-two, Elliott is the youngest present. "My boss presents the line in the meetings and we basically take notes so we know what's going on. In the first meeting we set colors. We might discuss how much fabric we have to buy, and generally work out problems." Elliott's opinions are only occasionally solicited. "At times they say, Okay, Carol, would you wear that?' and I'll say 'No, it's too old-looking' or 'I'd never wear that!'"

Phone work is a huge part of her day. "I'm calling up fabric salesmen all the time. If we have our own colors by this time, I'm looking for fabric for sample lines to be shown to meetings and to manufacturers. We buy fabrics with colors approximating the tones we've chosen so they have an idea what we're up to."

Once the fabric comes in, the designs go to patternmakers and samplehands. "I advise on what color thread to use or what size elastic fits. I used to run out and buy whatever we ran out of but now we have a freelance girl in once a week."

Few design assistants, like designers, work exclusively on one line. "There are always two seasons overlapping, if not three, and on top of that we're doing lines for two separate divisions," she stresses. "I also prepare and update the presentation boards, making changes with the illustrator. I answer questions from samplehands, patternmakers, salespeople, and the warehouse in New Jersey. Maybe something came in wrong. Because my boss knows I draw quickly she'll give me an unreadable sketch or a photograph and I'll do the sketch. I get my boss coffee if I have to but then again, she gets me coffee sometimes too."

Elliott feels school definitely gave her technical background. "But phoning fabric salespeople you don't learn in school. I've started going to the knitting mills and working with the production man there. You don't learn that either. And seeing actual designs for the first time is incredibly exciting."

That thrill also exists for Lola, a twenty-five-year-old designer at Albert Nipon who worked up from an assistant's job. Her experience personifies the foot-in-the-door advice of experts. She studied fashion design at Drexel University in Philadelphia and did a sophomore year internship at Albert Nipon. "I came in and asked the production manager if I could sew. He said yes and I stayed three months." She's honest about the experience. "It was very boring. I did side seams, set pockets, set loops, set waistlines, stitched tucks. I did different things every day so when I went to the design room I'd understand."

As luck would have it, Pearl Nipon needed a gofer and Lola was it. "I sorted threads, did little sketches, was a dress model, checked buttons, straightened up, anything," she admits. An assistant's position opened and she won it. Lola makes a distinction quite a few assistant designers make. "I was more of a designer's assistant than an assistant designer," she says. "I was a gofer for the designer. I kept records, did a lot of organizing, ordered buttons for the duplicates, kept the room organized, and did patterns. My boss let me drape a lot. She'd fit the dress on the form and I'd make corrections on the pattern."

As a head designer now, Lola looks for patternmaking skills when she hires assistants. One of her two assistant designers has a patternmaking degree and three years experience as a patternmaker. In Lola's view, future designers go wrong in ignoring patternmaking skills. "It's a good idea to know the technical aspects of what makes up a dress," she says.

A patternmaking degree is an acceptable credential for an assistant design job. An assistant is often the one who makes the first pattern, although there can be a separate first patternmaker or the designer may make the first pattern. The first pattern is the first interpretation of the garment, used by samplemakers and duplicate makers. It reflects style. It is not to be confused with the final perfect pattern done by the production patternmaker that reflects style and fit.

The best way to land a job as an assistant is with a fashion school degree in design or patternmaking. In some cases one-year degrees will do and in others they won't. Some people have liberal arts degrees and tack on a year at a fashion school or experience in the industry. You also can't go wrong doing time as a salesperson in a department store during holidays, summers, or weekends. Understanding the bottom line is an asset.

Stylist/Fashion Coordinator

Styling or fashion coordinating means many things to many people. At the highest level, usually at a relatively sophisticated company, the job is much like that of a fashion director in a retail store. It is a fashion coordinator's job to help plan the line, give it direction, research trends, and develop concepts guaranteeing the line a strong and salable image. Knowledge of color, fabric, and fashion are important. A fashion coordinator/stylist might well meet with buyers, attend fashion shows, visit the market, work on advertising and promotion, and give guidance to or exchange ideas with a company president and designer. In a small company with a limited design staff a stylist may explain trends and design concepts directly to the president of the company, patternmaker, or production manager. By no means, however, do most apparel manufacturers have such people. Those that do—mostly large firms—often produce groups of clothing which need an overall frame.

Dorothy Roberts is president of Echo Scarfs. Referring to Shelley Pfeifer, her vice-president of fashion, Roberts remarks, "I get more letters and calls for her job than any other." Pfeifer comes up with color ideas, selects fabrics with other staff members, "designs" the line and lends its overall direction, follows through to production, and does slide presentations for salespeople. Pfeifer went from *Vogue* to Echo ten years ago.

Albert Nipon design

Melissa Feldman is the assistant fashion coordinator at Albert Nipon. She works out of the factory in Philadelphia alongside the design staffs. Her boss, the fashion coordinator, is considered Pearl Nipon's right hand. A high-level fashion coordinator or stylist anywhere is likely to be considered the head designer's or design director's right hand if not the company president's to boot.

Albert Nipon design

"I first started working here during two summers in high school," says Feldman. "I sorted buttons and zippers, ran errands, sorted fabrics. I was a gofer." She went to a liberal arts college and started showroom modeling part-time the summer of her senior year. At graduation, Pearl Nipon offered her a job that typifies the grab-bag flavor of styling jobs. "At first I didn't know what the job was, nor did she," confesses Feldman. "I followed her around doing whatever she told me to do. I helped different people whenever they needed it, from sorting buttons to helping at fashion shows to going on fashion shoots to swatching fabrics to doing the cutting tickets." When the fashion coordinator needed an assistant to concentrate on helping with fashion shows, Feldman was it.

"My main job is doing the fashion shows on the road," explains Feldman. "Stores out of town give benefit performances for local charities. I go to the town, run the rehearsal, instruct the choreographer, do the fittings, and assist with lighting. I have my own music. I do all the accessories: the jewelry, the hats, and the shoes."

Feldman considers taste the most critical tool for a budding fashion coordinator/ stylist. "You just have to have a judgment, a feeling. What's right for the company? What's right for the model? You have to have taste because at two o'clock in the morning you're asking yourself whether a burgundy or blue stocking is better and you better know. Not why it's better, just what is better. You can learn but not without something innate to start with. A design or merchandising degree helps but isn't essential. Start at the bottom in a fashion office in retailing or manufacturing."

Starting salary for an assistant like Feldman would be in the neighborhood of $250 a week.

Piece-Goods Buyer

Researching the market for ideas and trends in fabric and deciding which fabrics to buy is the domain of the fabric or piece-goods buyer. The buyer also gives direction to the designer, who probably has researched the area as well. As we saw at Bill Blass, it is the piece-goods buyer who lets Blass know certain of his designs take the department over budget. Naturally, the process of buying piece goods requires paperwork and patience. Orders go wrong, shipments are late, fabrics arrive damaged or off-color. A mismanaged fabric department can close a business overnight.

A piece-goods buyer usually starts as an assistant to a piece-goods-and-trim buyer, handles mostly detail work for the buyer, and earns $250 a week. With experience, however, a top-notch piece-goods buyer can earn $40,000 a year.

Because this job is really part design, part merchandising/buying, and part textiles, a background in any of those areas is suitable. Add on some ability to handle figures. You can, however, count on your personality as an asset in a job interview, especially if you're outgoing and challenged by the opportunity to negotiate.

Samplemaker

Samplehands or samplemakers make sample garments based on first patterns. A second group of employees, called duplicate makers, may make the duplicate samples. As Oscar de la Renta pointed out earlier, samplemaking is a dying craft. Samplehands are generally well-trained seamstresses from countries where sewing and related skills are a respected tradition.

Although designers cherish top quality samplehands, even fight over them, pay them $400 a week or more, and rely on them for advice on whether a design works or not, this job is not recommended to anyone interested in moving on and up.

Despite the existence of those who have used the job as a steppingstone to assistant designer, samplemaker was a more acceptable and frequent springboard years ago than it is now, when technical fashion education is readily available, making it possible, in a sense, to bypass this job.

Indeed, school, particularly continuing education courses at night, is what some samplemakers are taking advantage of in order to pick up skills in draping, sketching, and design in order to become drapers or assistant designers.

OCCASIONAL OCCUPATIONS

Draper

Draping is rarely a separate job. The head designer, assistant designer, or first patternmaker usually drape.

Sketcher

Bill Blass started as a sketcher. He'd probably have a tougher time of it today. Positions are few and far between save those at top-of-the-line superexpensive houses. If you are interested anyway, the job requires strong illustration background. At these handful of expensive houses, a sketcher may also sketch for the licensees: chocolate boxes, shoes, perfume bottles. Albert Nipon has an illustration department consisting of three young women. These illustrators sketch the line for record-keeping purposes only. They also cut fabric swatches for record keeping.

Sketcher isn't a direct steppingstone to any specific fashion job unless you acquire skills in school or on the job commensurate with the fashion job you want.

On the other hand, you may want to pursue a freelance fashion illustration career or a more general illustration career (for corporations, ad agencies, etc.). See chapter 15.

Fitting Model

Fitting models are usually a size 8 for samples. Some houses have a full-time model although most hire from agencies. It is their job to let the designer or other appropriate person know what the garment feels like. At Nipon, the model is a smaller size 6 and Pearl, also a 6, acts as model as well. Heidi Thorner acts as her own fitting model. Bill Blass, as we've noted, uses a fitting model, size 8, for the samples, and hires a duplicate model who is a size 10.

Models can move into other jobs. It can be a foot-in-the-door. One picked up costing years ago while a model. "I was their size 10," says Peggy Vaughn now costing clerk and sample coordinator at Albert Nipon. "You can be very, very busy doing that, but once the line is done you have nothing to do except sit around all day and wait for new dresses to come in and try them on and work with the patternmaker. It didn't occupy all of my time. I helped out in the costing office awhile. By doing that I became interested in costing and I liked it a lot."

Jack of All Trades

Alexander Julian called it an all-around-everything, most call it a gofer, and the category could fill volumes. Particularly in young companies the first couple of employees—sometimes family members or friends—almost always have a hand in everything down to writing orders, packing boxes, and shipping garments. They'll show lines to buyers and the fashion press, organize production schedules, work on costing. They may also help develop a marketing strategy and sit down with retailers to talk display. Should the opportunity pop up, taking a jack-of-all-trades job may be the best way to learn the ins and outs of a wide variety of positions and pin down your favorite, or even allow you to move up into administration.

Whether or not to take a gofer job calls for serious insight. If the company is young, and you think it's promising, it has a history of gofers gaining responsibility, or is a place where you could learn a lot, this job may be an excellent choice. If, on the other hand, the opportunity to become part of a growing organization isn't mentioned in an interview and doesn't seem likely to you, and gofer seems to be a rigid, established, dead-end low-rung slot, skip it. To a great extent, your choice depends on your respect for, interest in, knowledge of, and research on the company. And, of course, of yourself.

At new and very promising firms like Andrew Fezza and Rebecca Moses (chapter 10), jobs for all-around everythings panned out for those committed to the project just as they did at Alexander Julian. It's always a measured risk.

CHAPTER 5

APPAREL PRODUCTION

Production has an image problem. "When I came here I thought, Oh my God, it looks like a garment factory—a sweatshop," admits one production assistant. "This is not work where you have a nice pretty office. The people here aren't those types of people," allows a production manager. As the least glamorous of the fashion fields, production is easily overlooked by jobseekers. Too easily.

Production boasts stimulating and responsible jobs for production managers (and assistants), industrial engineers, costing engineers, and production patternmakers. Such jobs can be lucrative, all the way up the ladder to a vice-president of production title and a six-figure income. "Where else can you get sixteen to eighteen thousand dollars to start with a one- or two-year production management degree?" asked another production assistant.

There is ample room for advancement too. For instance, one shipping clerk advanced to apprentice spreader, then to apprentice cutter, cutter, and finally assistant production manager with complete responsibility for seven duplicate lines. A plant's rigid eight-hour-a-day schedule can be a plus as well.

The manufacturing or production of clothes is either done in a company's own factory or is contracted out to an independently owned plant. It is in these factories that the production process begins and ends. In a nutshell, fabric is removed from the bolts on which it arrives, stacked in layers, cut, and then sewn into clothing, under the supervision of a plant production manager. But let's look closer. First a *production patternmaker* makes one final perfect pattern based on the final designs or patterns. In some companies where designs are relatively standard the production patternmaker

can be the "designer" as well. A *grader* makes patterns for different sizes, and then a *marker* decides how patterns are placed on the fabric before cutting so that there is very little waste. It is the *cutters*, then, who cut through the piles of neatly stacked fabric. Finally, the cut fabric is delivered to *sewing machine operators* who stitch the garments together. After the garments are sewn together, they're shipped to stores.

Whether a factory employs thousands or under a hundred, is highly mechanical or not, it will more than likely be organized into separate departments. There will be a patternmaking department, a grading and marking department, a cutting department close by, a stitching or sewing area, a pressing area, and sections for shipping and stock. A production manager/plant manager runs the show with a variety of floor supervisors for specific operations. In some operations, usually larger ones, there may be separate industrial and costing engineers backed up by a junior engineer. In others, as we'll see, the production manager and/or assistant may take on their duties. Generating efficient methods of manufacturing is the bailiwick of the industrial engineer, who is often associated with time-motion studies and methods analyses. The costing engineer breaks down the various steps in the manufacture of a garment to determine its final cost. But as we've heard, no two organizations are exactly the same and titles can be hazy indicators of actual duties, which can vary enormously.

Two career strategies stand out in production. One is to grow up in a company town and/or in a family where working in a factory automatically leads to apprenticelike positions early on. Another is to earn a degree in apparel production management, industrial engineering, or patternmaking technology and begin at a higher level. The standard route to production manager is junior engineer, senior engineer, chief engineer, and then production manager. As one successful production manager wisely cautioned those contemplating sidestepping formal degrees, "If you don't have the education, you can't take full advantage of what comes your way."

Finally, two terribly important trends continue to affect those after jobs in manufacturing. First, the bad news. More and more manufacturing is being done overseas, primarily in Hong Kong where labor costs are far lower. As of 1982 41 percent of our clothing was produced elsewhere. This means plant closings and far fewer blue collar manufacturing positions. Now the good news. Shops are modernizing to include computer grading, marking, and patternmaking. Cutting departments are increasingly automated, as are pressing areas, with more innovations on the way. There's also the data processing area where invoices, payments, and orders, etc. are handled.

Production Manager

Sometimes called production engineer or plant manager, production manager is a responsible job. A production manager can earn $40,000 or more—more than the company's designer—depending on skill, experience, responsibility, and the company. In simple terms, the production manager oversees the whole shop, making sure the production process from patternmaking to cutting and sewing and shipping runs according to schedule. He or she hires employees and works out schedules. If a company carries out its early production operations out of its main administrative offices rather than at the factory, there may also be a production manager there to oversee production patternmaking, marking, grading, and the sending of final patterns to factories here or overseas. In the latter case, the production manager may go to Hong Kong or Singapore to coordinate production. At the highest level, a production manager is a vice-president of the company, involved in crucial administrative decisions especially those concerning modernization and the enormous budgets involved in purchasing high-tech equipment.

A production manager for a small plant describes the job like this: "I'm responsible for piece goods through cutting, sewing, folding, and packaging. I make sure, via department supervisors, that operators follow correct procedure. People report to me on quality and I make sure the machines are maintained. I do costing, based on time-motion studies and methods analyses, and try to eliminate inefficiency and bad habits that creep in. At a large company, I'd evaluate the studies of an industrial engineer and probably an independent consultant."

Production manager is not an entry-level job. The production manager quoted has a bachelor's degree in home economics, a subject which she proceeded to teach upon graduation. Then, while a receptionist for a childrenswear firm, she went to night school in production management/industrial engineering. She garnered a position as a junior industrial engineer, moved to senior industrial engineer, and then to production manager, a standard line of advancement.

However, the vice-president of production at Albert Nipon, Edwin Jesberger, oversees a much larger operation worthy of twenty-seven years of experience. His old-fashioned line of advancement, typical of many old-timers, was, as one cutter put it, "The school of hard knocks."

His background is that of a master tailor who began as an apprentice in Germany in 1938. "You did everything in those days . . . cleaning the shop, learning the machines, going to school at the same time." He oversees 220 sewing machine operators in this plant (there are 1,000 elsewhere), floor help, supervisors, mechanics, pressers, etc. Of sewing machine operators, he says, "There is no skill in this country. Sixty percent here are Portuguese and Chinese, some with forty years experience. We have a multilingual relay system to tell people what to do. We take young learners, but Americans are not interested. No American wants to sit down and sew." He also attends European trade shows devoted to new technology and is instrumental in decisions concerning automation.

A good production manager masters skills beyond the technological and organizational. People skills are important. You must be able to communicate with people who may not speak the language without being patronizing. It also helps to enjoy math and to have an ability to evaluate. Finally, you may be asked to relocate if your area has few or no factories.

Production Assistant

At twenty-six, Monica Howard is a combination production assistant, industrial engineer, and costing engineer. She is fully responsible for the time-motion studies and methods analyses often associated with an industrial engineer, the costing associated with a costing engineer, and the paperwork and scheduling generally associated with a production assistant. She is fortunate that her boss, with whom she works closely on costing, has been more than willing to show her the ropes. Although her situation isn't typical, she is proof that one's preference for a small (and less sophisticated) operation can result in increased responsibility and the opportunity to pick up the skills of several people in a large operation.

"A big part of my job is to break down all the individual operations," says Howard. "Seams, bottoms, tops, everything—and to set prices." In the main office, where Howard works, there is a chart for every single style the company features in the current line, with pictures, a number code, and fabric swatches. For each of those styles, Howard keeps careful track of every operation from cutting to sewing and bagging. "The charts show exactly where something is as we go along from belts to seams. We pay operators so much for each operation and there are four hundred pieces to be done, so we always know where we are. My assistant puts the sum total on the boards outside. There's a skirt board, pant board, and a board for anything special. When a garment's complete, we erase it from the board."

For time-motion studies and methods analyses, Howard uses special mathematical techniques to evaluate operations. "I try to determine the most efficient way to do anything. Is it efficient to pick up scissors twice? We want to eliminate handling. Handling is time and time is money." To cost a garment, Howard adds up individual costs for trim, fabric, labor, incidentals like assorting and supervisory operations, to come up with a figure. To that is added the company's percentage markup.

But it would be hard to close the book on Howard, or production management for that matter, without mentioning enthusiasm. Indeed, young production managers and assistants I spoke with appear to be an especially satisfied lot. Perhaps it's earning good money at a young age. Maybe it's the personal sense of responsibility or feeling relatively secure in one's chances for advancement. Whatever the reasons, there is an unmistakeably sincere care for the factory and its workers that was infectious to this observer. Should you manage to finagle a guided tour of a well-run garment factory, grab it. Production will not only no longer be a mystery but you may sense its appeal.

Howard begins her tour for me with the patternmaking department, eagerly showing how patterns are cut from cardboard with shears. "The cutting supervisor still uses paper patterns to make the markers by hand," says Howard. "He also grades the patterns." The cutting room, walls lined with paper patterns, is home to the spreaders who lay out the fabric. "Spreaders should also be on the lookout for flaws," adds Howard. Nearby cutters slice through the layers of fabric. The assorting area has women at a long table gathering and bundling the pieces. On each bundle goes the bundle ticket that sewing machine operators tear off to keep tabs on pieces completed. A piece-work payroll person collects tickets daily.

"Angelina's a topstitch girl," says Howard, pointing out one of her operators. "Because it's a piece-work shop, we try to keep them on one thing, otherwise they don't develop speed." Table one does sample skirts and seams. Two does bottoms (pants).

There are sewers adept at linings, setting on waistbands or zippers. At the jacket table, there are those skilled at pocket flaps, others at jacket seams, facings, linings, or topstitching. At the fourth table, sewers use the multineedle machine for shirred waists, and a fifth table of operators hem bottoms and make buttonholes. Pressers are busy pressing seams open after they've been sewn. Cleaners and examiners clean and check racks of skirts and jackets for obvious flaws. Off to the left, a row of men press garments before they're put on hangers. Here, too, one man does the legs, another cummerbunds. One man runs the old-fashioned bagging machine which drops plastic bags over assembled outfits. In a huge area removed from production, garments are packed in boxes and readied for shipment.

Production assistant or assistant production manager is an entry-level job leading to production manager or plant manager. Today, hiring can depend on a technical degree in production management or industrial engineering. Howard's two-year degree in apparel production management from the Fashion Institute of Technology in New York included courses in data processing, costing, patternmaking, cutting, sewing, pressing, and marketing. The same degree can lead to entry-level jobs as a junior industrial engineer or even costing engineer. As we've seen all along, the scope of a production assistant's duties can vary depending on an operation's size, complexity, and extent of automation. Some companies distinguish between a workflow-oriented production assistant, like Howard, and an assistant production manager who's more of a hands-on assistant to a plant manager with duties concerning day-to-day operations of the plant itself.

A final word of encouragement for women contemplating this largely male field. "There's a shortage of engineers and they're still mostly male," says Howard. "For a female, this is a fabulous field. You can get fifteen thousand dollars to start as a junior engineer. Traditionally, women are sales clerks in retail. But women are the ones who buy the clothes. If you wonder why you pay eighty dollars for a shirt, this is where you find out. The next step for me is to own my own place."

Production Patternmaker

"The designer is concerned with the styling of a garment. The patternmaker is concerned with making the design work. A skilled and experienced patternmaker will know how a garment is put together, have an educated eye for line placement, and an understanding of all the components which are to be considered in order to bring the garment out within the price range of the manufacturer," says Phyllis R. Brodsky, Chairman of the Patternmaking Technology Department at the Fashion Institute of Technology in New York.

What exactly does a patternmaker do? In simple terms, a production patternmaker, as distinct from a first patternmaker on a design staff, makes the final or "perfect" pattern based on final approval of the designs. A perfect pattern is what the production staff at the factory relies on to make the clothes.

However unheralded elsewhere, a patternmaker's importance to an apparel company can't possibly be overestimated. A mistake in a production pattern can cost the company big bucks. Just imagine the consequences of ill-fitting garments hitting the stores. This is why experienced production patternmakers can earn as much as $800 to $1,000 a week.

Production patternmakers may end up working in different settings depending on a company's size and structure. In a small operation, like Howard's in the previous section, the production patternmaker may also do the marking and grading. Others like those at Calvin Klein Jeans, work closely with the designer and design staff in a location separate from the factory, and send the perfect patterns off to the factory overseas. Others may work at the factory itself. In some companies, there may not be a design staff at all. An owner may relay changes in style directly to the production patternmaker. In other situations, often smaller operations, the production manager may be the patternmaker.

Because patternmaking is a highly technical skill, there are relatively established ways to break in. The best way these days is through training at a good fashion school. Another is to apprentice yourself to a master patternmaker. As you might expect, examples of the latter are rare.

Entry-level positions that can lead to production patternmaker include assistant patternmaker, assistant designer, grader, marker maker, sample cutter, duplicate makers, and production assistant.

When it comes to advancement, a top-notch patternmaker may stand to become a production manager. Still others have become designers. If you're aiming for a design or an assistant design job, a patternmaking degree is a far less common route than a design degree, but you still stand a solid chance of breaking in.

Be forewarned: Computerized patternmaking is here. Keep an eye peeled for opportunities to pick up the skill. Check local schools.

Costing Clerk/Costing Engineer

A costing engineer cares about the cost of manufacturing. Peggy Vaughn is the former Albert Nipon fitting model who currently works as part production sample coordinator and part costing clerk. In the latter capacity, she does what costing engineers do elsewhere. "I total costs of all the fabrics, buttons, belts, labor, freight, and anything else that goes into the cost of a garment," says Vaughn. "I come up with figures and then I know what the retail price of your dress will be."

Knowledge of costing goes hand in hand with knowledge of production. We've noted a production manager and assistant involved in costing. Looking at it in reverse,

Vaughn stresses that costing leads to other areas of involvement because you're so involved with the original line.

For starters, take business courses in college, or later on to supplement your education. Liking math helps and a willingness to go into computers isn't a bad idea either. "Everything will be done on a computer so you have to be interested in that area. We computerized marking a while back. It's the future of this industry, I'm sure," warns Vaughn.

With the proper technical degrees, costing engineer can be an entry-level job. Otherwise, a costing department gofer may be your first job. Vaughn's assistant came in doing whatever was needed. She fetched and she ran and she fetched. Now she's keeping records of costs. She records every button that comes in so when it's time to cost the line her boss is ready to start. You recall Vaughn picked up costing while working as a fitting model. Howard picked it up on the job. Keep your eyes and ears open. A gofer can go far with the right attitude.

CHAPTER 6

APPAREL AD-MINISTRATION AND SALES

President

Administration and sales jobs comprise the business end of apparel manufacturing. They include the bottom line—and the top line—jobs. Administration includes a company's president and its vice presidents, often of marketing, merchandising, and/or production. Sales positions run from a national sales manager to regional and district managers and the sales force.

Let's start with characteristics industry leaders cite as keys to their own success. All top administrators mention leadership ability. This includes the ability to make important decisions, to troubleshoot on a daily basis, and to head up a team operation. Team size, structure, and hierarchy can vary enormously from company to company.

The team at the helm may feature the vice-presidents of any number of divisions such as sportswear, activewear, childrenswear, etc.; a national sales manager; and merchandising manager. Then again, a president of a tinier operation may simply go on input from individual salespeople, a small design staff, and production manager or even the production patternmaker. Administrators tend to put in long hours and to feel they "paid their dues" for the sometimes dubious honor of holding forth at the helm. Indeed, many started at the bottom. Alexander Julian said success has something to do with sticking with it, working hard, and, he assures us, luck. Colombe Nicholas considered people skills the key. "Treat people you work with as equals. You are not above anyone" is her motto. Top executives should be standouts in politeness, pleasantness, and personality. For Jhane Barnes, the designer who runs her own company, success has to do with a willingness to take risks. "You've got to be willing to take a chance and to be scared," she says. "And the thing is that a lot of people aren't." Others cite being able to cope with rejection and failure, to pick up the pieces and dive in again. Being in the right place at the right time or, moreaccurately, the ability to recognize and seize opportunity crops up, too. And for Jay Margolis, president of Ron Chereskin, a well-known sportswear company, getting there falls to those who "keep their eyes open." This ambiguous yet crucial quality means not being narrowminded. It suggests leading as well-rounded a life as possible. Travel if you can. Read. Maintain an intelligent perspective. As one company president quipped, "It certainly helps if you can think." These characteristics crop up in any gathering of top-notch managers. They're hardly the private domain of apparel manufacturing.

It would be folly to suggest a step-by-step strategy to a president's job. If one were forced to devise a "standard" approach, it might call for starting out as a trainee or assistant in sales or merchandising and working your way up. Jay Margolis took the merchandising route. However, he came to his first job, as an $8,500-a-year assistant merchandise manager, by absolute accident. He was playing basketball at a friend's house when his friend pooh-poohed a scheduled job interview at

Jay Margolis (l) with Ron Chereskin, the designer

an apparel company. Margolis went "for the hell of it." By his own admission, chances are he might otherwise be teaching high school. After assistant merchandise manager, he became associate manager, merchandise manager for the sportswear division of another company, president of one American licensee of a major European company, and finally president of Ron Chereskin.

The sales route begins with a job as a trainee in a showroom or in showroom sales. You theoretically then go into sales, become sales manager, then vice-president of a division, then president. You may also be able to progress via a retail training program. To judge by the media, the design route would appear the most popular path to the peak. For more on this route, take a look at chapter 10 on starting your own design business. None of these routes, you must remember, can be considered typical, fool-proof, or even blindly recommended. They are merely relatively common.

Educational routes can't be dictated either, although many executives are willing to suggest getting a solid business education and accumulating retail experience by way of summer jobs. College, as you might guess, is a must. Liberal arts degress abound, sometimes bolstered by business courses. Major subjects run from English and history to science and foreign language. Merchandising and marketing degrees come up somewhat less frequently. Some presidents do have MBAs and law degrees, although they claim advanced degrees to be neither demanded nor solicited in hiring. Advanced degrees certainly can't hurt, but experts will be glad to tell you that fancy degrees will never replace paying your dues and on-the-job experience. The goal, however you go about it, is to learn the business.

From designer and company president, Carol Horn: "I think it is very important to be a business person also. That's reality. It's reality to know who your customer is, what price range you're in, and what price your fabrics should be. You have to know how to make your clothes come out to the right price and how to make sure they're available. That's reality." Echoes Oscar de la Renta: "I'm tremendously involved in the business part of it. A great deal of my work has to do with promotion and licensing. There are a million things in business."

The job of a company president is to use his or her expertise in business to direct the company. This demands nothing more or less than a profitable and marketable product. Indeed, when Margolis was asked his favorite part of his job, he replied, "Product. Developing it, looking for new, different, marketable approaches so we can develop business. I enjoy seeing the big picture, finding a new niche, and then generating business. Like neckwear. I saw a niche and I knew we had a business."

Concern with product usually means a lead role in finalizing the line. Remember merchandise meetings in the design section of chapter 4? A president should enter a merchandise meeting armed with information from the widest possible range of sources. Primary sources include salespeople, who constantly fill him or her in on what people and stores do and don't want. He or she solicits information from merchandising, marketing, retailers, and customers. The president of one accessories company telexed his design studio after discovering, on a visit to a Texas store, that six shoppers loved a particular piece of jewelry which hadn't been included in the upcoming line. His instructions: Add the design to the line immediately! Similarly, the president of a menswear firm, after being told via his salespeople that the stores were looking for a certain jacket vent, ordered it be done. Indeed, some companies do not have a design staff, and a president/owner will feed design changes directly to production.

Because the buck stops with a president, the other half of a profitable product—profits—are his or her ultimate interest. For instance, when a president hires directly, it is no accident that he or she's more likely to hire the manager in sales, merchandising, marketing, or advertising than in design or production. Day-to-day routines involve constant attention to selling the product: meetings with salespeople, feedback from buyers and retailers (some in person), and some travel. Jay Margolis spends about four months traveling in Europe, Hong Kong, and elsewhere. "You know, our clothes are now in Harrods in London and Galeries Lafayette in Paris," he boasts of his many trips to retailers. To market the product, he works on promotions, advertising campaigns, may hire public relations and publicity people, and will involve himself with the presentation of the product in the stores. Poor presentation is something no decent apparel company president can stand.

A president bears the burden of top troubleshooter. For this reason, the skills of a diplomat and negotiator may just be a president's ace in the hole. Admits Carol Horn, "I constantly listen to people's complaints and solve problems that go on." Says a division president of another womenswear company, "Being president is a reactionary job. It is my job to react to the problems a large business generates. There are fabric problems, problems at the mills, production problems, delivery problems, problems with scheduling, allocations, projections."

ALBERT NIPON
CHAIRMAN

ALBERT NIPON, INC.

"I think the people who are successful in this business enjoy getting up in the morning, going to their jobs, and doing their work. There's constant exposure, constant excitement, constant newness, and constant pressure.

"My normal day starts at seven or seven-thirty and runs twelve to fourteen hours. It's been that way for almost thirty years. Even if I come to New York, I'll try to stop in the factory in Philadelphia first between seven and eight to touch base with a few people there.

"I always start out going through the mill, telling my secretary about appointments, making calls. Invariably I meet with all department heads in the company, my controller, my credit manager, my production heads, and my shipping heads. Then I'll be up in the design room with Pearl. Intermittently I'm speaking with customers. You just never know.

"Then I come in here [New York] and make contact with our customers and our sales staffs. Intermittent things always come in. That's why I like my desk clean when I leave at the end of the day because the next day I don't know what will be there—but I know it will be a lot.

"Because the business entails a lot of travel, I never found a great need for vacations. A two-or three-day weekend at home is like a vacation because half the year we are away on weekends at market or shows. Since a lot of my family is in the business, being together makes it enjoyable whether I'm working or not."

Vice-President

Depending on the size, structure, and philosophy of a company and its chief executives, the vice-president title can mean a variety of things. In some cases, a vice-president runs a division of the company. In others, the title goes to an employee with a longstanding track record. A production manager, for instance, may become a vice-president of the company. Maxine Forman, is a senior vice-president in merchandising (see page 68). Important in considering vice-presidents is that they are people that presidents want in their policy-making circles.

Anne Cole is executive vice-president of Cole of California, a prominent swimwear company. Of the job, Cole concludes "My job is achievable if you are willing to work. I think the main problem with young people I see is they want a lot of money early on and don't work for the result. But now is the right time for anyone who really wants to achieve. I would recommend some liberal arts, some fashion school, and some travel abroad. I talked to one recent art school graduate and I said 'Get yourself to New York, take yourself to Europe, somehow find out what the world is all about.' You're talking about being a big career person when you're talking about a vice-president's job. You can't be a big career person and be narrow. You've got to expand constantly."

Merchandiser

If I were to compile a list of jobs I wish more jobseekers knew about, this one would rank up there with production manager. It is not by any means an entry-level job, but there are starting assistants' positions as well as sales trainee jobs. In my view, it is certainly a job worth aspiring to. What makes a merchandiser's job so exciting is that it is one of the few jobs that blatantly combines the creative and business ends. Unlike the job of fashion coordinator on a design staff, it involves a heavier dose of bottom-line responsibility and marketing savvy. It is also of interest because it is one of the rare positions demanding a strong interest in and knowledge of fashion itself. Luckily for the merchandiser, he or she must know what the trend-setters are up to.

The word "merchandising" is defined in one dictionary as "sales promotion as a comprehensive function including market research, development of new products, coordination of manufacture and marketing, and effective advertising and selling." What a hodgepodge. Well, in a sense, merchandising is just that. A good merchandiser has a hand in every pot, including determining current trends and keeping tabs on all the sources of new ideas we've discussed—from visiting the market to observing the economy to checking out what we're wearing on the streets. A merchandiser feeds information to the design staff. He or she, as you recall, is present at merchandising meetings in which the line is discussed and whittled down. A successful merchandiser must know production well enough to price a garment. How else does he or she know whether or not it's feasible? A merchandiser is a key member of the company policy-making group and considers ideas for promotions, advertising, and retail displays.

At Cole of California, like many companies with merchandisers, there is a merchandiser for each division. "Merchandising is the coordinator for the whole effort today," insists Anne Cole. "It's a very important job and a big career. The merchandise manager puts the entire line together. That doesn't mean designing it but rather bringing it together and discussing concepts with the designer. What is the focus and philosophy going to be? In my own personal collection I know I want it to be individual bathing suits expressing either a lifestyle or a type of person. For me, style is a personality thing. We have regimental stripes for the tailored person. We have novelty stripes for the fun person. We even have cashmere for the outlandish person. By no means is every line merchandised in the same manner. In the Cole line, the company's general line, we think quite differently because the line represents a larger audience. So we focus on fabrication. We take a group of fashion knits and we do that as the active look. The 'after five' look will be more glitzy stuff like sequins. Sedate prints go for the average woman who isn't looking for anything wild and crazy."

When Anne Cole hires a merchandiser, she looks for "taste, style, and an eye." "No specific experience in the business is necessary," she says. "You can learn from retail and you can learn from the wholesale operation. I would never let anyone merchandise without some kind of sales experience. I would send her out to the showrooms and let her deal with the product and see what it looks like from a customer's standpoint. You can say, 'I like it or I don't like it,' but to perceive it through the eyes of your customer is to really know it. We also like to find people in retail, because we think they have the experience of looking at merchandise and knowing the difference between something ugly and pretty. They have a taste level so they can bring out the best in the product and aim it toward the customer with some degree of appeal."

In reality, Cole's merchandisers, as those elsewhere, hail from diverse backgrounds. At Cole, one came from sales. (This route often begins in the showroom or as a sales trainee.) Another worked behind the scenes at a competitive swimwear firm. Another merchandise manager started as a gofer in the design room.

The most sought-after entry-level precursor to merchandiser is assistant merchandise manager or merchandising assistant. One merchandising executive with an apparel firm hits the nail on the head when she says she looks for someone who can handle detail work. "There is an enormous amount of detail work," she reiterates. "We make master boards and the amount of information that goes on these boards is staggering. The kind of button that is going on, the kind of stitching, the color of the thread. When you start to add up a hundred and sixty garments in a line and each one may come in three colors, the amount of work that goes into each board is really enormous." Her assistants also shop the stores. "I'll find out whether or not [a garment is] selling," says the executive. "But they should be aware of which looks are happening." And she continues, "I also expect them to read fashion magazines. I basically try to give them as much information as possible so when we all sit down and talk they can make smart judgments. It sounds silly, but believe me, in just discussing a blouse collar you can get crazy.

"I also let my immediate assistant go out and do trunk shows (fashion shows in stores) for me and she calls salesmen every week to find out what is and isn't selling. If something isn't selling, maybe it isn't selling just in North Carolina because the sleeve is too long or the neck too high. But maybe it's not selling in North Carolina,

California, and one other state and I have a bummer on my hands. So my assistant tries to understand why something is good as well as why it is bad. She also follows up with the buying offices and does follow-up everywhere."

The executive says she chose her assistant because she was dedicated, interested, caring, able to listen, bright, and inquisitive.

One popular way to prepare for a first job as a merchandising assistant is with a retail training program preceded by a degree in liberal arts, merchandising, marketing, or buying. Our expert believes her program at a top store paved the way for her flourishing future. "It's opened doors to me and I've been able to grow like crazy. If I were starting off again, that's exactly how I would start."

Maxine Forman, another high-ranking female apparel executive, entered a training program at Bloomingdale's, after a liberal arts degree (English). She moved on to assistant buyer (handbags), then to Macy's corporate office as an associate buyer (robes and daywear), became a buyer for a chain of twenty-four stores in the South and West, moved into merchandising for a fiber company, and then into fiber sales. It was as a fiber salesperson—the first, and at the time the only, woman selling for the company—that she met her current employer and was offered a key merchandising position. Forman is currently senior vice-president of merchandising for a $120 million division of a $227 million company. On the following pages she describes her job.

Maxine Forman

SENIOR VICE-PRESIDENT, MERCHANDISING

RUSS DIVISION, RUSS TOGS, INC.

"When I arrived here, the company was exclusively producing double knits for main floor departments. While our sales were solid, they were static, and the main floor industry was, as a whole, suffering.

"After exhaustively studying the marketplace, we came to an important conclusion. Growth potential for the kinds of styling, designs and fabrications the company had been producing was severely limited. What we saw as our challenge was to produce a new type of main floor line, one that would appeal to the tastes of contemporary working women, that would offer them the kinds of designs they wanted, yet at prices they could afford.

"Our first move was to upgrade the line through color, use of different fabrics, and more fashionable styling. Next came what was perhaps our most important decision: to introduce a group of wovens, using a blend of synthetics and natural fibers. The initial reaction of buyers was excellent, so much so that we had to purchase additional materials just to satisfy the orders we'd booked. Then, when the clothes finally hit retail stores, they all but flew off the hangers.

"We did what we believed in, and were proved right. Just because a woman has a limited budget doesn't mean she should be forced to dress unfashionably. We work very hard to make certain that doesn't occur by offering the most up-to-date contemporary styles, and selling them at prices most women can afford.

"That's the key to merchandising—knowing what your customer wants, and then giving it to her at a price she can afford. As head of the team which produces our lines, I'm personally involved in everything from the selection of fabric, colors, and designs to volume projections and production quantities. Working with an unbeatable team, I put my experience, knowledge, taste, and marketing instincts on the line every day. I'm committed to producing the finest, most affordable contemporary women's clothing possible.

"Assemble and back a collection you believe in, that's based on a sound knowledge of the look your customers are after, and chances are it'll perform well in the marketplace."

SALES

Sales is a field with tremendous potential. Sales experience is an asset to any fashion career and crucial if you're out for an executive position or to start your own company. On the other hand, sales is a perfectly satisfying career in itself, perhaps because the financial rewards can be sufficient—if not overly sufficient.

Sales offers several options. You can work in showroom sales, presenting the line to buyers in the company showroom. Most companies have a showroom in New York City and in many or all of the apparel marts that have sprung up in urban areas like

Los Angeles, Dallas, and Chicago. Second, you can also work in road sales, traveling assigned regions and selling directly to stores. Finally, you may end up as an independent sales representative, or "sales rep," independently handling anywhere from one to a dozen or more lines in a specific geographic region. Beginners in showroom or road sales usually start in the showroom as an assistant or sales trainee, earning in the $15,000 range. It's the prospect of fat commissions down the line that attracts jobseekers in droves. Commissions, of course, depend on your skill, the company, and its product.

Running the whole show is a sales manager. If a company has several divisions, each will most likely have a sales manager under the guidance of a national sales manager and several regional managers. In other cases, depending on the size and philosophy of an operation, the owner and/or president of the company will do the work himself.

In chatting with salespeople and industry leaders about sales careers, one point surfaces again and again. The mere mention of "salesperson" brings personality traits immediately to mind. "Outgoing" is mentioned most often, followed by "personable," "charming," "aggressive," and "the type who doesn't mind smiling all the time." One employer cites "a certain aloofness, a sense of timing, and an ability to listen." One successful rep says his key is "perseverance, and an ability to be convincing in a nonpushy way." He also thinks the most important personality trait for a salesperson is an ability to be diplomatic. To yet another employer, sales requires instinct and intuition, organization and impeccable appearance.

To salespeople, however, the key ingredient is product. Whether budget men's suits or sexy jumpsuits, successful salespeople claim little would be possible without their personal beliefs in their individual products. "They must be totally into clothes of this nature," says Gene Ewing, who heads up her own $24 million California-based womenswear company. "If they weren't, how could they put in the hours or handle the customers?" Ewing receives as many applications for sales jobs as she does for those in design. She has four salespeople in New York and two in Los Angeles.

Although employers are open to outstanding candidates, whatever their backgrounds, you're better off stacking the deck in your favor with at least an undergraduate degree. And more and more salespeople are walking in with advanced degrees. One administrator likes at least a liberal arts degree, if not an advanced degree, because he feels it gives a salesperson more tools to work with—such as a wider range of subjects to chat about with a high-powered customer, particularly when selling over dinner and a show. Another point about sales is that many companies seem to enjoy promoting from within, so that one finds many salespeople and sales managers who began as assistants.

To be fair to those without formal educations, several administrators report hiring young assistants they describe as self-taught. Moreover, sales ranks include former housewives, receptionists, administrative assistants, gofers of all bents, models, merchandising and design assistants, teachers, and buyers. The list is virtually endless.

Showroom Sales

An initial stint in the showroom, often as an assistant or as part of a training program, is considered the backbone of a sales career. A typical showroom includes a showroom manager and a staff of salespeople who present the line to buyers and write the orders. Indeed, everyone in this chapter (including administrators) has done time, one way or another, as a showroom salesperson. Anne Cole insists on it for merchandisers. Chantal White, who was on the road showing Betsey Johnson's latest line in a California hotel room, put it this way: "To be in sales, unfortunately you have to get a job in a showroom fetching coffee—hanging out. There's one person I know who started out doing this as part of a work-study program in college and now she's in sales a little earlier than she might have been, but she did it just the same." A showroom assistant or sales trainee can expect to learn the ropes, from taking inventory to writing orders, keeping the showroom organized, showing the line in a pinch, and doing a range of follow-up phone and paperwork. Pay for assistants is in the $250-a-week range.

One sharp former receptionist I spoke with pressured her boss long and hard enough to reap a showroom manager's job. Like most managers, she made sure samples were in-house, appointments intact, and models and magazines just so.

She recently attained the more lucrative position of showroom salesperson, where her experience to date reflects that of her colleagues elsewhere. She's charged with three major accounts (three major department store chains). The job promises two main responsibilities: servicing their buyers and servicing the stores themselves. Servicing one's accounts includes a good deal more than showing the line to the buyers, filling out orders, and sending them off to the factory. Some salespeople may take the time to wine and dine buyers and/or retail executives to win an account in the first place. Our newly promoted salesperson tries to make sure her merchandise moves out of the stores. In order to do that, she visits every branch once a month, which adds up to eighteen stores in all. She even counts stock when she's visiting the stores and tries to convince buyers to write fill-in orders. She speaks to department managers to make sure her merchandise is presented so as to catch a customer's eye. As we've seen, salespeople also give crucial input to merchandisers, administrators, and designers on what is and isn't selling.

Road Sales

Road sales is a field in flux. Time was when the road salesperson did just what the title indicates. He packed his company's line in his car and traveled store to store.

Admits Bill Borenstein, a thirteen-year road sales veteran, "The day of the traveling salesman is coming to an end. It's too expensive and time-consuming and inefficient to keep someone on the road. The smaller stores know if they want your merchandise they can go to the nearest mart, and the major buyers are in New York." Indeed now that apparel concerns have showrooms in the apparel marts across the nation, road salespeople can save time and energy by presenting their lines to buyers from a single convenient location rather than travel store to store.

There are several other ways a roadperson displays his or her wares. One is by opening an office in his or her region and enticing buyers to visit there. Another is showing the line from a centrally located hotel room. Borenstein does this in Washington, D.C. That's what Chantal White was doing in the California hotel room with Betsey Johnson's line. "The big stores get you in New York," she reiterates. "Principally we come for the specialty stores on the West Coast. We want to build a clientele among them."

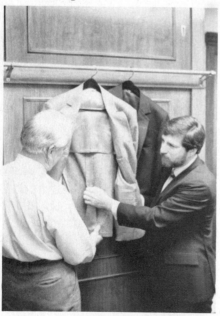

Finally, a roadperson is capable of negotiating a wide range of financial arrangements with an apparel company. He or she may work on straight salary, on salary against commission, on commission or on a dozen variations in between.

Bill Borenstein took the tried-and-true route to road sales, beginning with a sales training program with a large, reputable manufacturer. After a brief stint for a menswear company in showroom sales, a territory opened up at another menswear company and he moved into road sales.

The president of this company opts for a unique setup featuring twelve high-caliber salespeople who often function as national managers of sorts with great leeway to resolve problems themselves. "When he hires you, he expects you to know what you're doing," Borenstein emphasizes. What Borenstein does, beyond showing the line, is feed the president crucial information on what's selling, what isn't taking off, and how production can facilitate changes to generate sales. "The smartest way to sell is to convey information to piece goods and production so you get the right thing to the customer," he stresses. A few years ago Borenstein discovered in his travels that leisure suits were going like hotcakes. He wired an SOS to the factory, via his boss, to shift gears immediately or the company stood to lose its shirt.

Currently, Borenstein handles the territory from New York to Virginia with accounts numbering over 200 and an income that puts him at the top of his field. But its the getting there that novices must heed. "When I started thirteen years ago, I first took our swatches and samples and drove to Atlantic City," he recalls. "I started at the north end and walked into every store until I reached the south end. In every one I said something like, 'How do you do? I'm Bill Borenstein and I want to show you what we make.' I opened my first account about halfway down the strip and landed three by the end of the day." He adds this postscript: "At one I was turned down for credit. Another burnt down and the third still buys from me today."

For this roadman, like the sales rep in the forthcoming section, the key issue for the successful salesman is longevity. "An excellent salesperson can sell anybody once," Borenstein says. "But we want to sell for many years." Borenstein feels confident this requires the type of person who can develop quick and lasting relationships. "You have to be able to establish relationships and gain someone's confidence fast," he concludes.

Independent Sales Representative or "Sales Rep"

Independent sales reps are self-employed individuals, with or without a staff of assistants, who are hired to sell a company's line. A rep is hired when an apparel company doesn't have sufficient sales coverage in a specific part of the country to supplement a company's staff. A rep usually lives in the region he or she represents.

Repping is one of the most attractive options for those preferring autonomy, freedom, and a flexible schedule. "My lifestyle comes first," said one sales rep. "I wouldn't work for people I don't like." Indeed, the joy of repping, once you're established, is the pleasure of picking and choosing the lines you represent. Some rep only one line, either because it generates enough business by itself and/or because the company insists the rep handle its line exclusively. Borenstein is technically a rep who handles one company's line. No company allows a rep to handle competitive lines.

One California rep in his late thirties lives in Los Angeles. He enjoys an office in the California Apparel Mart, relaxed hours, international travel, and a lineup of clients he admires for their "high quality." But going out on one's own is rarely a smart risk without years of experience and solid contacts, especially among buyers.

For eleven years, our rep held a variety of staff jobs in his family's menswear businesses. "I swept, sold, dealt with fabric, was vice-president of a company, everything," he says. He opted for repping, he says, because he saw he was good at selling. He has been on his own eleven years. A company hit him with an offer to represent them in the thirteen western states and he chose to give it a go because he "related to the owner." He was contracted exclusively to them.

The company had never had a California rep, and he had the make-it or break-it opportunity to knock on the rarefied doors of finer stores in the region and attempt to strike up longstanding relationships. He succeeded and in 1978 became a fully independent rep handling five menswear companies, each run by talented young designers he says he "believes in."

In a typical day our rep splits his time between giving in-person presentations and sales-related phone calls. Phone smarts are a big part of success on the sales job. "As time goes on," he says, "you develop a sales presence on the phone. You have to learn to be smart enough not to be a nudge but you also have to be persistent." Rude encounters with reluctant retailers is a hazard of the job not reserved for novices, although the goal, as in all sales jobs, is to solidify relationships with the stores. "In many cases," he offers, "reps make a lot of money fast and then the line goes under." As Borenstein stressed, anyone can sell a store once. The goal is knowing a buyer well enough that he or she simply places orders with you automatically or, at least, returns your phone calls.

A closely related concern and the job's biggest drawback is economic security. Reps say it can take anywhere from two to twenty years to rest on your laurels—or it may not happen at all. At any moment, an account (company) you've been successful with can leave you cold. "The goal is to get to a position where economically you're not feeling cheated when a company leaves you," warns the rep.

As for payment, a good salesperson should know how to negotiate a contract on his or her own behalf as well as on that of the companies he or she represents. Some reps are on salary, others on commissions ranging anywhere from 2 percent to a whopping (and rare) 20 percent. Some are given an advance against commissions. Expenses may or may not be covered.

Showroom sales is an ideal way to begin accumulating experience, confidence, and contacts. Some reps hire assistants. "If you're together, honest, and smart, you can pick up anything," he says of the former teacher he hired as his first backup. When you've decided to shed the shackles of a salaried staff position, he advises caution. "First, read the trade publications," he says. "Then go into clothing stores and see the taste level you like and the clothing you like because selling goes far better if you like the product. Then call up the companies and see if they need help selling."

Good luck.

C H A P T E R 7

RETAIL

Retail is the universal springboard of the fashion business. There's virtually not a single position where previous retail experience isn't an asset. Indeed, fashion is chock full of successful individuals in a wide range of jobs, from apparel manufacturing to textile sales, who started in retail, either behind the counter or, more likely, in an executive training program. Designers Ralph Lauren, Perry Ellis, and Alexander Julian started in retail. Julian still swears by it as the perfect design prerequisite. Department store promotion, publicity, public relations, and special events departments are filled with retail graduates.

And luckily for jobseekers, top retailers agree on the pluses and minuses of retailing. Just snag an assistant buyer, a buyer, merchandise manager, or any insider. They'll give you the dirt.

Right off the bat, they're likely to tell you about the crazy hours: Christmas, Thanksgiving, Sundays. Nancy Kirby, our woman in textile sales, referring to her early days at Montgomery Ward, puts it this way: "You're on your feet all day long. I used to come home exhausted. And you never take your vacations when other people do." "The perception of my people is you live above the store," says the corporate training director at a major department store. "A lot of people are turned off by long hours," concludes Helen Galland, former president of Bonwit Teller. "It's a field full of opportunity if you're willing to work, but it's a sacrifice."

Digging further into the minuses bag, expect to hear about physical stamina. Warns Marvin Traub, chairman of the board at Bloomingdale's, "Retail is demanding and not everyone is prepared." Galland agrees. "Know what you're getting into," she says. "A lot of people are disappointed because there's lots of drudgery."

Frequently mentioned disadvantages run to on-the-job pressure, low starting salaries, and having to relocate in order to reach upper corporate echelons, especially in chainstore organizations like Sears and J. C. Penney. Retailers, however, are increasingly suggesting that as more and more stores open suburban branches, possibilities of staying put increase.

A look at the virtues of retailing, however, show why this business is so addictive, why some buyers call themselves "retail junkies," why books have been written with titles like "Department Store Disease." Stimulating, exciting, and exhilarating are big adjectives in this business. One career counselor we heard from in chapter 2 says if her clients like "adrenaline charges" they'll like retail. Indeed, energy, "metabolism," and drive top lists of qualities sought in job applicants.

Other consistently cited personal qualities include flexibility, maturity, assertiveness, an outgoing personality, and excellent people skills. Bloomingdale's Marvin Traub says he looks for intelligence, a positive attitude about oneself and one's career, leadership, flair, and style. Helen Galland seeks "a self-starter, someone with taste." Other winning characteristics include integrity, pragmatism, quickness, eagerness, and a sense of urgency. For buying jobs, fashion sense, a good image, a facility with figures, and analytical ability crop up.

Chief among these qualities, however, is excellent people skills, especially an ability to communicate. Said one merchandise manager of her initial one-year department manager's slot at Saks in St. Louis, "Because it's a national chain, I learned how to communicate on a national basis, which is wholly different from having all stores in the same town. That really put me in good stead."

When all's said and done, it boils down to whether or not you have a _real_ interest in retailing. Indeed, when Bloomingdale's rejects training program applicants, Traub says it's most often due to doubts about genuine interest in retailing. Before one exec talks about résumés, he talks about "people who demonstrate a characteristic interest. . . . They tend to have some experience," he says. "Either from working or through their parents." Indeed, get thee a summer or Christmas selling job to test and then to demonstrate interest. Strong interest is, in fact, what Traub and other industry leaders consider the ultimate key to their own successes. Silly as it sounds, a top New York fash-

Marvin Traub

ion coordinator specializing in juniors, may have said it all. "If you're meant to be in it," she says contentedly, "you'll be in it."

What are the important pluses to working in the business itself? Tops among them are immediate recognition, responsibility early on, and a fast track to upper management. From the exec.: "It's an open kind of business. If someone brings up an idea, it happens overnight. If you need instant feedback, it's here. On Saturday a young merchant feels terrible and on Tuesday he has a display. It's exhilarating." "It's easy to see how you're doing," adds Bloomingdale's Traub.

There is indeed rapid promotion in retail—a fast track, so to speak. An assistant buyer who hasn't been promoted to buyer in two or three years is one disgruntled assistant buyer. Helen Galland thinks there's too much moving up too fast. "There's security in knowing what you're doing. I was a buyer ten years and each year I learned more and got better and better." But times have changed. Hand in hand with rapid promotion goes responsibility very early relative to other businesses. The numbers of buyers in their twenties, handling million-dollar-plus budgets, better known as open-to-buys, is startling. As a cosmetics buyer, Colombe Nicholas, the current President of Christian Dior–New York, negotiated a $24 million open-to-buy.

Organization of a Retailer

CORPORATE HEADQUARTERS

Chief Operating Officer and Senior Executives

Merchandising Staff	**Operations Staff**	**Control and Credit Staff**	**Personnel Staff**	**Publicity Staff**

Oversee the respective functions of the entire store network.

REGIONAL/DISTRICT OFFICE

Regional/District Manager

Merchandising Staff	**Operations Staff**	**Control and Credit Staff**	**Personnel Staff**	**Publicity Staff**

Oversee the respective functions of a group of stores in a particular section of the country.

RETAIL STORE

Store Manager

Merchandising	**Operations**	**Control and Credit**	**Personnel**	**Publicity**
buying	store maintenance	accounting and finance	employment	advertising
selling	security	planning	training	sales promotion
merchandise management	customer service	inventory control	labor relations	public relations
department management	warehousing and distribution	payroll	employee services	publicity
	receiving	data processing		special events
	shipping	systems and methods		display
		charge accounts		

In addition, retail is relatively "easy" to get into. Retail executives, including Marvin Traub, enter "easy" in the book of retail pros. What they mean is that retail—and this is relative to other businesses—has wide-open entrance requirements. For the most part, stores are looking for four-year liberal arts degrees; your major doesn't matter, with the exception that some stores may prefer business majors. The executive training programs to which all these graduates are applying have their exceptions, too, in an occasional dancer, actor, or former football player. A two-year associate's degree is less valuable and may put you at a disadvantage in stiff competition, although occasionally stores offer two programs—a junior executive one for those with associate degrees and the executive training program for those with B.A.s. There is considerable debate in retail as to the value of an advanced degree, particularly the M.B.A. (master of business administration). The concensus seems to be that an M.B.A. may help earn quicker promotions and salary increases but that it is neither a guarantee nor a necessity.

A typical department store has five divisions: merchandising, operations, control and credit, personnel, and publicity and promotion. Because 60 percent of management positions are in merchandising (the "power's in merchandising," said one buyer), because the overwhelming majority of jobseekers want to be buyers, because the other four divisions often hire nonfashion outsiders, we're concentrating on positions in the ever-popular merchandising line and how to land them. The best way is to apply to a solid executive training program after college.

The Executive Training Program

This is the best way, the fastest way, and the best guarantee of promotions and pay raises later. There are two basic types of training programs. One is a pure merchandising or buying program leading first to assistant buyer, then buyer, divisional merchandise manager, and general merchandise manager. Some stores have a vice-president, merchandise manager job between the last two posts and/or an associate buyer position between the first two. The second is a store management program. Here the emphasis is on "management," on running the show, and as might be expected it has been largely a male bastion. A typical store management program leads to a first job as department or sales manager, followed by group manager, division manager, assistant store manager, and manager of the entire store, and maybe even regional and national headquarters for a top executive position.

Some stores have separate merchandising and management programs. Others combine the two. In the latter case, your first job is either assistant buyer or department manager, and you can pursue the program of choice afterward.

Programs usually combine classroom work and on-the-job training, last anywhere from three months to a year or so, and begin several times a year, say in January,

June, and September. They're very competitive. Macy's New York hires 240 trainees and receives 15,000 applications. Bloomingdale's New York store gets about 5,000 for 250 positions. Starting salaries are in the neighborhood of $14,000, and occasionally go as high as $18,000. For the most part, pay increases are based on an annual review, taking into consideration, among other things, your department's gross margin and the store's established percentage increases for raises.

To get in, you can do what most do: Send a résumé and cover letter to the store. You may also end up as most do. "We're talking about six thousand résumés!" says the corporate training director. "The only difference is the color of the ink. There are kids who spend lots of money on résumés. One kid had the most beautiful résumé! The only thing that differentiates you *is you*." Amen.

Avoid résumé-itis. Yes, you need one. No, it's not an end in itself. The idea is to get through the door and get an interview. "Absolutely the best way is to be there. Live on peanut butter for a week. If you live in Alabama, go to Burdine's in Miami," says the training director.

So you're intent on the résumé. You drop into your college placement office, pick up a copy of their *College Placement Annual*, or use *Sheldon's Retail Book*, copy the names and addresses of the nation's top retailers (many of which are gigantic corporations owning handfuls of name stores). There are fifteen or so in all and you dash off a résumé and cover letter to the likes of Federated Department Stores and J. C. Penney, among others. Federated lets you know you must contact their stores individually and sends names and addresses of respective recruiters. The list includes I. Magnin in San Francisco, Bullock's in Los Angeles, Rich's in Atlanta, Burdine's in Miami, Filene's in Boston, and Bloomingdale's and Abraham & Straus in the New York area. You'd like to try New York but don't feel up to tackling Bloomingdale's or Macy's, so you send a cover letter and résumé off to Abraham & Straus. Meanwhile, you've received an executive training booklet from J. C. Penney.

Let's pretend we read booklets thoroughly and realize they tell us in a clear-cut, step-by-step manner every single thing we need to know. The booklets begin as this chapter does, enumerating personal qualities the stores desire and making sure you have a strong interest in retailing. Indeed, the glossy yellow full-size number from Abraham & Straus is literally subtitled "Rate Yourself as a Retail Executive." Inside, on the first page, is a checklist of "attributes required," of your desire to be in retailing. Stick your checks in the blank boxes.

The booklets tell the type of program they offer and give you a little chart showing which job you'll land first, second, third, and so on. Abraham & Straus says it typically has two programs: a central merchandising line beginning with assistant buyer and ending with general merchandise manager; and a store management line, going from department manager to store manager and even group vice-president. An A & S chart (see page 84) shows that individuals on programs spend time as a suburban department manager after initial slots as assistant buyer and department manager respectively. You then pursue your program line of preference. The J. C. Penney chart tells us its program is atypical, offering one program combining merchandising and management and that the first job will be merchandising manager, the next senior merchandising manager, followed by general merchandise manager, and then store manager (see page 85).

Booklets explain exactly what you'll be doing in every position surprisingly well and accurately—down to how long you should expect to remain in a position before a promotion. Indeed, relative to similar materials from other industries, these function as basic career guides in themselves—despite the requisite photos of employees enjoying themselves.

As for training programs themselves, recruiting materials carefully describe program lengths and content. Abraham & Straus informs you that a typical trainee on the merchandising line starts out with ten weeks of on-the-job training in a buying office assisting a buyer, while a store management trainee has a fifteen-week stint assisting a department manager in a suburban store. During this time, you'll get two assignments, one in home furnishings and one in apparel, and you'll have weekly seminars run by A & S executives. Two performance reviews by buyers and department managers with whom you've worked and one by an executive development manager follow. Within three months you should be an assistant buyer with full "responsibility for an entire merchandise classification." By the way, the materials say over 85 percent of executive positions are filled from within. J. C. Penney insists their program is "one of the most intensive and thorough in the industry." It lasts thirty-four weeks. The first twelve weeks you're a "sales associate" in a store, selling and operating a cash register "to find out, right at the beginning, if you've made the right career choice." During the next twenty-one weeks you'll be indoctrinated in the ways of merchandising, "building a merchandise assortment that appeals to customers in your market, presenting it for sale, determining what should be reordered." Your final week takes place in a regional training center in Atlanta, Chicago, Dallas, or Los Angeles, learning management skills in the classroom. Afterwards, it's back to a selected store for your first assignment to a specific department and some responsibility. In twelve to fifteen months you'll be promoted to merchandising manager, with responsibility for a department with significantly increased sales volume and additional sales associates to supervise.

These recruiting materials always give the how-tos of applying on the last page. They give names and addresses of executive recruitment directors and regional offices, and suggest scheduling interviews with college placement offices.

By the way, booklets are awash with retail trivia. Did you know that Abraham & Straus is New York State's second-largest department store and the fourth largest in

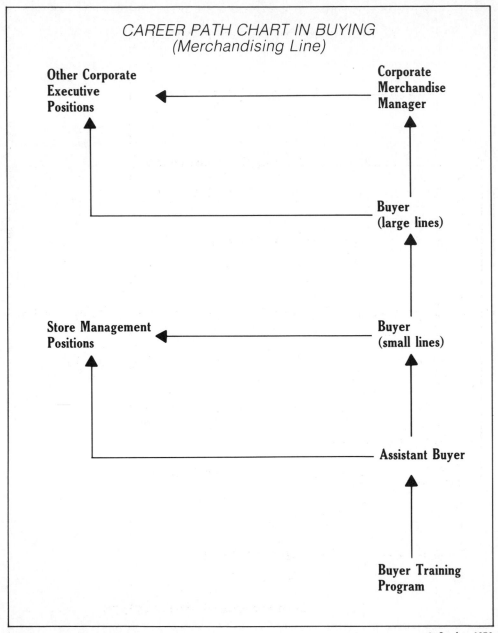

CAREER PATH CHART IN BUYING
(Merchandising Line)

Other Corporate Executive Positions ← Corporate Merchandise Manager

↑ Other Corporate Executive Positions

Buyer (large lines)

↑ Corporate Merchandise Manager

Store Management Positions ← Buyer (small lines)

↑ Store Management Positions

↑ Buyer (large lines)

Assistant Buyer

↑ Buyer (small lines)

Buyer Training Program

↑ Assistant Buyer

© Catalyst 1976

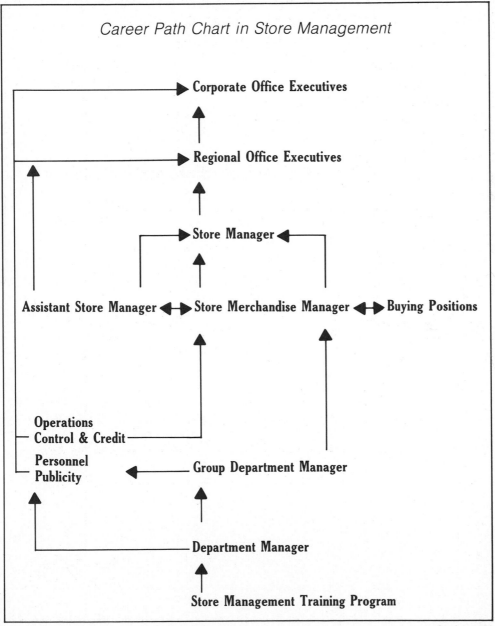

Career Path Chart in Store Management

Corporate Office Executives

Regional Office Executives

Store Manager

Assistant Store Manager ⟷ Store Merchandise Manager ⟷ Buying Positions

Operations
Control & Credit

Personnel
Publicity

Group Department Manager

Department Manager

Store Management Training Program

© Catalyst 1976

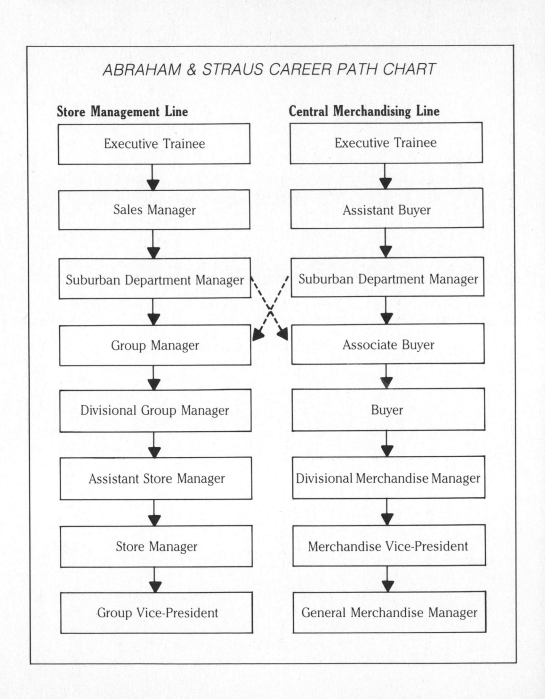

ABRAHAM & STRAUS CAREER PATH CHART

Store Management Line

| Executive Trainee |
| Sales Manager |
| Suburban Department Manager |
| Group Manager |
| Divisional Group Manager |
| Assistant Store Manager |
| Store Manager |
| Group Vice-President |

Central Merchandising Line

| Executive Trainee |
| Assistant Buyer |
| Suburban Department Manager |
| Associate Buyer |
| Buyer |
| Divisional Merchandise Manager |
| Merchandise Vice-President |
| General Merchandise Manager |

J. C. PENNEY CAREER PATH CHART

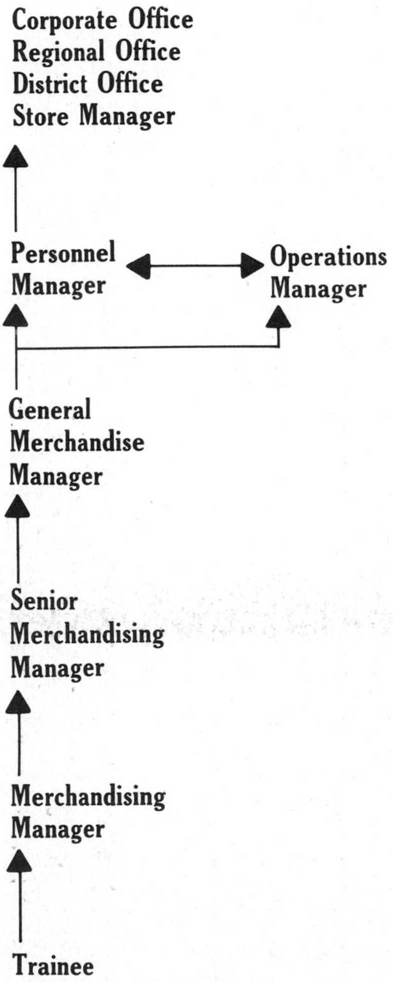

Corporate Office
Regional Office
District Office
Store Manager

↑

Personnel ←→ **Operations**
Manager   **Manager**

↑   ↑

General
Merchandise
Manager

↑

Senior
Merchandising
Manager

↑

Merchandising
Manager

↑

Trainee

the United States? That it's averaged one new store opening every two and a half years since 1952 for a total of fifteen? A & S has 1.5 million charge and credit account customers. J. C. Penney dates to a 1902 one-room store and now has 1,700 stores nationwide and annual sales of about $8 billion. J. C. Penney takes up more space in shopping malls than anyone. They hire 1,500 trainees every year.

Assistant Buyer

An assistant buyer—in an executive training program—is typically assigned to a buyer in a specific department and helps the buyer plan, buy, price, analyze sales and inventory reports, and go into the market. He or she also helps in developing promotions with special events, publicity, and promotion people, and displays with the display department. Another duty is supervising the sales staff.

An assistant buyer usually gains responsibility in increments. It has been said after six months to a year of training one should expect to be an assistant buyer, and after three years, at the latest, a buyer. In some stores, you'll be given an associate buyer title in between. Industry executives, however, stress following your own tempo and adding responsibility only as you see fit. Indeed, many choose to be career assistant buyers. Salaries are whatever you earned at the start of your executive training program with increases at the end of your first year and each subsequent year. Career assistant buyers, therefore, might be making $18,000 or more.

The reminiscences of Colombe Nicholas on an assistant buyer's life are particularly amusing, as they are on that of buyer, and on up the ladder. The conversation also illustrates one typical way in which retail can lead to senior management positions, both in and outside of retail. In Colombe Nicholas's case, that means the presidency of Christian Dior's U.S. corporate licensing office, whose sales hit $250 million in 1982.

COLOMBE NICHOLAS

A RETAIL REMINISCENCE

Nicholas was born in New York City and moved with her parents to Piqua, Ohio, when she was just a year old. Subsequently she lived and went to school in Montreux, Switzerland, ending up at the University of Dayton with a degree in hand at nineteen. She then became the sole woman in the freshman law school class at the University of Cincinnati, from which she graduated at twenty-two. Nicholas is married and lives in New York City. Her favorite hobby is collecting art and attending museum exhibits. She has no children.

When did you first become interested in this industry?

My sophomore year of college I went to work for a store in Dayton. That was the first exposure I had to retailing. I never really gave it much more thought other than that I was dealing with customers. The following summer I was a waitress

and I never thought I would be in a department store situation again. When I graduated from law school I went to work in the family business for two years on tax issues my father had. Unfortunately that was in Piqua, Ohio, and in Piqua, Ohio, to be single and over twenty is a disaster. I then told the family that I was moving to New York and that I had no intention of practicing law because I found it boring. I didn't know what I was going to do.

What happened in New York?

I came to New York and went on many job interviews, from research analyst to positions at Charles of the Ritz working for Yves Saint Laurent Perfumes. Anyone who even gave a remote lead for an interview, I followed up. Since I had no idea what I wanted to do, I thought I'd talk to everybody. If a friend had a friend who suggested I see so and so, I went. I felt in talking to these people that I got a little bit of insight into what jobs were available, what aspects of those jobs interested me, and what I wanted to eliminate. On one of these interviews, someone suggested I go and meet the head of personnel and labor relations at Macy's. She was also an attorney. I credit her with getting me started in the field of retailing. When I had a conversation with her, the first of many, she said there was great opportunity for women in retailing. I was also a little shellshocked, gun-shy of the fact that I had started college at fifteen, graduated from law school at twenty-two, and looked ten. People were always saying, "When will Mr. Nicholas be back?" and I had to say, "Sit down, you're talking to him." She explained that retailing had been open to women for some time and there was very little age discrimination. She also said you were promoted on achievements very quickly and with an advanced degree I had a chance of getting into upper management. I decided it sounded very challenging and interesting. I would deal with people, use skills I had learned in school in terms of discipline and negotiations, as well as skills I thought fit in well with my personality.

How did you know it was right for your personality?

I think when you are considering a job or career path, you have to take a very critical look at yourself. If you're not outgoing it would be very difficult to be a salesman. What are your qualifications? What are your pluses? What are your minuses? Try to equate that with the job you are trying to seek, so you don't get shot down because you're trying for something that just does not relate to you as an individual. I was also prepared when I took the job to really start at the bottom, because I wanted to learn. I didn't want to stay at the bottom forever, but I wanted to learn all aspects of the job. I started in a training squad. I was made assistant buyer in the silver department.

What did you do as assistant buyer?

Well, on the main floor of Macy's they sold forks and spoons at twenty-five cents a piece. We used to call those things "chop suey," because people would fight over these knives, forks, and spoons and try to make sets. Here I am with all my degrees, up in the stockroom dumping knives, forks, and spoons into baskets to take down to the main floor, so people could fight over these twenty-five-cent things. And I did this for a certain amount of time.

What was your next job?

I was promoted to the towel department where I expertly learned to fold towels. I would spend half my day on the floor straightening stock. I'm saying this because there is a big misconception when retailers give you a title. "Executive" means you can sweep the floor and you can also write an order. What comes first is not a matter of importance, but you have to be prepared to do either. You will get recognized faster if you're willing to do anything. Don't be a prima donna, just get the job done.

What were your titles after assistant buyer?

I was promoted to buyer of small leather goods. I must admit I moved faster than most people moved, but by the same token I did have a law degree and they were paying me more than they were paying comparable people on the training squad.

Would you recommend that a person who wants to be a buyer obtain an advanced degree?

No. I think you have to decide where you want to go, what level you want to achieve, and have an education that is commensurate with that level. I'm not saying that you are locked in if you don't have an advanced degree, but if you want to be chairman of the board or chief executive officer or president of a company in the framework that is in existence today you really have to earn an advanced degree. I think what has happened, though, is that a college degree has gotten to be what a high school diploma was thirty years ago. Most people have it. The next level, be it an MBA or a law degree, puts you apart from the crowd. On the other side of the coin, I'm sure there are other presidents of companies that didn't get advanced degrees and got there by being very skilled in the area that they chose to go in. A person can be a marvelous designer and sketch beautifully and not have any formal training. It's a situation where the talent was in them. To be a good lawyer, a good CPA, you have to have gone to school.

When you were at Macy's as an assistant buyer did you have it in mind that you wanted to make it to the top?
Absolutely. I knew that from day one. That was the most important thing.

It sounds like you couldn't imagine it any other way.
I'll never forget when I got this job, my boss looked at my résumé and said, "It looks like you couldn't keep a job." And I said to him, "What do you mean?" He said, "Every year you were promoted." I literally thought if I wasn't promoted every year, that I wasn't trying hard enough and I wasn't doing something right. Now that's my own personal pressure that I put on myself. It doesn't work for everybody—but it doesn't have to.

What jobs did you get after leather goods buyer?
Subsequently I became a buyer in several departments at Macy's. I worked there five years until Bloomingdale's stole me away. It's a very small world, the New York retailing world, and if you've acquired a good reputation people call you up and say, "Are you happy?" I worked as a cosmetics buyer.

What were your duties as a buyer?
Selecting merchandise to be sold, writing orders, following up on orders after delivery. You have various branch stores that also get merchandise and you have to make sure that that gets delivered. Another aspect is advertising. Department stores spend a great deal of time either advertising in their own catalogues, in newspapers, or on radio or television. You have to negotiate the vendor contribution to help pay for the ad. How the ad is going to be photographed, what color it's going to be photographed in. All of that is part of the job. You also have to work with the selling staff and pay attention to how merchandise is presented on the floor. You spend time

on the floor to hear consumers' reactions to the product. Maybe a blouse was terrific because the price was right and the color was great, but why aren't people buying it? Maybe it wasn't cut right. The armhole's too tight. So you live with your merchandise.

How large was your budget?

I think, on an annual basis, about $24 to $25 million, which is quite large. That was my cosmetics buying job.

Did you aim for as large a budget as possible?

Oh yes! You negotiate with your boss. It's called more open-to-buy. It's a vicious cycle generated by sales. You have to make sure what you buy sells or you end up with a backlog.

What are the virtues of retailing?

The thing that is so exciting about retailing, and why you become a retail junkie and why people are so dedicated, is that it's the only business I know where every day you get a report card. Every day you look at the sales sheet and you see how you're doing. There are such gratifications, you think, Oh my gosh, I picked up or why did I drop? Then, there's a snowstorm, the store's not going to open, and I'm going to lose a million dollars. In most companies you have to wait for quarterly reports. You don't see every day how things are checking. It's very stimulating.

What pitfalls should people who are dying to become buyers try to avoid?

There's a great deal of physical work involved. I don't think people realize that. Fifty coats arrive on the floor and there's no one to put them out. Guess who does it? There are long hours. Department stores are notoriously open at all the wrong hours. Christmas, Thanksgiving, Sundays. As a result you end up initially being married to your job, because you're either too tired when you're not working or you don't have the time. I think you have to get a lot of satisfaction out of the job because you don't have time for anything else.

What was your next step after buyer?

I was promoted to branch divisional merchandise manager in Stamford, Connecticut which meant I had to drive to Stamford every day. I decided I wanted to be back in New York, so I left and became the vice-president, merchandise manager in accessories at Bonwit Teller. I was at Bonwit Teller for two years and decided to leave when I remarried and planned to move to Philadelphia. I didn't have a job for six weeks when I went on an interview to be president of Dior and four months later I was hired.

Department Manager/Sales Manager

Even on the merchandising line, you may cross over and work as a department manager. A department manager doesn't buy merchandise and is best thought of as a floor manager. He or she works on the floor making sure merchandise is presented properly and the sales staff is functioning well which includes figuring out their schedules. A department manager works with customers on occasion as well as with advertising, promotion, and publicity. Perhaps the biggest part of the job is getting along with the department's buyers in order to facilitate reorders, plan for incoming merchandise, move goods doing poorly, and occasionally make recommendations on markups and markdowns. Like assistant buyers, the beginning department manager earns whatever he or she earned as a starting trainee. Career managers can make $20,000 to $25,000.

It's probably fair to say the department manager slot gets a bum rap from those on a merchandising line who'd just as soon skip it altogether. One merchandise manager begs to differ, but only in retrospect: "Without the experience you don't really know what the urgency is on the other end of the phone when a department manager calls and says, 'I need.' If you're going into buying, I highly recommend it. Most stores plan it that way."

Here's a rare inside look from someone who did go into buying and quickly at that. She says when future buyers are typically confronted with six months apiece as an assistant buyer and department manager, it's to their advantage to do department manager first. Assistant buyers work in the office daily, she says, so administrators notice them when a promotion comes up. According to our ambitious buyer, the department manager is on the floor so he or she doesn't get noticed. She claims it's an advantage to be a department manager first so that when you're an assistant buyer you're ready to spring when something pops up.

If real-life power plays fascinate you, listen to what our buyer writes in a personal letter: "As with many corporations, the lines of power don't really show much. The poor department manager is a case in point. Technically she is accountable to the store manager and assistant store manager (see chart on page 121), but as a department manager she is also responsible for the performance of each department under her, to its buyer, divisional merchandise manager (DMM), and general merchandise manager (GMM). She may have nine buyers and two or three DMMs on her case, plus the store manager. Either ladder (store or merchandising) can make or break her, but if she wants to go into merchandising (which she does) the opinions her buyers and DMMs and GMMs have of her are more important (in real life) than those of her actual superiors (the assistant store manager and store manager)."

Good luck.

Buyer

According to 1980 statistics there are in the neighborhood of 34,000 buyers in this country. It's probably the most popular fashion career.

Training program materials bend over backwards to stress the buyer as business-person. The A & S booklet reads: "A retail executive is a well-rounded business manager. Control of sales volume, deliveries, distribution, promotions, and merchandise quality are all a vital part of a buyer's job."

In general, buyers shop the market, work with vendors, and write out purchase orders, based on an overall plan they work out. A buyer is given a budget, or open-to-buy, which can run to the $24 million that Colombe Nicholas had as a Bloomingdale's cosmetic buyer. Indeed, top buyers are tops at negotiating substantial open-to-buys from administrators. In smaller stores a buyer may have a wider range of duties from placing orders to helping get merchandise distributed, supervising sales-people, and working with promotion and publicity on sales promotions and special events. Buyers also work with presentations and with the sales staff and department managers on individual department presentations. In addition, a buyer may work out deals with manufacturers (vendors) to have items made exclusively for the store. As to facility with figures, much of what a buyer does is carefully recorded on a computer. So buyers study research reports and sales records. Salaries go from around $20,000 to as high as $60,000 for very high-level buyers.

Now listen to a twenty-five-year-old accessory buyer for a prominent specialty store who graduated from Indiana University in marketing and joined Abraham & Straus's executive training program. Her first job was department manager in accessories. She stayed there for about a year before being promoted to the store's Brooklyn branch as department manager in childrenswear. After three months she joined her current employer, Bonwit Teller, as assistant buyer in hosiery and sunglasses. She remained in that position from May until the following August when she was promoted to buyer. We're chatting just a month later.

Does she think it's typical to be promoted so fast? "Bonwit's is a smaller operation and as a result you're more visible," she offers. "In a big organization like A & S you can get lost." Her boss, the divisional merchandise manager, says privately the reasons for her promotion to buyer, "I sense she has fashion flair and she's mechanically good. When I say mechanics, I mean the running of your business. That's analysis, controlling your money, launching merchandise."

Merchandise managers are also cautious when moving buyers from a "basic" department, say brassieres, to a more complex area like hats, that require more "fashion sense." Another critical consideration is the volume of the department. Confided one buyer, "Assignments are sometimes power plays."

Does our accessory buyer have any idea *why* she was promoted so quickly? "I've always thought of myself as a workaholic," she says. "And I was in unique situations. For instance, the first buyer I trained with left and I had the opportunity to work on my own." She was given greater responsibility again after a new buyer was brought in. "I was noticed more than if I had been working with a buyer who had been working many, many years," she says.

Indeed, increased responsibility and getting noticed are crucial to the would-be buyer. Says Maxine Forman, vice-president of merchandising for Russ Togs, whom we meet in chapter 5 and who began in Bloomingdale's executive training program, "I worked as an assistant buyer for this incredibly fabulous woman to whom I attribute a great deal of my success. She had self-confidence and experience and wasn't threatened by a woman. She gave me a lot of responsibility." Forman goes on to detail that responsibility. "I had a lot of buying power. She went off to Europe several times a year and I bought. She was there for me one hundred percent and when I made a mistake she was supportive."

Our accessory buyer describes her major duties as "planning, analyzing, developing a growing business with fourteen stores within my area." Here's a "typical" day: "Mondays are busiest. I go through reports, see what's selling, what's not, what to reorder. We also have markdown days, so depending on my stock situation, I go through my reports for markdowns. Then I go into the market and see some lines. There are still a lot of manufacturers I haven't seen because I'm new. This week I'm concentrating on the millinery market. There are a million and one things to do like answering calls from thirteen stores about their needs."

Buying for thirteen stores requires knowledge of each one. "You have to know what kind of customer you have in each city and each store," she says. "There are a lot of stores I haven't been to yet. You have to know your geographic areas, your median income, the size of the store, what percentage of your total is planned for each store. You know if your store is planned to two percent you're not going to put in an assortment like a New York plan where it's twenty-seven percent of your business. Basically, I would say when I pick a line and sort a line out, there'll be things I'll drop for smaller stores in different areas. For the most part they all carry the same merchandise but not as assorted as the big stores."

In order to buy, she relies on a sales, stock, and receipts plan. "Then it's up to you to break it down by store," she says. "But you are given one figure and every six months, fall and spring, you break it down."

How responsible is she if things in her area don't sell well? "Very" is the answer. "You must work in the market to solve problems. You have to work with the manufacturers negotiating profitability."

On pitfalls of a buying career, she echoes industry leaders. "People get frustrated

**BACKSTAGE WITH A BLOOMINGDALE'S
BUYER**

Accessories Buyer in her
department

Looking over ads in Advertising Department

Reading Selling Reports in her
office

With her Department Manager on Selling Floor

**With her Associate
Buyer in Receiving
Department**

**In her department
again**

too fast and they give themselves time limits. If they haven't been promoted by a certain time they give up and go elsewhere, most likely in the same position. That sets them back because they lose seniority. I've seen it happen a lot. I'm not going to give up."

What does she like best about retailing? "It's exciting. For a woman, well, clothes have always meant a lot to me. A lot of it is personal taste level but a lot is being able to interpret the kind of store you're buying for. It's exciting to see if it works and if it sells when you put it together." If you haven't gotten tired of hearing it, here goes: "If you are not willing to sacrifice a little, I wouldn't recommend it. If I don't get my work done here I take it home and work till midnight. It's a time-consuming career."

Her goal: to be a fashion coordinator.

Market Representative

Besides stores there are merchandising organizations or buying offices, either independent or owned by the stores, that give advice on what's hot and what's not. They're almost always in New York and they work closely with store buyers. A variation on the buyer, called a market representative or market rep, works in these offices, the best known of which are Associated Merchandising Corporation (AMC) and Frederick Atkins, Inc. Sometimes reps are given the go-ahead to buy, in which case they'll arrange and negotiate volume purchases to get better prices and delivery dates for large groups of stores. Bernie Ozer, Vice-president of AMC, is extremely influential. Most reps have previous buying experience. Pay is generally lower than that of department store buyers.

For those with wanderlust, there are important import/export houses with offices all over the world. When a subscribing store's buyer arrives overseas, these agents take them to the resources for what they're buying. Once again, they are expected to know what's new and hot and best and successful and cheapest within that buyer's market.

Merchandise Manager

The next step after a buyer is divisional merchandise manager (DMM), a job involving taking charge of a group of departments, usually organized by merchandise. Salaries can go from $30,000 to as high as $80,000. The next step (the DMM's boss) is general merchandise manager (GMM), a top executive in charge of the entire merchandising division. After GMM you may move on to jobs in regional or national corporate management. Salaries can reach $90,000. Incidentally, some stores have a "vice-president, merchandise manager" between DMM and GMM (see A & S merchandising line on p. 84).

The number of GMMs, DMMs, buyers, even departments themselves depends on sales volume and/or emphasis on that particular aspect of the business. In a lot of stores there's just one DMM for, say, menswear and home furnishings and perhaps more than one for ladies apparel and cosmetics (see p. 83).

The merchandise manager primarily coordinates and oversees the efforts of buyers. The DMM, in coordinating the buying effort, develops a merchandising plan, divides up the buyer's merchandise assignments, and reviews their selections. He or she keeps up with the market in the same way. The DMM will also visit manufacturer showrooms and travel abroad.

Analytical skills are even more crucial because the DMM is totally responsible for the bottom-line success or failure of the division. Profit and loss statements, sales figures, and computer reports play a starring role.

Glenda Price is vice-president, merchandise manager for Bonwit Teller and her career path is not only typical but is what she recommends for aspiring retailers.

Price attended a liberal arts college, the University of Kansas, and started off in a training program in a St. Louis department store. Her first step was a two-and-a-half-year stint as assistant buyer for better sportswear, followed by a department manager slot in a branch store for six months. Next came Saks Fifth Avenue's St. Louis store as a sportswear department manager for a year. Her original St. Louis employer hired her back as associate buyer, after six months of which she finally became a buyer. She stayed almost three years before winning a coveted blouse-buying job at Bonwit Teller in New York. "It was kind of unusual to hire someone from the Midwest in a New York store," offers Price. She was promoted to merchandise manager after three years and stayed five more.

As current vice-president, merchandise manager, Price manages three divisions: accessories, intimate apparel, and gifts. "I can best describe the merchandise manager's role as administrative," insists Price. "I oversee eight buyers and twenty-two departments and, in simple language, I run a company within a company. In overseeing these buyers, I'm responsible for planning and giving them both fashion and financial direction.

"When we talk about a budget, we're really talking about a six-month merchandising plan. I plan sales, inventory, and marketing by store, based on the turnover we want to achieve. This gives us our inventory levels. We make sure when sales go up we have inventory to support it, and if sales go down we adjust inventory to counteract that. If we plan properly we avoid too many markdowns. "We also plan markups, and the trick is establishing a price point on each item at which it'll sell more, even if I sacrifice a little markup. A lot of markup isn't important if it doesn't sell. Then we have an operating statement that comes out giving us our gross margin or the bottom line we're responsible for. If I give the operations division a good gross margin and they're watching their Ps and Qs, we all come out with a nice profit.

"That's what it's all about."

Fashion Coordinator/Fashion Director

An envious gift buyer for a California department store called this job "fashion-fun." Not all stores have a fashion coordinator or director, and ones that do are usually large. A fashion coordinator normally specializes in a particular market, so, for instance, Macy's has a fashion director for juniors. At a higher level is the fashion director who guides an entire store or group of stores. Like Melville, she or he is often a vice-president of the corporation as well.

A fashion coordinator or fashion director coordinates and plans the overall fashion statements for a season. This prevents one-third of the store from doing an elegance story, one-third doing Japanese, and one-third doing country casual. To do this, a fashion coordinator or director goes to all the major markets in his or her area, and tries to win the support of buyers.

Catherine di Montezemolo (r) and Peggy Kaufman, Vice-President of Public Relations (see p. 183), discussing an upcoming promotion with a merchant

Catherine di Montezemolo is vice-president and fashion director of Lord & Taylor. As such, she's a prominent member of the national if not the international fashion circuit, as are her counterparts at other prestigious department stores like Saks' Ellin Saltzman.

Becoming fashion director for an entire store takes years. In di Montezemolo's case, it took thirty, starting at *Vogue* in a variety of editorial jobs. (She began as editorial assistant, became a fashion editor, covered the French and Italian collections, and moved to special projects editor.) Saltzman was a *Glamour* editor.

Di Montezemolo prefers to preface her comments as she does when addressing Lord & Taylor's executive trainees, and that is by explaining that in years past a fashion director was unheard of because stores were single units. "Now a buyer with thirty or forty-some-odd stores has so much to worry about what with inventory, having sales, opening new stores, windows coming up, problems with deliveries. She's got a day that's packed and not many assistants. She doesn't have time to think about whether sleeves are getting deeper, skirts a little longer." Di Montezemolo concludes with the purpose of her job: to guide buyers, but not to tell them what to buy.

Six times a year and nine months in advance of a season di Montezemolo does a projection focusing on fashion, color, and fabric. She will eventually present comprehensive sketches and models of everything she feels should be in stock, in catalogues, and in windows. Di Montezemolo shows her fashion projections to general merchandise managers and divisional merchandise managers on the first day they're available. On the second, she shows all buyers in the store's divisions. Moreover, di Montezemolo is constantly approached for related fashion guidance by designers, buyers, divisional merchandise managers, and manufacturers. "They call and want to come in to discuss what kind of direction they should go in," she says.

Di Montezemolo gets color and fabric direction from "how we feel," from fabric markets, and from ready-to-wear shows in Europe and the United States. She also stresses display department input. "We work very closely with display people on the look of the windows months and months in advance. We try to balance them. Say one week is junior, the next sportswear, the next dresses, and so on."

In addition, di Montezemolo has an assistant in charge of branch stores. "We tell the branches' display managers how mannequins should look, how we like the hair, skirt lengths, color of stockings, and so on at least twice a month," says di Montezemolo. Another apsect of working with branches involves films. "We do films for branch managers, say for Fall when they're getting Fall merchandise in, showing how they should display and promote it. Once again, we dress mannequins and do themes."

A fashion director is intimately involved with advertising. "We work very hard with buyers on all ads," explains di Montezemolo. "They bring ads to me ahead of an ad meeting and we try to create something that's us. We work further in advance on double-page spreads."

When Lord & Taylor opts for private label merchandise, as many department stores do, di Montezemolo plays a lead role. "When merchandise is sold directly from the contractor to us, we're very fussy about what gets our label," she says. "I'm involved in color, in sizing, in everything the store buys."

The ideal first job for an aspiring fashion director, according to di Montezemolo, would be in a fashion office like hers in charge of a specific market. Unfortunately, di Montezemolo and others like her don't hire entry level, although she hired two secretaries and promoted both into fashion coordinator slots. One became fashion coordinator covering fabrics in the American market. "When we want special private label merchandise, she goes into the market or to a fabric library and brings back prints," says di Montezemolo. "I work closely with her, as do all the buyers." Another secretary became the coordinator in charge of branch stores. Under di Montezemolo's direction, she pulls together those branch themes and coordinates the films. In addition, the fashion office is home to someone in charge of display, a fashion coordinator working in the market on accessories and loungewear, and a stylist who styles ads for publications like *Vogue* and *Women's Wear Daily* and works closely with display to tie-in with advertisements. Beneath her is an assistant stylist.

To get a job with a top-notch fashion director like di Montezemolo, "enthusiasm and a taste level" are paramount. "Most applicants don't really know what they want," cautions di Montezemolo. "They should come in and say: 'I want to work in a fashion office.'" As preparation, she suggests a training program at a high-quality store preceded by a four-year liberal arts or retailing degree or even a fashion design degree from a top school like Parsons School of Design in New York.

Starting salaries vary tremendously depending on the nature of the position. An assistant fashion coordinator or fashion coordinator can earn $13,000 or $14,000. If the position is powerful and heavily involved with advertising and promotion, $40,000 to $50,000 is possible.

Retail—The Entrepreneur

There are two million retail outlets in the United States. That's the good news. The bad news is that few thrive. For that reason, opening a store is never to be done thoughtlessly, matter-of-factly, and without knowledge of the business.

First, opening a clothing store requires capital to pay managers, salespeople, rent or a mortgage, advertising bills, insurance, supplies. Don't expect a profit the first year. That means you need enough to operate year number one and possibly beyond.

There's no excuse not to research like hell. Libraries have dozens of books on the subject. Local schools offer courses on the how-tos of opening your own store. Banks give advice and loans. The Small Business Administration, 1441 L Street, NW, Washington, DC 20416, provides loans and information. Catalyst is a good source of information for women, available by writing Catalyst, 14 East 60th Street, New York, New York 10022. Ask for a list of local chapters. Once your business is underway, the American Women's Economic Development Corporation, 60 East 42nd Street, Room 405, New York, New York 10165, is a good source of support, information, and seminars. Several of the designers mentioned in chapter 10 are members.

Work experience is crucial. At the very least, work in an establishment where you can pick up the ins and outs of the business. Experience as a salesperson is good for starters, and probably the smaller the operation the better in terms of the opportunity to learn several aspects of the business.

Most successful entrepreneurs have an individual interest or talent that becomes the focus of their store. Consider it an identity similar to that required for a clothing design business (chapter 10).

For instance, the focus of Betsey Johnson's two stores happens to be her own designs. Her "mod zoomy little showcases," as she describes her boutiques, are as mod and zoomy as Johnson herself. Admittedly, the purpose of store number one was "a dump for unsold merchandise." Her second store, however, is meant to be a lively showcase for her designs. Now Johnson dreams of franchises across the country. "We'd be great in L.A.," she says. Her first two are in Manhattan.

Geraldine Stutz, president of Henry Bendel, the New York specialty store, is perhaps the best-known, most influential, and frequently imitated entrepreneur in the country. On the importance of an identity, Stutz says of Bendel's, "This is the last of the entrepreneurial specialty shops, which means this is truly a projection of what I see and judge and like and feel and am all about."

If you manage to keep up with *Women's Wear Daily,* you read in-depth coverage of hundreds of new retail operations coast to coast. One thing *WWD* retail articles illustrate brilliantly is just why people take the plunge.

In Dallas, we see that a carpenter, dental assistant, and former retailer open a vintage clothing shop based on a "partnership of friends and mutual love for old clothes."

In Boston, a couple, one with a sister in fashion design, opt for the high-fashion clothing of top international designers like Armani, Montana, and Issey Miyake. They have a trendy clientele. The store's a fantasy for them.

In Little Rock, Arkansas, two women fill a vacancy in the city's retail roster with a shop selling "big city" looks. They choose to sell Anne Klein, Adele Simpson, Blass III, and Halston. They do not, however, sell the ballgowns already popular in neighboring Texas stores. They say their customer is "the well traveled, well-educated woman with a moderately comfortable to affluent income, the wife of a professional or a professional herself." Women, no doubt, with whom the owners identify.

In Chicago, a thirty-seven-year-old woman buys a small specialty shop endangered by big-time competitors, a slow economy, and a quiet location. What she brings to her store, according to *WWD*, is a "winning concept," a "minimart of affordable fashion." Nothing in the store costs more than $100 (with a few exceptions) and the customer is a professional or homemaker aged twenty-five to forty-five. A former salesperson, the entrepreneur says, "I had some of the greatest bad times in my life, but now that I've established my niche, I'm aiming for six turns a year and a five hundred thousand dollar volume."

In Newport Beach, California, the look of the sales staff as well as the clothing is preppie, casual, and traditional. The entrepreneur, who also owns a nearby shop, selected a "jeans-type store with sophistication" and extensive computerization of records.

Meanwhile, in Santa Monica, California, a woman decides to open the "number one swimwear store," In eight years, she runs a four-store chain and million-plus business. Big selling points are allowing customers to mix sizes, locations near the beach, and an emphasis on service. Her regulars are "junior fitness-oriented types."

In Manhattan, stores catering to female business executives are proliferating. Someone takes it one step further with petite sizes. Another is a bit more updated. Another more upscale. Another more high fashion. Another budget. Another the older sophisticated woman. Another the large-size woman.

So you need capital, experience, an identity, managerial ability, and a snippet of entrepreneurial verve.

GERALDINE STUTZ

THE FIRST WOMAN OF ENTREPRENEURIAL RETAIL

In the national if not international retail community, Geraldine Stutz—Gerry or Stutzy—is a household word. She is best known for Bendel's main floor "Street of Shops" concept, originated twenty-one years ago, two years after Stutz took over as president.

The Street of Shops refers to a series of freestanding individual "shops" devoted to everything from hosiery, hats, and belts to travel accessories, stationery, food, and housewares, all on either side of the store's central aisle. "When we first opened the Street of Shops I invited every retailer in town to a party because I was so thrilled," says Stutz. "But because I had been quiet as a mouse since taking over Bendel's, I had been very criticized. It was just an indication to the retailing community that, of course, I didn't know what I was doing. So one of the retailers shook my hand politely at this party and said, 'Well, Gerry, at least you've got guts,' and then they all sat down on the curb and laughed and laughed and laughed. They said it was an impossible idea because what you needed was open countering and catch-a-customer-every-place-along-the-line. Madness. Of course, it has since become the most imitated form of merchandising in the second half of the twentieth century."

Geraldine Stutz says she was interested in fashion "from the womb." "My mother was a very chic woman. She had a strong personal style so I was always aware of clothes," she adds. Moreover, Stutz was an overachiever. "I went to a long series of Roman Catholic schools in Chicago," she says. "I spent my time making every effort to please my mother, mother superior, and mother church. In other words, I was really trained to achieve."

Stutz received an acting scholarship to Mundelein College in Chicago, moved to New York after graduation, landed a job as fashion editor for a group of movie magazines, then worked as an editor at *Glamour* magazine for seven years. From there she was hired by Genesco, the retail giant, to oversee all I. Miller shoe operations, and then, in 1957, to head Henri Bendel, then owned by Genesco.

"When I joined Genesco," explains Stutz, "I was the first woman they'd brought in. I was lucky enough to work for the one American tycoon [Genesco Chairman W. Maxey Jarman] in the fifties who honestly believed that women's businesses might best be run by women."

The personality of Henri Bendel was from the start the personality of Geraldine Stutz. As she already said, the store is a projection of what she sees and judges and likes and feels and is all about. And she doesn't mind reiterating, "The general ambience and the character and the statements this store makes are all mine." Because Stutz is a super-chic size 6, the store carries only small sizes. Like Stutz, Bendel's is "avant garde without being fashiony, full of daring and original style." Indeed, Stutz doesn't believe aspiring retail entrepreneurs have a crack at a position like hers unless they have strong personal style. "Fashion says 'me too,'" stresses Stutz. "Style says 'only me.' It takes individual character and style and originality to be successful. If you've got it, you're a specialty shop; if you haven't, it doesn't make any difference what else you've got."

That specialty shop comes about by "what I'm all about rubbing off on the enormous talents of the people who work here. There is not a single soul in the store I don't work with. I'm involved with advertising, publicity, credit collection, mail order, catalogues, buying, accounting, personnel, customer service," says Stutz. She writes all of the store's advertising copy as well.

As you might expect, Stutz looks for people whose heart and soul are akin to hers. In an advertising manager, she seeks someone who likes the same kind of advertising she does. When hiring buyers, she looks for people who like a "Henry Bendel type of look."

Bendel look or not, the store has very few buying jobs. "Our buyers stay anywhere

from five years to a lifetime," says Stutz. For those fortunate few, there is only one instruction: Buy what you like. "Since I wasn't a retailer I could only make the kind of store I wanted to shop in," explains Stutz. "Twenty years later, twenty-five million dollars worth of people like what I like." Accidental or not, Bendel's is famous for introducing new designers. Among those with Bendel beginnings are Mary McFadden, Cacharel, Sonia Rykiel, and Rei Kawakubo, a major Japanese designer.

As Geraldine Stutz tells it, the only terrible time in her life was when Genesco put Henri Bendel up for sale. "I recognized four years ago that I labored under the delusion that the store did belong to me, and acted as if it were mine when in fact it wasn't mine, and the minute Genesco decided to put it up for sale I realized it wasn't mine. I wanted to buy it outright and it was the only terrible time of my whole life."

In the summer of 1980, Geraldine Stutz succeeded in raising $8 million from foreign investors and beat out the competition to buy Henri Bendel. She is the first woman to own a major fashion specialty store.

For novice entrepreneurs, Stutz offers an off-the-cuff litmus test: How do you feel about working when other people are on vacation? How do you feel about the pressure of an enormously competitive business? How do you feel about the layer of glamour being very thin? How much satisfaction do you get from conceiving an idea, working it through, and having it succeed?

Indeed, seeing how a project turns out is Stutz's favorite part of the job. "That means at two in the morning, seeing a just-completed

Commes des Garçons shop that has had buyers, the advertising department, painters, and display people involved for three months. It's the satisfaction of looking at it and finding it terrific!" Stutz is bubbly now. "After it was decided I wasn't a passing fancy in fashion, people used to say to me, 'What are you going to do next?' I should move on from Bendel's to something large and world-shaking. I listened and I finally said, 'What makes you think bigger is better?'

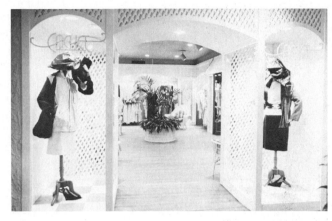

"I said I'm here because I'm a power maniac. There's no place else in the world where a person exercises my absolute control. It stretches and uses every talent and muscle I have. Henri Bendel is my platform. It is my theatrical production. It's given me a handsome living. It's given me pleasant celebrity. It's given me a chance to say no and have it clear. What more could you ask? And, now, it's mine, all mine."

Salesclerk

In a small store you may just begin as a salesperson and rise to buyer and store manager or act as a combination of both. From there you may be kicked upstairs to a main office, if there is one, or you may opt to open your own store. In any case, sales experience—whether in a small operation, department, or chain store—is excellent experience. And the earlier the experience in your career, the better. It's particularly useful in testing initial interest in retail.

A salesclerk job is not recommended, however, in a department store as a stepping-stone to assistant buyer and buyer in place of an executive training program. Rather, it works well as a complement to school, to caring for children at home in anticipation of a fashion career, or as an interim position between school or home and acceptance in a respectable training program.

CHAPTER 8

TEXTILES

Unless you've lived in the Southeast, parts of New England, or the mid-Atlantic region, have a family member in the business, or have worked in textiles yourself, chances are textiles doesn't grab you. Moreover, if "fashion" is your focus, you probably never gave textiles a thought, unless a teacher or other textile enthusiast broached the subject.

The textile enthusiast immediately informs the novice that the textile industry is responsible for far more than clothing fabric. "I've never been so thrilled in my life," said one textile designer, of the time she first spotted her patterns on train and airplane seats. A textile department chairman, is particularly proud of work as research supervisor for the Office of Naval Research developing cold weather clothing. After a super-successful space shuttle mission, kudos (and an award) went to the textile company that created the crew's phenomenal spacesuits. And Jhane Barnes is just one Coty-Award-winning fashion designer who has signed a lucrative contract to design home furnishings fabric.

Textile applications are, in fact, boundless. There are 25,000 products made for the military alone. Industrial uses include filters to trap soot from coal-burning power plants and covers on riverbanks to prevent erosion. Medical applications include artificial arteries and burn dressings. There are typewriter ribbons, tires, and bulletproof vests.

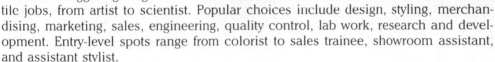
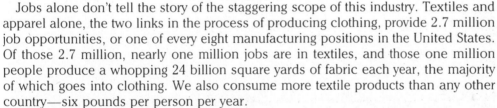

Textile enthusiasts can go on about the staggering range of textile jobs, from artist to scientist. Popular choices include design, styling, merchandising, marketing, sales, engineering, quality control, lab work, research and development. Entry-level spots range from colorist to sales trainee, showroom assistant, and assistant stylist.

Jobs alone don't tell the story of the staggering scope of this industry. Textiles and apparel alone, the two links in the process of producing clothing, provide 2.7 million job opportunities, or one of every eight manufacturing positions in the United States. Of those 2.7 million, nearly one million jobs are in textiles, and those one million people produce a whopping 24 billion square yards of fabric each year, the majority of which goes into clothing. We also consume more textile products than any other country—six pounds per person per year.

Ninety percent of the 7,000 textile plants are on the East Coast, mainly in the South, seconded by the mid-Atlantic states, and ending with New England. Most jobs in design, styling, merchandising, marketing, and sales are in New York City, where the business employs about 23,000. These jobs are in companies ranging in size from giant corporations like Burlington Industries, Inc.; J. P. Stevens & Co., Inc.; Milliken & Company; and Cone Mills Corporation to tiny converters with just a few employees.

Converters are one type of textile operation. The other is a vertical operation. Vertical operations, usually major textile mills, do every operation involved in making fabric from spinning the fiber into yarn up to the finished fabric. A converter buys unfinished fabric, often from the major vertical mills, and contracts the finishing and drying out to plants. Converters—most of whom are in New York—have far fewer employees, no equipment, less overhead, and can service garment manufacturers with smaller orders or special needs that the enormous vertical mills won't handle.

In fact, company size seems to be a job-hunting issue in textiles. A veteran of a huge company put it this way: "In small companies you'll do more things, learn more faster, and have a harder time. In large ones you usually do one thing, get lost, but are more secure."

Ask up front about your specific duties should you win a job. There are myriad interpretations of any single job title depending on company size, focus, management, organization, and philosophy. A frequent example is the textile design graduate lucky enough to hook a job with a prestigious major mill. She or he then discovers the company concentrates on manmade fibers, does no prints or "fancies," and the job isn't so much one of "design" as of technical coordination or marketing analysis. If you want to exercise your creative muscles and actually invent patterns, a small converter or design studio concentrating on decorative fabrics may fit the bill. Or perhaps assisting a freelance fabric artist in hopes of going out on your own will suit you. Of course, there are large mills, like Lowenstein, that do a big print business. The key: Open your mouth and know yourself.

STYLING AND DESIGN

Textile Stylist

Popularity-wise, styling seems to be the textile equivalent of fashion design. A typical hierarchy begins with the assistant stylist who supposedly advances to stylist and then head stylist. In a large textile company, every division from menswear to womenswear, childrenswear or knits will have a hierarchy of stylists within it. A stylist may report to a technically oriented product development manager in a mass volume house, a head stylist, styling manager, or perhaps a fashion-oriented merchandise director in a fashion house. Whatever the hierarchy (and it certainly varies), a stylist is best viewed as resting on the marketing line. Indeed, it's worth a reminder that to a great extent the textile industry is run by people with marketing and merchandising backgrounds, that a good design is one that sells, and that much opportunity exists through marketing and merchandising.

A stylist is an overall coordinator, an overseer of the design studio, who guides designers and colorists. Ideas come from conversations with fashion directors, merchandisers, marketing people, salespeople, customers, administrators, textile technicians, travel in the market and abroad, personal ideas, and experience. He or she makes sure textile designs move out of the design studio and get off to the mills, then works with the mills to get fabrics out of the mills and to the customers on time. Most stylists visit mills in person and make more than enough phone calls down South. As coordinators, they work with the broadest possible range of people.

Like fashion coordinator in chapter 4, styling is another wonderful job that combines the technical, creative, artistic, esthetic, and fashionable—and requires knowledge of each. Stylists working with knits generally require more technical knowledge because knits are machine-made as compared to wovens, which are done on looms. But in increasingly sophisticated times, technical training is a must. Ditto for training in business, especially sales and marketing. Background in design, art, or fashion isn't nearly so crucial.

Styling is unusually open to advancement. In a large textile firm, a stylist can become a styling manager, a product development manager, a director of development, or a fashion director, as June Roche did in the upcoming section. Some have moved into sales. Since a stylist is essentially part designer, colorist, production assistant, marketing analyst, merchandiser, and even salesperson, and because the position straddles the creative and bottom-line jobs, ingenuity and work can put you on the training track to any of those jobs. In a small converter a stylist may work only with the company president or opt to start a converting business of his or her own.

But what a hodgepodge the title "stylist" is. Depending on the philosophy and size of a company the duties of a so-called stylist, never mind the title, can vary. Let the above stylist-as-coordinator serve as a guideline, but keep in mind, as the people we'll meet prove, that a stylist may wear more than one hat—or perhaps half a hat.

Brenda Burris is a stylist for one of the country's major textile companies. As usual with big corporations, she is stylist for one department or division, in this circumstance, knitted womens outerwear apparel. Because of the department's smaller volume relative to other departments, Brenda wears the hats of styling manager (head stylist), assistant stylist, and stylist.

She is a coordinator who plans and finalizes the line, attends development meetings, sets and approves colors, does presentation boards, follows up with the mills all along, constantly meets with customers, and gets input on the market. Indeed, Brenda, like many stylists, learns quickly that this "marketing" input is the ultimate key to development of the line. In other words, fabric development works "backward" from us and our likes and dislikes to textile stylists via market researchers, merchandising analysts, the sales force, and product development managers. Indeed, on a day-to-day basis, her time is typically spent evenly divided between phone calls to the sales force and mills, paperwork, and doing the presentation boards and selling to customers.

Here's a typical cycle. Burris styles two lines a year, Fall and Spring/Summer. She begins work about six months before garment manufacturers (customers) purchase fabric and about a year and a half before we see clothing in the stores. Other company departments may begin as much as two years in advance. Her first step is development meetings or what elsewhere might be called merchandising meetings. She reports to the product development manager of her department. Because the company is a "polyester" house, development meetings involve textile technicians who fly in from the South, marketing people, and Burris. "Here we're really talking about technical interpretations by the mill," says Burris. "We don't call anyone 'designer' and don't do patterning or prints. If I 'design' at all, it's with computers or technical knitting machines." Burris then submits "suggestion sheets" based on recommendations from sales and marketing people, customers, fiber companies, and any sources she deems useful. About two months later, her suggested fabrics come in from the manufacturing plants in the South. Burris shows them to salespeople who in turn show them to marketing people who test them out for customers' reactions. The fabric line is now ready to be finalized.

Meanwhile, Burris sets colors. She decides which colors go with which fabrics. Beyond her own ideas, Burris makes up her mind based on color direction and input from marketing and salespeople, maybe fiber companies, color associations, and the corporation's fashion director. Because the fashion director does a color story too, Burris quickly distinguishes between their respective, ofttimes misunderstood, responsibilities. "The fashion director talks concept, color, the latest print," explains Burris. "I talk price, yarn, machinery, the cut of the machines, whether we can do it. Something may be really hot, but what if we don't run that blend and don't have the yarn?" Moreover, Burris is typical of stylists, with gigantic mills producing commodity fabric in mass for volume customers, in that many of her colors are predetermined. "We'll meet their colors," says Burris, referring to her customers. "A lot of fabric you carry over and just recolor. Or a customer has a fabric that's doing well at retail and they just need something a bit new."

Once colors are set, the coloring process is then carried out by colorists, under Burris's aegis. Colorists send the lab dips south, assign color numbers, do the requisite bookkeeping and filing. Burris then approves the colors and follows up with the mills. On occasion, Burris goes to the mill herself if she needs something in a hurry. "If I'm not sure a color will be right, I'll work closely with the technologist down South." She may even work on knitting machines herself. Once sample fabric is complete, Burris assembles her division's presentation boards and does presentations for customers.

Indeed, selling to the designers and merchandisers from garment manufacturers that are the company's customers is her favorite part of her job. "I enjoy sales presentations and working with customers because you get feedback on what you're doing," says Burris. "You're in a vacuum otherwise." She continues, "For some big customers, salesmen want me to do the presentation." As for presentation jitters Burris confesses she's rather adept at presentations. "Customers are looking for security and I've gained a certain proficiency at making the show organized and professional so customers can just sit and take notes." A typical line might include forty fabrics, maybe all lightweight women's knits, divided evenly between staple fabrics and new ones, with twenty-odd different patterns on each.

Another young stylist prefers small firms because "they're quick to notice accomplishments and mistakes." Moreover, she works closely with the company president, and is learning new constructions and costing. The New York office only includes the company president, his assistant, an assistant she shares with the home furnishings stylist, and two salespeople. The duties of this contented stylist are, however, on the order of Burris's. She chooses yarns, colors, weaves, sends designs to the mill, checks on yarns with the mill, makes sure the weave is correct, gets the designs out of the mill, and presents fabrics to customers.

For another young yarn stylist for a yarn spinner and weaver, the perk of the job is "styling the lines and seeing what the trends are." She too gets ideas from fiber companies and color associations with which she shares information on color trends, the economy, the market. So, too, she meets with customers by phone and in person, makes sure orders make it from the mills to customers, checks inventory, gives instructions on what to ship and to whom, and visits the mill down South a couple of times a year. There are six in her department, including three in sales, a secretary, and vice-president of the yarn division with whom she's in constant contact.

Entry-level styling positions range from assistant stylist to colorist, designer, even production assistant or sales trainee. Perfect educational preparation combines textile technology or engineering, art/design, and marketing. "He or she is equally facile with the esthetic and technical, much like an architect," says one professor of textile science, "and has a keen understanding of what's happening in the marketplace."

Our first stylist, with the major mill, began as a sales trainee (see Sales). Major textile companies offer training programs and may recruit on college campuses. Our stylist arranged an interview upon graduation from North Carolina State University with a two-year degree in textile technology and a minor in design. Before this, she obtained a four-year liberal arts degree in music. She also landed a summer internship with the company during college. Although she knew she wanted a styling career, she requested sales and marketing because she thought it was "easier to get a sales job than one in styling or design." Our second example transferred out of a college buying program into textile technology while at school and landed her present job right after college based on a teacher's recommendation. "Right place at the right time" is her explanation. The last of the stylists has a degree in textile technology and is going for a B.S. in marketing. She first did freelance handweaving.

Assistant Stylist

An assistant stylist might put together swatches for the swatch book, run errands for the stylist, and handle paperwork. One merchandising and styling trainee with a shirt manufacturer explains, "I work with the stylist on fabric alterations, swatch fabrics, will look for a specific detail like a stripe or plaid, keep in touch with the mills to track down goods, and do a lot of paperwork recording sample garments, working out patterns on specification sheets, writing weekly sales reports." He sometimes programs the computer to compare goods sold, check deliveries and purchase orders, and cost the garment. His degree is in fashion buying and merchandising and textile production management.

Summer jobs in high school can't hurt. Possibilities include mounting swatches for a local company, making up salesmen's sample books and sending them out, working next to and doing detail work for stylists, doing detail work for market researchers, or working alongside cloth inspectors of damaged materials. Check for internship programs with major textile firms and with your school.

But what are these employers looking for? "Smarts," says the chairman of one textile science department. "They want people who can think. All school can do is prepare you to begin learning."

Textile Designer

The designer is best thought of as an artist. He or she is the person who physically makes the fabric designs. Design is a visual and highly artistic position, usually requiring some drawing or illustrating ability and patience to sit for long periods of time drawing repeat or intricate designs. Good textile designers know fiber and yarn manufacturing, fabric construction, dying and finishing processes, and which designs lend themselves to mass production if necessary.

Designers generally specialize in knits, wovens, or prints. The first, as we saw in styling, demands the technical know-how of knitting machinery; the second is somewhat less technical and involves weaving samples on looms; and the third calls for painting prints on paper, a job calling for more drawing ability than technical expertise. In a printing operation, a designer may do the actual design, after which it goes to an engraver who interprets its feasibility before it is printed. A large company like Lowenstein corrects the whole thing on computers. A knit operation may involve a knit grapher as well as a designer. All three types of design can and are frequently done on a freelance basis, perhaps from one's home or a design studio.

To break in, go to a qualified textile school for the basics. A department store sales job isn't a bad summer job during school. Neither is a gofer in a textile design studio. If you can afford it, offer your time to a small company where you can learn or at least observe routines, or apply for internship programs with major firms.

One chairman of a textile design department describes the ideal design candidate this way: "He or she should be verbal and able to sell him or herself. It's a selling job to sell your ideas." After that, she stresses "knowledge of the whole market." For a job interview, she underscores the importance of a portfolio of designs that are applicable, practical, and usable.

The more you know of bottom-line considerations—production, costs, merchandising, sales, customers' demands—the better your chances of advancement once on the job. This is not to say design itself can't be a satisfying lifelong occupation. A four-year degree, however, may enhance your chance of becoming a stylist, director of creative services, head of studios, fashion coordinator, or executive of any kind. Computer graphics is an increasingly important skill, as are merchandising and sales. A one- or two-year degree is enough for entry-level positions as a repeat artist, colorist, or designer.

There are designers, some of whom we'll meet in this chapter, who entered the field by way of an art background, teaching themselves, and/or working in a crafts studio. They often open their own studios and sell high-quality home furnishings fabrics through interior designers and decorators. This is a major way textile designers can be at the cutting edge of fashion, although it is by no means a big part of the overall industry.

Another way to be at the cutting edge may be to work for a mill producing high-quality fabrics for sale to finer department stores at $20-plus a yard, or through decorators at as much as $100 a yard. As one professor of textile science summed up, "With home furnishings, customers are more likely to follow their own taste than with apparel and besides, there's no rush to development."

The key is homework (see chapter 16). Research the mills and research yourself. Lowenstein is a giant firm with a big emphasis on prints. Giants like Milliken do no prints at all and concentrate on manmade fabrics for a mass audience. Another giant,

Cone Mills, focuses only on corduroy and denim. Indeed, it's the largest producer of corduroy in the world. Orinoka Mills, on the other hand, is a tiny operation devoted to high-quality decorative fabric. There are fancy grey mills or those that produce unfinished fabric for apparel. A converter may be closer to the interface of fashion. Check it out.

Colorist

If you're ambitious, colorist is a steppingstone to designer, then possibly to stylist, maybe head stylist, or perhaps your own consulting or design business. It can just as easily be a lifelong occupation. Whatever your preference, colorist is a technical position, generally requiring one or two years of textile school, perhaps combined with merchandising, marketing, art, and/or liberal arts, especially if advancement is a goal. A colorist does what the title implies. She or he colors in the designs with paints or dyes and generally works under the direction of a textile designer or stylist.

"I love talking colors with customers and coming up with color concepts," says one twenty-two-year-old colorist at a yarn company. "I meet with customers here or at their offices, go over what they want, help them with their color line, and help them coordinate color from the color library." Garment manufacturers "match" colors in the company's color library, after which the company in this case custom dyes the yarn to meet specifications. "I make sure there's a good match so the customer buys," she says. Call it selling. Indeed, she constantly meets with salespeople for feedback from customers and works alongside them in the New York office.

The second part of her job is forecasting colors. If the idea of initiating the fashion process thrills you, this is it. Colors are forecast a whopping two years before a season hits; Spring of 1984 was complete by December of 1982. To forecast colors, she gathers information from major fiber companies, from color services devoted to color research, and from customer needs. This colorist's first forecast for Spring 1984 received rave reviews. "The best feeling of all," she says shyly, "is knowing you're on the right track."

The third aspect of her job is keeping the company's color library up to date, taking down old colors and putting up new ones. Her goal: to become involved in fabric development.

Repeat Artist

Just as it reads, a repeat artist works out the repeat design. It is considered entry level and requires much of the same training required for textile design and coloring. From here, one can move on to colorist or textile artist and possibly stylist.

Decorative Fabrics and Wearable Art

There is an individualistic, nonconformist, and expressive design path that often begins with an art or crafts background. Many designers or fabric artists don't relate to the mainstream mass-volume textile industry, didn't learn in technical school, and are glad for it. Many begin by freelancing and some grow into thriving studios; others work for a design studio, or go to work for converters with design studios devoted to decorative fabrics by the yard to be made into curtains, pillows, and upholstery. Their fabrics may be sold in department stores or through interior designers, decorators, and architects. Indeed, Susan Starr, a super-successful "fashion artist" who creates tapestries, rugs, clothing, and accessories in her Roswell, Georgia, studio, markets her work through art galleries and art consultants to banks and hotels.

What's newsy is that since the late seventies, some of these folks have found their endeavors increasingly profitable. Indeed, some are being pursued to create fabric collections under their own names by textile companies or even apparel manufacturers. J. G. Hook, a well-known sportswear company, hired a designer to do a "Collector's Edition" that was sold at Bloomingdale's. In reverse, clothing designer Jhane Barnes, known for her textiles, was chosen to design a line for Knoll International, a company known for designing and manufacturing fine furniture.

The two fabric designers we'll meet shortly run thriving businesses with approximately five employees each. Before the studio stage, however, most worked from their homes, maybe with a loom in an apartment or garage if they're weavers. They bravely carted yardage to local decorators or fabric showrooms, made an initial sale, and kept going until orders became large enough to warrant additional space and hiring assistants.

Anya Larkin, who does handpainted fabric for couture designers and home furnishings, prefers to hire assistants (of which she has five) from the Rhode Island School of Design because textile design graduates "understand the concept of more than one yard and don't get bored." A painter, on the other hand, "wants a new image all the time," she says. Her advice to budding fabric artists: "Work for a small fly-by-night entrepreneurial company and learn everything, or take a better paying job and do your creative work at home."

Larkin says she encourages her assistants to train with her and then start their own businesses. "I've found truly creative people don't want to do exactly what you do but want to do something a little different," she says. One of her employees does silk-screened evening jackets and kimonos on the side, another creates handpainted floor coverings, and a third paints wallpaper after work. Similarly, Susan Starr thinks ideal training for those interested in expressing themselves through their designs is to work as an assistant for an entrepreneurial effort like her own. Many would-be fabric designers contact Starr for jobs. "I look for personality," says Starr, "because we work so close to each other." She also says too many applicants "want to play here." "You have to be the type who weaves on vacation!" she quips. Starr currently has one supervisor, an expert weaver with a degree in history and ten years of experience who applies colors, organizes the weavers, and talks to customers; a rug and tapestry weaver who graduated from Clemson University in textile engineering and worked as a designer for a major firm; a beginning weaver; bookkeeper; and someone to handle correspondence.

ANYA LARKIN

HANDPAINTED FABRIC DESIGN

"I always painted and sketched and knew I'd be an artist. I came to New York after going to school in fine arts and worked as a gofer in the film business. When I left film for fashion, everyone said I was too old to start at the bottom picking up pins,

but I left a high-paying film job for a low-paying fashion job. I worked for a low-end high-volume garment center manufacturer and I hated it. Then I went to work doing a little of everything for two young dress designers.

"I started making fabric for Mary McFadden, the womenswear designer, in 1974. All along I had been making handpainted suede clothing and selling it to Henri Bendel, and I brought it to Mary because I knew she was interested in handpainted fabric. She commissioned four suede coats for her next show. They were a big hit and she said she'd buy as much as I could possibly manufacture. At that time I worked three days for the dress designers and three days painting fabric.

"The first year I painted every yard myself before it dawned on me I could make patterns. Last year I got out of fashion altogether and started concentrating on up-holstery fabric.

"Usually, I get a call or letter from a decorator or interior designer, all of whom have my samples. For instance, I just got an order for sixty-five yards at $75 a yard from Mrs. Trump of Trump Tower. That's a good order. In this case, they took two samples and created a third so basically we're designing a new fabric for them.

"First thing, I do a 'strike-off,' a one-yard piece just to clarify the design. I check all dyes and mix enough for sixty-five yards. I make sure I have enough ground fabric in the house. An order takes eight weeks, so I'll order a new bolt if I think I'll need it. Then I call the decorator to find out what yard lengths to paint the fabric in.

"To paint the fabric, we use an enormous eighteen square foot lightbox. I have five people working for me, each of whom has a project from the beginning to end. I lay the fabric on paper patterns I've made and we outline the pattern with hot wax and brushes. We just stand there with a pan of boiling wax and trace the pattern just like a paint by number. Wax acts as a resistant, so when we start painting the dye won't go beyond those points. At the end of the day the fabric goes to a special dry cleaner to remove the wax. I pick it up and it goes to a curing factory where they heat set it so the dye won't run. They send it back; I wash, dry, and iron it. Then it's ready to be shipped."

SUSAN STARR

TAPESTRY-RUG-CLOTHING ARTIST

When she was eight years old, Susan Starr started weaving. As an art major at the University of Wisconsin, she was still at it, leaving periodically to establish Starr Studio, a weaving studio in her native Roswell, Georgia, to weave in a factory in Mexico, and to start selling her tapestries to galleries in Atlanta and San Antonio. Upon graduation, she applied for a highly competitive grant from the National Endowment for the Arts and the George Arts Council "so I didn't have to support my art as a waitress." Starr won $12,000 grants for seven consecutive years.

Starr Studio became headquarters of a thriving custom-designed tapestry and rug business, and in 1983 she introduced her first clothing in an exhibit focusing on one-of-a-kind woven and/or knitted sweaters, jackets, handwoven shawls, handbags, belts, and boas. Her handmade sweaters, made by a team of thirty knitters, go for $300. Handbags average $200. Of thirty pieces in her first exhibit, Starr sold twenty-five. For now, Starr prefers to sell to individuals by way of galleries "so they feel they're buying a 'Starr.' I set up shows in a gallery or home and I'll get a well-respected social type or a group or a fund-raising situation," she explains.

Starr also sells her tapestries to banks and corporations. In the lush lobby of the Southeast's Bank of America headquarters hangs a Starr, a six-foot-square handwoven tapestry. "They gave me total freedom," explains Starr. "In other cases, I consider colors in the room, other artwork, the rug, but this time my piece was right in the lobby with nothing around." Ninety-five percent are commissioned originals and run $100 to $120 a square foot. Starr is contacted by art consultants, corporate interior design departments, and architectural firms, most of whom have seen her work elsewhere (in a gallery, private home, or at her studio). "Sometimes the bank president sees my work and contacts his design firm," says Starr. "We sell about twenty percent to New York, twenty percent to San Francisco, probably forty percent in this part of the country."

What makes a Starr distinctive and popular? The answer involves the same ingredients successful designers deliver in chapter 10. For one, a Starr is recognizable by virtue of its unique concept. For instance, Starr weaves with strips of fabric instead of yarn. She does all her own dyeing. Moreover, her sweaters mesh knitting and woven fabric in stunning ways.

Now that Starr owns her much-desired fly shuttle loom she plans on weaving capes. Whatever her commercial success, Starr remains an artist at heart. "My real work is tapestry," she emphasizes. "Art . . . I want it to be very big."

ADMINISTRATION

Although the president of a textile firm may physically sit in the company's southern headquarters, the industry is generally run out of New York City by people with marketing, merchandising, and sales backgrounds. The simplest possible road map is the classic one with the company president at the top. Reporting to him are the sales manager, merchandising or marketing manager, maybe a product development manager, and a manufacturing head. Beneath them will be the design/styling staff, market researchers, and account executives (sales). In a large firm with a more formal structure, each department or division will function as a self-contained unit run by a vice-president of the company or a general merchandise manager, who then oversees merchandisers and production coordinators, while sales people will be responsible to the sales manager.

In a small company, an employee may do more than one of the jobs. In a converting firm, for instance, there may be just the converter, an assistant, a stylist, and a liaison with outside companies.

Whatever the company size, sales, merchandising, and marketing are the backbone of the textile business, even if that business turns out to be a one-man converting operation. Whatever the hierarchy, merchandising, marketing, and sales functions tend to be complicatedly intertwined. No matter what, there's flow back and forth as well as team effort.

A senior partner with a prominent executive search firm, a twenty-year veteran of the business whose job it is to place people in executive positions in the fashion industry, summarizes tools for the top. "To be president of a company you either know how to make a product or you know how to sell a product. Selling skills should be very good at a high level."

SALES

A typical sales department setup in textiles is as it would be in apparel or any other business. There's a national or general sales manager, a regional manager, a district manager, a staff of sales representatives or account executives, and sales trainees. Members of the sales staff are usually assigned a territory or specific accounts.

Sales is a so-called line or bottom-line position, and as such can lead to senior management—if not the top spot—and substantial salaries and/or commissions. The president of Cone Mills, a company with over 11,000 employees and net 1980 sales of $730 million, is just one executive who started as a sales rep. Ditto for the company's executive vice-president.

Sales is also considered the "fast track for women." Experts invariably advise women with management in mind to start in sales.

A college degree is virtually a must. In large prestigious firms, a four-year liberal arts degree is what they're after. Some look for an MBA (Master of Business Administration). College major doesn't seem to matter. As a rule, the more sophisticated the company the more they prefer a broad background with some business, some retail, some marketing, and some math.

There are grumblings in the industry, however, that the MBA has been oversold and that what the industry needs most are more technical managers. The grumblers feel too many textile sales people are hindered by their lack of technical knowledge, and too often merchandise managers and others have to provide technical sales assistance. Whether these are the gripes of a few or a growing industry trend remains to be seen. No matter what, a combination of a broad liberal arts background, textile engineering or technology, business or marketing courses, and a training program is ideal educational preparation.

The personnel director of one large textile company says his company looks for someone "intelligent, promotable to management, stable, career oriented and loyal, with sales aptitude." Many interviewers measure your career orientation and ability to work hard by your work record in school. Want to know how to blow an interview? "Come in and want to know what we can give, not what you can give us. Ask 'Will I be a vice-president in two-and-a-half years?'"

The Executive Training Program

One of the best ways to get into sales is through a training program. You can contact the company yourself for application materials or check with your college placement office for companies that recruit on campus. In one typical program, which can last from three months to a year, trainees are initially assigned to members of the sales force for one day each for a period of two weeks. After that, each trainee spends time in the showroom learning the lines, followed by time in the company's various departments or divisions. Once training is finished, trainees are given accounts one personnel director called "the pits," and they must check in regularly with the sales manager. To develop their selling skills in this particular program, trainees are shown tapes and given case histories by top members of the salesforce. On the manufacturing end, they spend one week at the mill getting an overview. Finally, a corporate orientation comes "after we know they'll cut it." At this stage the trainee spends time with executives (heads of each division), who present programs, after which they spend a week touring the company's plants to view the latest equipment.

Salesperson

Members of the sales force obviously sell a company's fabric line(s) to customers and service those accounts. That could mean anything from supplying fabric in a pinch, setting special colors for a big account, or just calling a customer with congratulations on the birth of a child.

Salespeople are crucial members of the marketing-merchandising-product development team. In an industry where customer input ranks number one in planning a line, salespeople play an important role, directly or indirectly, in developing the line and new products.

All of this requires abilities to build longstanding relationships quickly, and to take rejection well. A good salesperson relates to the product. If you don't believe in your product, you can't sell it.

SAMPLE CORPORATE ORIENTATION SCHEDULE FOR SALES TRAINEE

Date	Department
6/21 A.M.	Personnel—Personnel Director
6/21–7/1	Sales—Vice-President & General Sales Manager
7/6–7/9	Corduroy—Assistant Vice-President
7/12–7/15	Vice-President
	Assistant Vice-President
7/16	Converting #1—Merchandise Manager
7/19–7/22	Converting #2/Shirting—Vice-President
7/23	Converting #3—Assistant Vice-President
7/26 A.M.	Greige Goods—Vice-President
P.M.	Credit—Vice-President
7/27 A.M.	Systems—Office Services—Office Services Manager
P.M.	Technical—Director of Technical Services
P.M.	Advertising—Director of Advertising

* On conclusion of orientation, product knowledge and department functions will be reviewed by sales management.

How One Sales Rep Did It

Nancy Kirby handles out-of-town accounts for Cone Mills, the world's largest producer of corduroy and a close contender in denim. Her accounts include giants like Levi Strauss, the country's biggest apparel manufacturer. Of landing the job, Kirby said, "I nearly died and went to heaven!" For Kirby, however, the outburst indicates far more than excitement. It tells of hurdles overcome. (See chapters 12 and 13 for further details.)

Kirby's current duties include showing the line to customers, doing follow-up work, booking orders, submitting and following up on lab dips with colorists, and working with merchandisers. "I have an ideal job," she says, "because I do everything from meeting with presidents of companies to working with designers." She adds, "You build up rapport with customers so it's very easy going to the theater or for drinks."

Kirby was most worried about relating to the other sales trainees in the company's training program. "I'm forty and they're twenty-three," she said. "My age turned out to be a plus because guys in their twenties weren't threatened and older guys weren't threatened either." Her first-hand thoughts on tackling a male field: "If women just remember to be themselves they don't have to compete with men. Men play sports. Men get together. Men aren't afraid to ask for help or advice in business."

Kirby also lives by the advice she offers beginners. "Once you make a contact, keep it," she insists. "You never know where your paths will cross. I've lived all over the country and it's unbelievable how many times I've met someone and we've known a name in common."

Kirby has drive. She never finished college because "I never knew what I wanted to do." She worked in a department store for a while and did some modeling. After ten years of marriage and two children, Kirby wanted to go to work. She admits it wasn't necessary financially. She just wanted to. So Kirby headed over to a store in Greensboro, North Carolina, and asked for a job. "When they asked why I wanted the job," she quips, "I said, 'To prove women over thirty lead happy, healthy lives.'"

Kirby started as a part-time salesgirl and after six weeks was offered the job of manager of the sportswear department. "What I had was maturity. I commanded respect from the younger girls on the floor. I had a flair," she says. "I had the opportunity to run fashion clinics, to make commercials, to help choose the lines."

Then Montgomery Ward, the well-known chainstore, asked Kirby to run their women's departments. "I was surprised they called," is all Kirby says. There she supervised nearly thirty women and learned profit sheets. "I had my background with people going for me and I had a daughter the age of the people on the floor," she says. "You sell your soul to the store. Days, nights, weekends—you'll never take your vacations when everyone else does."

No career wings its merry way without emotional stresses. Kirby was getting a divorce at the time her feet were killing her on the salesfloor. She wanted to go to New York. Her best friend, on a train ride, happened to plop down next to Cone's vice-president of sales who, in conversation, said, "Have her send me a résumé."

Kirby followed her own advice about contacts, got the sales job, and went through the training program. Kirby was at Cone three months when the man in charge of out-of-town sales left and Kirby won the job.

MARKETING AND MERCHANDISING

If there has been a major change in the textile business in recent history, it is in an increased emphasis on marketing and merchandising over manufacturing. This is an area of the future.

"Marketing and merchandising" covers all steps involved in developing the product line(s) from measuring consumer demand and behavior to launching marketing campaigns and initiating new products. The process includes the work of stylists who style the line, product development experts who plan for new lines (backed by research and development staffs), market researchers who study current trends and attitudes, and a merchandising or marketing manager who reports to the vice-president of marketing or merchandising.

At Cone Mills, for instance, as in many large textile concerns, a vice-president and a merchandiser (merchandise manager) are in charge of each product line or division. So, in the denim division, a vice-president oversees the department. Reporting to him is the denim division's merchandiser. In Cone's corduroy division, an assistant vice-president oversees the division; beneath him are three merchandisers. There is a need for three merchandisers in this division because Cone ranks among the largest manufacturers of corduroy in the world. So important is merchandising, in fact, that Cone's personnel department goes to the trouble of spelling out the division's merchandising function—"to develop new markets for profitable sales of existing and future product lines"—in its information sheet for trainees.

A vice-president or merchandise manager has a high-level job requiring a great deal of experience. As Robert Nesbitt, a senior partner with Korn Ferry International, the nation's largest executive search firm and a man who has placed many in high level textile positions, puts it, "Experience counts a great deal. The merchandising head is close to the same job as president of the company. He also works with the customer base. He doesn't have sales responsibility exactly, but the customer wants to talk to a merchandise manager with product knowledge." Adds Nesbitt, "He sometimes has a good esthetic sense as well." As for educational preparation, Nesbitt says "An engineering degree is now the prestigious degree, not the M.B.A." Others, however, swear by the M.B.A. A combination of business and technical is ideal.

If there is a route to the top, it is the one that starts in the sales force as a trainee and includes the continual acquisition of product knowledge. Eugene Trout, vice-president of the denim division at Cone Mills, represents a case in point. After a degree in marketing and a stint in the Air Force, Trout eventually took a thirty percent pay cut from an unrelated job to come to Cone as a trainee "cleaning up showrooms," because he considered Cone "a company offering a great deal of opportunity." After only a few months, Trout became an assistant merchandiser in the towel and bed-spread division. "Normally," says Trout, "they don't put someone in the assistant merchandiser position without two years selling. However, I did have selling experience in my previous job." After two and a half years in bedspreads and towels, where Trout says he developed promotion packages, worked with the mill on development of the line, planned the line, traveled a lot, did "overselling" or backing up salespeople, Trout won the title of merchandiser with what he calls "more authority and the same duties." Stresses Trout, "One of the keys to being a success as a merchandiser is having a good relationship with mill employees. I have to be able to tell them what I want, and get it," says Trout. After a year and a half, Trout became merchandiser for the smallest of the company's three denim mills, then became general merchandise manager for the denim operation, and, finally vice-president.

In a typical day, Trout says he spends much of his time on the phone with out-of-town salespeople and with the mills concerning problems with upcoming lines. During marketing season, Trout says he meets with the "big customers." In this case, the meeting might involve negotiating a contract or working with a customer who wants something special. "Or I may go on the road for four days and the next day fly to the mill down South. I travel twenty-five percent of the time but my wife says ninety percent." Trout also says he spends a lot of time planning. "We usually meet early in the morning or late at night or have lunch in," he says. The "We" here is Trout, the division's merchandisers, assistant merchandisers, and stylists. Finally, Trout puts in financial forecasts and deals with any personnel problems.

He reiterates: "For any job in marketing you have to start as a salesman. You've got to carry the bag. I think a business background is better than a technical one, but my assistant has a technical background."

At a small textile converter, the merchandising job generally exists minus the sophisticated backdrop of market researchers, product development engineers and other personnel. At one converter specializing in prints, for instance, a young assistant with an associate degree in fashion buying and merchandising from the Fashion Institute of Technology and a B.A. in production management and textiles works closely with a team including the company president. This comes after a year in "executive training." She's involved in pricing, costing, and buying grey goods. She spends about forty percent of her time dealing with the mills, helps develop computer systems, and works with the president on fabric development and with stylists on new prints and textures. (Grey goods are fabrics in undyed state before finishing.)

Product Development Engineer

At major textile firms where this title exists, it can be a popular management job. Routes to this position include assistant stylist to stylist to product development engineer, or designer to stylist to development. A textile degree is good preparation. Said one veteran product development expert for a major company of his duties, "I travel around the world, talk to people, make fabric that sells and make money for the company. "I do this by seeing, by traveling, by knowing what others do, by working with customers. A new product starts with a guy like me or maybe one step before."

One step before can mean getting ideas from the work of top European designers likes Yves Saint Laurent. "We go to all the shows," says our veteran. It also means visiting European textile shows, talking to yarn company consultants, apparel manufacturers, European mills, Japanese mills. "Travel, search, ask," he advises. "Keep aware of everything." In this technical idea game, if YSL is a force, two years later we may find YSL in practical polyester.

Product development experts also supervise stylists and colorists, and visit mills to work with finishing and dying processes there.

As for the future, our veteran says, "The introduction of new fibers is where I think there's a big challenge. We're looking for better performance, lower cost and durability." In one instance, he helped develop a fabric with the feel of wool that's washable, wrinkle-free and crease resistant for use in men's, women's, and children's garments. "We initiated it four years ago," he says. "And started producing it two years ago."

To accomplish this, "we go to a fiber company and say 'We need something that feels like wool,' and they come up with the fibers. I make an evaluation and have fabric made at the mills. We work with dying and finishing very closely. We meet frequently. There are specialists down South in certain areas and we brainstorm." Technical knowledge, especially textile chemistry, is crucial. Then our expert presents his new fabrics to the marketing people. "It's creative but very technical," he concludes. "A fabric has a certain hand or feel to it but there's also supply and demand."

Market Research

Sophisticated market-research departments are usually found in large vertical companies. It is the job of a market researcher to do just what the name indicates—research the market to find out what the buying public wants and doesn't want, what the trends are, how large the market is, where problems are. Doing this kind of work involves research tools such as calling trade organizations, interviewing appropriate experts, interviewing consumers, sometimes via time-saving "focus groups," and writing elaborate reports.

One typical 1981 report from the market research department at Milliken & Company is titled "The Petite Sportswear Market" and aims to "explore the viability and potential market" for petite sportswear. The study involved extensive interviews with department store executives in fourteen cities and with buyers from New York buying offices. It called for audits of petite sportswear merchandise, a thorough reading of articles on the subject published from 1978 to 1981, monitoring the purchases of 7,000 demographically balanced households and analyzing vital and health statistics and Census Bureau reports.

Twenty-six-year-old Suzanne Hofford was the market researcher in charge of this report. She is a 1978 graduate of Clemson University with a B.S. in Management, a minor in English, and an M.S. from the same school in Management Science with a concentration in marketing and market research. Indeed, a graduate degree, usually an M.B.A., is a virtual must in market research. Hofford is one of four market research analysts working from the New York offices. She reports to the Director of Marketing Research in the company's southern headquarters.

Hofford's sportswear study was one of her major projects. Once it was finished, she presented it to the womenswear marketing staff, then on a grand scale to garment manufacturers and retailers. As for results, "people like Levi-Strauss did open petite divisions and retailers did get a lot of direction," says Hofford.

At the moment, Hofford's eye is on automotive upholstery. For this study, ten months in the works, she's already talked to over 80 managers at auto dealerships to find out what's selling. What's the ratio of vinyl to fabric? She's finished 800 interviews with consumers for which she hired an outside consumer research firm. She wanted to know, among other things, what's important when you purchase a car? Hofford then went to Detroit, where she presented her findings to upper management at Ford, General Motors, and Chrysler.

Before commencing the study, though, Hofford developed an initial proposal based on the outcome of development meetings at southern headquarters and submitted it to Milliken's automotive managers. After all agreed on the proposal, Hofford submitted a budget, selected the outside research firm and got the mills to make the necessary samples. "As soon as we see Detroit turning in favor of fabric," says Hofford. "We have to start ordering machinery." She presented her final report, which includes marketing recommendations as well as her findings, to the automotive business staff. Then Hofford put the results on slides and set out to make formal presentations to the directors of purchasing, styling, and interior design at Detroit's auto corporations.

Of her career, Hofford echoes a familiar refrain, "Traditionally, textiles hasn't been involved in marketing. It's been a manufacturing business. This is one of the areas of the future."

Of her daily routine, Hofford offers, "I'm always here at eight A.M. and many nights till eleven. I travel a lot. If I'm in New York three days a week, it's a big week in New York."

Of the pressure, she remarks, "My deadlines are always tight. I don't consider myself a procrastinator but the first three days of compiling a report I always know the pieces but I just can't pull them together. It's depressing. Statistics can take forever."

Fashion Director

In large firms there may be a separate person with the job of giving the line (s) its "fashion" look and coming up with a "fashion-conscious color story." This person gives major, even glamorous presentations to apparel manufacturers, retailers, and potential customers. The idea is to lure them with shared information on upcoming trends, particularly color. In many cases, the fashion director utilizes "idea" garments in making presentations, garments whose look predicts that of two years hence. From these shows garment manufacturers and retailers may indeed get some ideas. In any case, it's a marvelous service for the company to offer its clients.

This service is just what June Roche, the much-touted Corporate Fashion Director of Milliken & Company, does. To garner ideas, Roche goes to the European shows, to museum exhibits, to color associations, to fiber companies, to designers known for influencing fashion. She travels (her favorite hobby) to the Middle East, Europe, the Far East. And on those trips she's paid to exercise her other favorite hobby, photography.

Roche began in the company's styling department as an assistant stylist of wool dress fabric. Before that, however, when the company came recruiting at the New Bedford Institute of Technology (no longer in existence), from which Roche graduated with a B.S. in textile design, she says the company was looking for a man. Roche insists the only reason she was hired was that her marks were so much higher than any of the men's. That was twenty years ago.

Roche not only worked her way into the fashion director's job over the course of twenty years, but she created the job. In the beginning she could be found making samples on a handloom by her desk, creating patterns on power looms down South, and showing the lines to customers. She styled the important sportswear fabrics eventually, set yarn dye and piece-dye solid colors, worked with the big customers, flew to cities across the country to make increasingly elaborate presentations and continued to come up with fresh ideas and colors.

The name of the game for Roche is always color. She is best known for her annual show for which she does the producing, directing, coordinating, writing, and editing. She does one show, held in a custombuilt theater in Milliken's New York headquarters before an audience of 5000 industry decision-makers. Until 1982, however, Roche coordinated two shows, the current one and one for which she virtually became a household word in the industry. Known as the "Milliken Breakfast Show," this former fashion extravaganza was held at New York's Waldorf Astoria hotel, had a three-million-dollar budget, a cast of Broadway stars, and of course, a "who's who" guest list. Once Roche presents her current show in New York, she takes the show on the road, to Detroit (for automakers), to North Carolina (for the home furnishings industry), and to the apparel marts in Los Angeles, San Francisco, and Chicago.

A movie, *Road Warriors*, was the inspiration for her Fall 1983 show, held in October 1982. Roche felt there was a solid chance "Road Warriors" aggressive clothing would be all the rage come fall and winter of 1984. The success of lingerie mail-order catalogues selling sexy undergarments at the height of the recession was the source of her Fall 1984 show, an extravaganza held in October/November 1983. Roche felt there would be a desire for more feminine office-wear or what she calls "executive femininity." Roche has a sense of fashion, of American taste, of current events, and much instinct.

When not on stage or travelling for research, she might be found hidden in a laboratory in a windowless building in the South developing the 120 colors that form each season's color story for womenswear fabrics for this billion dollar company.

If you want to be a fashion director, the typical route begins with a designer's or colorist's or assistant stylist's job and a move to stylist, styling manager, or head stylist. You can also try finding a job as an assistant to a fashion director. It is the same route that, with solid technical preparation, leads to product development with sales or business background, swerves into marketing or merchandising. A textile degree is a good idea. On the other hand, a liberal arts degree supplemented by technical training widens one's outlook, as does travel.

CHAPTER 9

THE FASHION SHOW AND ITS SHOWPEOPLE

By 10:00 A.M. the limousines are three deep outside the Pierre Hotel on New York's Fifth Avenue. Inside the hotel the fashion press, buyers, celebrities, and society clients are beginning to congregate outside the Cotillion Room, where at 11:00, the first of Bill Blass's three Fall shows will take place. It is the last Monday in April.

What these veteran showgoers expect is a glittering, glamorous, dramatic, and sophisticated parade of clothes, 100 samples to be exact, expertly worn and worked by the world's top models whose faces are easily interchangeable with magazine covers, commercials, ads, and European shows. Veterans know the show will last only a little while, under half an hour; that the clothes will be grouped by fabric, by style, by overall look; that different music will accompany each little group but that song flows into song as group flows into group to create a collection. Some anticipate

the flashy finale, that last sensational, super-smashing group Blass always saves till the end. It will be eveningwear. It will be beaded, glittering, sparkling, dazzling. Flashbulbs will burst in quick succession. TV crews will move in for a closeup. Blass will walk ever so dignified and almost shyly from behind the curtain, flanked by his favorite models, nodding to the clapping crowd, cigarette in hand. Well-known fashion writers and editors, those who know Blass personally, run for a quick snappy quote. Devoted clients, wives of corporate czars, Nancy Kissinger, Barbara Walters, nudge in to give Blass a peck on the cheek and mention dresses that struck them as appropriate wardrobe additions. Some members of the press, particularly from *Women's Wear Daily,* snag buyers from top department and specialty stores to record their impressions. "His best collection ever," one can be heard saying. "Wearable," says another.

What some elegant showgoers probably don't know is that inside the Cotillion Room at 10 A.M., Bill Blass is watching his one and only cursory run-through of an event whose price tag is enormous. This day of the show the Blass collection is insured for one million dollars. It is the one and only time the cast of characters, from the producer/director to assistant directors, set and lighting designers, stage crew, models, hair and makeup artists, and backstage dressers meld to create what is to be a gala spectacular, a one-shot Broadway show of sorts.

Designer

As you may recall from chapter 4, Bill Blass goes to Europe for fabric, his "inspiration," about six months before the show, a year before items reach stores. All along, Blass has been sketching. Coworkers, like promotion director Tom Fallon, say Blass sketches every available minute—on planes to charity functions, late at night, waiting for lights to change. After finalizing the line, samples are made in the six weeks or so before the show by a staff of samplehands and one assistant. Models drop by for regular fittings with some designers. They don't always with Blass (see Models). Meantime, collection samples may be in the works up to the day of the show.

Blass has the final okay on everything—from the pros and cons of carpeting the runway and, the color, cost, and delivery time of the carpet to whether his society clients would be happier seated on risers in the rear or in the first row, which models carry off his collection best, and which music, lights, and sets best project the Blass image.

Blass is in close contact with his promotion director and liaison man, Tom Fallon, who hires a reliable group of professional freelancers that includes Tess Sholom, a jewelry designer, with whom Blass met the previous December because Sholom's Fall collection premieres at the same time Blass's does. Fallon contacts a theatrical designer to construct and design sets and lighting, a music coordinator to come up with tapes for the show's segments, thirty models, and two hairstylists. Everyone involved returns to the office periodically to watch the collection progress. On the day of the show, Blass is nervous as hell. He's seen one dress rehearsal just hours before. His saving grace is confidence in his people.

Promotion Director

It is clear to Tom Fallon that piecing the fashion show puzzle together belongs among a promotion director's myriad responsibilities. "The fashion show is one of the most important aspects of promotion," says Fallon. Indeed, the purpose of the fashion show is to promote and publicize a designer and his clothes. Why else cater to the press and celebrities?

For years Tom Fallon produced, directed, and coordinated the Blass shows himself in-house. As he describes it, the more the fashion show became a professional production, the more he and Blass "just had to hire someone professional to produce it." They handed Michael Arceneaux the producing reins in 1981.

But Fallon's current liaison function is still no small job. "Bill may have an initial meeting," says Fallon of the outside professionals hired, "but he needs a liaison." The music consultant and set designers schedule their appointments through him. He meets with them to plan and make adjustments later as the show nears. He calls the agencies and books the models. Because the group of "world-class models" who

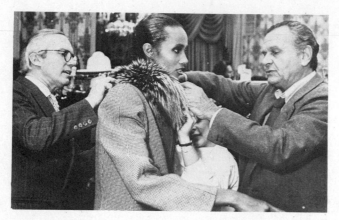

do the major shows is shockingly small—about seventy "girls"—he generally knows exactly who works the clothes well and who Blass likes.

The critical part of Fallon's job is knowing Blass himself and the image he wants to project so intimately that he is virtually a surrogate Blass where freelance personnel are concerned. "I watch his fittings. I watch the collection build. I can talk to him, work with them, and then talk to him," explains Fallon. "So much tension is put on the show. Choosing the right girl for the right dress. I second-guess him. I know the right attitude." He continues to explain his role in show preparation. "I work the lineup with Bill, then Michael [Arceneaux], and I adjust it. Bill has specific ideas but he doesn't have time. I know his thinking. It's all filtered through me. When I have a question that has to go to Bill, I can ask him when he has a minute without appointments that take his time."

The promotion director plays an important role the day of the show too. He is a critical contributor at the early morning dress rehearsal, at which he sits with Blass. "I sit and edit with Bill," he says. "Even if it's just to tell a girl, 'Don't pull at the skirt,' or maybe we thought four girls in red dresses would look snappy with white hats but once we look at it it's overpowering."

Bill Blass, like other designers, videotapes his show and Fallon is a go-between here as well. "A lot of stores use the tape for selling," explains Fallon. "They'll have the tape running at the point of sale. I also take it when I travel across the country."

Fallon's travel involves another type of show, the kind that complements a big charity bash or "do." Blass does anywhere from twelve to fifteen a year in this country. He has also done shows in Japan, Paris, and Berlin. "When he goes out it's for a big charity event," says Fallon. "I go, I fit, I stage, and I rehearse." He uses show videotapes as a training tool for any new models.

At this stage in his career, Blass doesn't do the third type of show, the popular minishows in department and specialty stores often boosted by a heavily advertised personal appearance. "Trunk shows are selling shows," insists Fallon. "Our salesforce does that."

Fallon started as an assistant designer for Halston, then became menswear design assistant for Blass. Of interest to jobhunters is how Fallon went about landing his current spot. "I worked for Blass's menswear company and we had a show in Boston," he says, smiling. "So I'm looking through his women's collection in Boston one day. I was disappointed and told these two guys, who told him! Then Blass says, 'I'm looking for an assistant in my womenswear.' In two months I came to work here. I took over producing the shows."

Fallon's words of wisdom to jobseekers: "Design students must be made aware that creative talents aren't reserved for the design room. We have a model who became an assistant designer. Ralph Lauren was a salesman. Perry Ellis was a salesman. If you have talent, position yourself and it will come out. A production manager, a sales manager, a fabric buyer all have to be esthetically sensitive." And, of course, so does a promotion director.

The Producer/Director

"The problem with my getting into fashion was that it didn't have enough show biz," says Michael Arceneaux, the producer and director of the Blass extravaganza. "So I brought show biz to fashion."

Indeed he did. Arceneaux, like a handful of freelance producer/directors, is hired to coordinate the efforts of the designer, models, set and lighting designers, and music

coordinators in much the same way a theatrical producer/director does. "This is an industry where people applaud a dress!" Arceneaux says with a smile.

Arceneaux, like the other fashion show freelancers, has a rather rarified job of his own creation and one that has only come into its own in the late seventies and early eighties. When an apparel company opts for a splashy show, it may use in-house people to produce and direct the show, as Tom Fallon did until 1978.

When an outside producer is brought in, that producer is often Michael Arceneaux. Besides Blass, he has done shows for Calvin Klein, Geoffrey Beene, Fendi, Giorgio Armani, Murjani, Valentino, Evan Picone, Ferragamo in Italy, and Issey Miyake, the Japanese designer.

In late 1981, after doing the Monsanto (a major fiber company) and Fendi shows, Arceneaux wrote Bill Blass a letter saying he'd like to do his show. Tom Fallon called Arceneaux. Once called in, Arceneaux instinctively considers whether a show is to be a "presentation" or "an introduction," each calling for a different approach. When the collection has been seen elsewhere, such as Europe, the "presentation" is the thing. Case in point: one breathtaking event for Japanese designer Issey Miyake's collection aboard the aircraft carrier *Intrepid* with enough models to sink a ship. Case in point: Valentino's smashing spectacular up and down the grand staircase of the Metropolitan Museum of Art.

When a collection has never been seen by press and buyers, as with the Blass Fall collection, the clothes are the thing. "This type of show is intimate, slick, clean, fast paced, pretty, and sophisticated," explains Arceneaux. "It's important not to over-power the clothes." So as not to detract from the clothes, introductions are usually held in relatively understated surroundings: theaters, design school auditoriums, or a designer's own showroom. Because Blass considers the Pierre Hotel's Cotillion Room ideal for his collection, location isn't an issue. On other jobs, Arceneaux may suggest appropriate spaces, although he doesn't actually rent or contract space.

In the case of the Blass show, the set and lighting designer, music coordinator, models, and hairstylists come part and parcel with Blass. In other instances, Arceneaux may be asked to hire them himself. Arceneaux is also assigned a production budget to cover the extensive hiring costs and incidentals.

For the Fall show in April, Arceneaux starts about three months earlier discussing ideas for sets and lights with freelance theatrical designer Michael Hotopp. The two then build a model stage set (see Theatrical Designer). "It's a *lot* of work. The best part of working with pros is that they know how to collaborate," says Arceneaux of his little team. At least one more meeting follows, after which Arceneaux meets Hotopp and Blass to fiddle with the model stage and finalize the sets.

Similarly, Arceneaux discusses music with another longstanding team member, music coordinator Tom Dillow, who meets with Blass about a month before to toss ideas around. They firm things up about three weeks before the show. If Arceneaux changes the models' lineup the night before, he'll call Dillow, who makes adjustments.

What follows is an interim period during which the collection is being done and the samples finished. From March into April the collection is finalized. During this period Blass, Fallon, and sometimes Arceneaux determine which models will be hired (see Models). Hotopp is at work on set construction. Tom Dillow is taping.

All along Arceneaux stops in to check on the progress of the collection, as do other freelancers. He meets with Blass initially and later if necessary. As time goes on, he'll have a solid idea how the clothes are to be grouped, a crucial element in his two scripts. Dillow's music carefully follows these clothing groups. A change of clothes can equal a change of music.

As soon as Arceneaux knows what the collection looks like, he starts staffing the show. Before he's done, what with stage crew, set and lighting designer, music coordinator, and models, he'll hire 250 people. He uses five assistant directors for the Blass show, all of whom he hires three days before the show but all of whom expect this last-minute routine. His assistants are all dancers and "theatrical people," and two of these work full-time throughout the show season. His right arm, Renee Baughmann, was in the original cast of *A Chorus Line* on Broadway. Another crucial assistant

handles production and functions as stage manager. The five supporting players will read Arceneaux's script for the show and make sure all goes well, from models to set arrangements, on the day of the show.

About two weeks before the show, Arceneaux puts together two scripts. One features lighting, music, and staging cues. The other features a diagram of the stage with arrows showing where each model walks. Arceneaux is a choreographer of sorts. Each assistant director gets copies of both scripts. Arceneaux usually finishes the scripts about two days before the show. The so-called run of show, or who wears what in what order, is figured out with Blass.

Says Arceneaux of the real preparation for the show just hours before the press and buyers file in: "It's like cooking a meal. You spend hours cooking it and twenty minutes eating." The show's called for 11:00 A.M. and the models must arrive between 8:00 A.M. and 9:00 A.M. From eight to ten, "We work the girls," says Arceneaux. This amounts to a quickie run-through based on the show's script, while hairstylists are at work. Arceneaux instructs the models where to enter, where to walk, to count to ten as they stop in certain parts of the stage to "work the clothes," and when to return. In each case, he insists the models repeat his instructions back to him. That's about it.

Each model has a rack of clothes, each with a card prepared by Arceneaux indicating by color whether to enter stage left or stage right. It carries a diagram with arrows showing the step-by-step route onstage as Arceneaux noted previously. The five assistant directors help zip zippers, button buttons, fix flyaway hair. The lights dim. The music sounds. The lights come up. The glamorous meal is served.

"Knowledge of show business and knowledge of fashion" is as close as Arceneaux comes to a career formula for potential fashion show producers. Arceneaux has a background in dancing, acting, fashion design, and illustration. He was also creative enough to concoct the job and lucky enough to enjoy good timing.

Arceneaux was born in Louisiana and moved to New York City in 1964 to study fashion design. He also danced and acted off-Broadway. He admits he had no idea what he was doing. He also remembers others saying he "had guts." He worked as a womenswear designer for a number of important designers in the late sixties. Of one of those jobs he says, "It was the wrong place at the wrong time." In 1968 he was chosen as one of three most promising young designers in the business. Calvin Klein was another.

In 1969 he turned his hand to illustration for clients who included major fiber companies. As a consultant to an ad agency he also designed three lines for a fur account and fell into doing shows for the first time. His first big one was for a fur company, starred Debbie Reynolds, and was held at the Plaza Hotel in Manhattan. He continued to try his hand at directing and producing. In 1974, he relocated to Los Angeles. There he designed menswear full-time for a year or so until returning to New York in 1977, where he started doing shows again, this time for fiber companies. Shortly thereafter, the fashion show as the essential dramatic accompaniment to a couture collection took off. In 1981 he approached Blass. We know the rest.

Jobhunters do contact Arceneaux. Most want to know how to do what he does and most beg to assist him for nothing in exchange for the opportunity. He has very occasionally taken a few up on it and indeed believes getting a job working close to people like himself combined with studying fashion magazines is one way to start. "Just convince me," says Arceneaux of what he looks for in hiring newcomers. "I remember sitting in Bergdorf Goodman and saying I was the only person in New York who understood the Giorgio Armani show and what it should look like. I just said, 'I know what to do. I'm your man.' I was also an unknown." Then there was Arceneaux's jobhunting behavior on a much earlier occasion, while tracking down an assistant design job with a major designer. "I begged him. I said, 'I want to do this! I am good. I want to be here!' I was twenty-four at the time and at twenty-four when I wanted it I knew it. I couldn't bear to hear no. Just give me something with people who inspire me—I love it."

His advice: "Ask yourself what you want to do. What is your life experience? I was a dancer young. I figured out how to put together a portfolio and pounded the pavements for illustration and design jobs. Just do it. There's no magic."

He continues, "You go in and audition and be as good as you can be. Tomorrow's another day. When you get the job, you have a glass of champagne, and when you don't, don't worry about it and don't wait till people call you. Then much later you're a star and everyone thinks it happens overnight. I'm thirty-eight!" He's even smart enough to continue to keep his eyes open. "I know there's a fashion pendulum," he says. "Fashion means change. The pendulum could easily swing back and all this fashion show business could be over." What would Arceneaux do then? "I will change too," he says.

Theatrical Designer

What do the Bill Blass show, the Osmond Brothers' Las Vegas concert, Barry Manilow's apartment, the Broadway show *Oklahoma*, and IBM's television commercial have in common? All were staged by Michael Hotopp and his company Associated Theatrical Design, Ltd. Minus a partner, he is now Hotopp Associates.

Blass is Hotopp's sole fashion account. His biannual path to the runway begins about three months earlier with an initial meeting with producer/director Michael Arceneaux to "kick ideas around." Arceneaux has already met with Blass, gotten an idea of the look and focus of the collection, the "idea" to be strung through the show's scenery, lights and music. Arceneaux will be at any meeting Hotopp attends. At their second meeting, Arceneaux and Hotopp check out the rough sketches Hotopp has done since their initial meeting, and they choose a concept for Blass. The next time the two meet is in a taxicab on the way to Blass's Seventh Avenue office for meeting number three, where Hotopp presents his pasteboard and paper "sketch model" of the stage. The three physically tear apart the model, putting an exit here, an entrance there, levels here, models there. He goes to a final model ten days later, which he and Arceneaux finalize with Blass. All along he checks out the growing collection for color, pattern, and texture.

Hotopp moves now into construction drawings, selects materials, and gets Blass's approval. For instance, he chose carpet to match the color of the Pierre Hotel's Cotillion Room, where the show is held, and brought carpet samples in for Blass to see. It will take four to five weeks for the actual manufacture of the stage, a job he contracts out to "reliable companies."

Next, Hotopp works up a "lighting plot." Although the overall purpose of his job is to highlight the clothes, he must also carefully consider any negative effects on video equipment, photographers' flashbulbs, and audience members.

Blass is the only fashion client for whom Hotopp provides "full technical production services." So Hotopp contracts to have the scenery built, arranges trucking for set delivery the day before the show, and hires the take-in crew and stagehands. Installation takes twelve to twenty hours and is usually done anytime from noon to 9:00 P.M. the day before the show.

For the show, the crew arrives at 11:00 A.M. the day before to assemble the stage and lights, carpeted stairs and runway. They even have time for a quick dress parade with two models Blass brings along. Bill Blass is always present the night before. Clothes are put in order on the racks. On occasion—but not this time—Polaroids of models are taken and attached to each model's rack so she'll have a visual game plan. The day of the show, Hotopp is out with the press and buyers, watching.

Hotopp's two biggest catastrophes were a thirty-second power failure which he mended with a mad dash for the chief electrician (there's always a standby staff), and the time he opted for mirrors and all the flashes went straight into them, masking the clothes.

If you're seriously considering a theatrical design career with an emphasis on fashion, you probably don't need to be warned of the competition. "It's extremely difficult," says Hotopp. More surprising might be that Hotopp considers himself to be just getting started in as much as he hasn't done much Broadway or film work. For beginners, he sees no route other than going to school in theater as he did. He also emphasizes the necessity of expanding beyond fashion, because two fashion shows a year don't pay the bills.

Hotopp attended Carnegie Tech (now Carnegie Mellon University) in Pennsylvania and transferred to New York University. He studied theater design, scenery, costumes, and lighting at both schools. Hotopp grew up in Charleston, West Virginia. After college, he got a job teaching at North Carolina School of Arts, was drafted into the military, and then came to New York to work for a production firm that packaged shows for then-popular dinner theaters and summer stock. In 1973 he and a partner started their own company, Associated Theatrical Design, Ltd. That company employed five full-time in model making, drafting, illustration, and general studio assisting chores. The company designed scenery and lighting and worked with carpenters using blueprints, sketches, and models. A company that once did shows for Blass brought Hotopp in when Blass needed a set for a Blassport division show at the famed Four Seasons restaurant. "That was seven seasons ago," says Hotopp happily. "One of the reasons everyone stays around is Blass is a wonderful person to work with."

Music Coordinator

Living one's life as a music coordinator or programmer for fashion shows is a rarified existence and Tom Dillow, music man of the Blass blasts, is the first to admit it. "It's a small class but I'm at the head of it," he smiles.

Dillow hails from Virginia, attended Georgetown University, dropped out, and says he's never been interested in fashion. His love is music and he's played everything from piano to violin and harpsichord going back as long as he can remember. After quitting college, he came to the Big Apple and landed a job that bears no relation to anything he's done since. Knowing his intense love for music, a friend set him up in a business putting together tapes for parties, dinners, restaurants, or any social event for which people are willing to fork out money for professionally made tapes. It was a simple freelance operation calling for a soundproof corner in his apartment where he could put together cassettes and reel-to-reel tapes. In 1978, a model friend who knew Blass brought Dillow, who had never dreamed of programming music for fashion shows, to Blass's attention.

Dillow's initial encounter with Blass was amusing. "Blass said he wanted 'red music.'" He laughs. "So two days later I came in with the reddest music possible, a big orchestrated tango to match Blass's twenty-two [orchestrated] red dresses." It won Dillow a freelance job he still maintains and launched a reputation as well as a new career option. Dillow's since done music for Christian Dior and Yves Saint Laurent in Paris, Michaele Vollbracht, Carolina Herrera, Fabrice, and numerous department stores.

As for Blass, Dillow talks much like Arceneaux. "I know what to expect," he says. "I'm always looking for ideas. I'm always prepared. It takes a couple of months to get the bulk done." He's quick to add that the last-minute rigamarole hardly excludes him. "They change the lineup and I make adjustments the night of the show," he says. This could mean adding fifteen seconds more to the Stravinsky and taking ten seconds away from the Thornhill.

Dillow first meets with Blass about a month or so before the show. "He'll have an idea or say, 'I want new stuff,' or he'll say a word or something that gives me an idea," he says. "We firm it up about three weeks before the show, but it's all subject to change." So, too, Dillow's in touch with Arceneaux "note for note . . . we spend hours

here picking music," he says, referring to his combination apartment and studio. "A good three days within the three weeks before the show."

Rehearsal the morning of the show is Dillow's tape tryout. He acknowledges, however, that timing is never the same for every run-through. According to Dillow, the key is to make sure he doesn't run out of music. To guarantee this, he includes an additional couple of minutes in each segment. If he knows Blass is going to have seven groups of clothes, he puts together seven separate musical segments, and figures a segment's timing by walking it through himself. If one segment featuring six models takes four minutes, he includes eight minutes on the tape. An asset for Dillow is the enormous talent of world-class models. If one girl spots the one preceding her milking the cameras, she'll shorten her promenade. "There's no reason for me to be more than two minutes off," says Dillow.

There is not only different music for each clothing group or segment, but transitions within segments. "There may be five minutes with Stravinsky, Donna Summer, and Gershwin together and it sounds like one piece. I spend days on it," he says. During the show itself, Dillow is backstage running the tapes.

Dillow keys his success to knowing so much about music. "I can't imagine anyone wanting to do this," he says, thinking back to his rarified niche. "It's not something for someone who's ambitious and wants to branch out, although creatively it's limitless."

Within minutes, Dillow laughs—he seems happy in his work. This time he's talking about the enclosed studio in his home. "I'm often working at five A.M. because the pink dresses are short," he quips.

Models

There are no more than about seventy "girls" who travel the globe doing couture shows. Bill Blass culls his models from this world-class group. Moreover, like other name designers, his girls come from the name agencies that tend to represent these models: Ford, Elite, Wilhelmina, Zoli.

No one is better known among agency czars than Eileen Ford of the Ford Model Agency. The Ford agency offers open interviews from nine-thirty to noon, five days a week, in their New York office. Girls from across the country (if not the world) can be seen stopping in, snapshots in hand and occasionally their mothers in tow, hoping to break in. Ford herself is known for putting girls up at her Manhattan apartment.

On a television talk show one night the host asked Ford a typical question: What do you look for in a model? Ford's response: wide-set eyes, big eyes, not-too-deepset eyes; straight nose; nice long neck; slender body with long sleek proportions especially from the knee to the ground; good legs; healthy hair; a generous mouth with full, luscious lips; light eyes, no brown eyes, please; five-foot-eight is the cut-off height; seventeen, eighteen, nineteen preferably, twenty to twenty-one years of age is the cut-off.

That host asked another appropriate question: But what about becoming a *top* model? Show up at the open interviews, says Ford. It's the only way, she reiterates. Take a train, a car, a plane. Bring snapshots or send measurements in advance with a self-addressed stamped envelope. For one of the agency's highly publicized gala searches, "The Face of the Eighties," 10,000 eager girls showed up for a crack at the title. What agencies are less likely to publicize is that most models are recruited. "They're scouting all the time," says Dianne de Witt, one of the top models in the world. "If they're not identified on the street or the beach, it's the grocery or department store." Confirmed one agent, "A lot are off the streets."

But the real stars, recruited or not, have "something else." Eileen Ford says she saw it in Lauren Hutton. Dianne de Witt has it. If you go to a Blass show, you might be as surprised by models who aren't pretty as by ones who are. "They've got something else," says Tom Fallon of Bill Blass. Maybe it's style or self-confidence or elegance or charm.

Dianne de Witt is reluctant to conjecture just why she's managed to stay on top for over five years. Said Oscar de la Renta of de Witt in *The New York Times Magazine*, "I don't usually like apple-pie blondes, but I do love Dianne de Witt's looks. She has great elegance, an interesting face, and she certainly knows how to walk." Said Bill Blass in the same article, "Good models are actresses, such as Dianne de Witt, who can wear anything. She's just as good in sportswear as in evening clothes."

Dianne de Witt is a Houston girl who always loved fashion magazines, music, and drawing. She wanted to be an illustrator. In high school, she did some modeling for the Sakowitz department store. "He kind of molded me," she says of a former Sakowitz's art director. "He had faith in me." She's quick to add that "school was always primary." She went to Southern Methodist University and majored in music.

In 1975 de Witt finished college, came to New York, and signed with the Ford Agency. In five to six weeks she was in Europe where she was to stay for eight often lonely months. "It's typical for the agency to send new girls to Europe. My Texas pictures were no good," explains de Witt. "You have to get your book together to be a working model." So de Witt went on "appointments" set up by the agency, and her picture appeared in Italian *Bazaar*, French *Vogue*, and *Marie Claire*, among others. She was moving into the international set. "It was sad," says de Witt honestly. "I was in a little hotel in the sixth *arrondisement*, in the San Michel area of Paris. There were lots of days without work and you can't call home without money." De Witt began to do shootings in Greece, Tunisia, Hamburg, Munich and the loneliness lifted. "After that I was set. I had a book and the support of the Fords."

Until 1980–81, de Witt concentrated on print, meaning magazine and newspaper editorials and ads and catalogues, in part because so-called photographic models were never used for runway work. Indeed, Bill Blass was the first to use print models on the runway in 1980–81 and everyone followed suit. It's been rumored that de Witt was one of Yves Saint Laurent's favorite models. In modeling circles that's an accolade without comparison. "The European shows are a big deal. It was a fascinating experience walking down the runway," she says, referring to Paris shows she's done for Karl Lagerfeld of Chanel and Claude Montana. At present, de Witt's time is split between runway, print, and television.

De Witt arrives at the Pierre Hotel's Cotillion Room for the 11 A.M. Blass show between 8:30 and 9:00. "Only in Bill's case is there a small rehearsal," says de Witt of the morning walk-through. "Oscar doesn't have one." For Blass, there are no prior fittings. "For Oscar there are," she says. "We also do our own makeup and for most others we don't." Although Osmani Garcia and Christiaan are around to do hair, de Witt has great leeway. She adds, however, that in the Spring 1984 show "Christiaan gave the runway a new punch." As Garcia said, "The high-paid cover girl has a sense of what's happening."

In the brief rehearsal, director Arceneaux runs through the "blocking" for the show, demonstrating to the thirty-odd models where to go when, where to stand and exit. A card on each girl's clothes hanger maps out where she'll enter, exit, and walk. At most, de Witt will have four garment changes.

"What happens at eleven, when the lights dim and slowly come up, makes you the model you are," says de Witt. "What happens on the runway is impromptu. If the designer decides something's no good on you, you switch with someone else. Your job is to sell clothes."

To do that, models "work" the clothes and "working" simply has to be seen to be believed. It's what de la Renta meant when he said de Witt "certainly knows how to walk." It's pure professional theater—part training, part "something else." The way de Witt moves her hips forward and tosses her head back. How even the dreariest garment looks sophisticated.

The highest caliber models know all the tricks of the trade. That makes rehearsals unnecessary, slipups rare, and justifies $2,500-plus-a-day salaries. "If the cameras are clicking on the girl in front of you," says de Witt, "you give her more time and cut yours short." If the music skips a beat or repeats there's an impromptu game plan. If a garment's too big or small and a model can't switch with someone else, she knows how to work it. If four costume changes are in close succession, she might wear four pairs of panty hose and peel each off in order of appearance, depending on their colors.

De Witt's personal game plan is "have a normal life with normal dating." She smiles. "I like being a girl from Texas. I'm very close to my family. If being a student appeals to you, get an education because modeling is short lived." She adds, "Get an agency! Freelance models give the business a bad name."

When all's said and done de Witt is probably typical in that she considers television commercials more challenging than print and runway "because I deal with copy and acting." De Witt's résumé includes T.V. commercials for Ultima II lipstick, Vidal Sassoon shampoo, Black Tower wine, and Pierre Cardin men's cologne. "The only bad thing," she says, "is that you can't work for a competing product until the commercial's released." Unlike many models, however, de Witt hasn't set her sights on Hollywood. She is open to the possibility, she says, "but who knows? . . . I'd like a husband and family and maybe to go into business with friends."

Hairstylist

"It was just like in the movies," says Osmani Garcia of his 1979 selection to style the tresses of Blass's thirty stunning models. He was joined in April 1983 by a second and trés chic hairstylist, Christiaan.

Garcia came to the United States from Cuba in 1974 and went to work as a clerk in the garment industry. One day on the subway home he spotted one of those ubiquitous subway ads promising a lucrative career in hairstyling. On this particular day, Garcia tore one off.

Garcia attended the hairstyling academy nights for fourteen months while clerking in the garment center. He laughingly admits his performance wasn't first-rate. "I never thought I had talent," he confesses. Garcia figured school was meant to help find him a job so when the hairstyling academy had an opening in one of the top salons on Madison Avenue, Garcia jumped at it.

After a four-week trial, he got the job. A short time later, the owner's assistant left and Garcia stepped in. Of his jobhunting success, he makes one helpful point about his own personality. "It was not in my head to go to the small operators. I will go to all the big salons." Interestingly, Garcia notes that the Madison Avenue job opening was available because recent graduates were "afraid" to interview at top spots. "You have to put your head in higher places," he says. "If there is something good out there I will try it. What I admire about actors is they go to so many auditions. If they don't like your work, you're just not right for the part. Don't take it personally."

While at his salon job, Garcia was introduced to people at the Fashion Institute of Technology, where he styled for shows and exhibits. Here's the big break of which

movies are made. Garcia was shlepping equipment for the hairstylist doing the Blass show. In
a rare twist of fate, the hairstylist pooped out at
the last minute and Garcia found himself, equipment in hand, at the Pierre Hotel at rehearsal
time. Blass already called in another hairdresser
but asked Garcia to get started in the meantime.
"I did five models before the hairdresser arrived," he says.

He joined the Blass show team in 1979. For
that show, Garcia meets with Blass a few weeks
before, looks at photographs of the models, the
hats, and the dresses. In some cases, with name
models, Garcia knows what to expect because
he's worked with them year after year. No matter
what, he works with what the models show up
with, according to season and the image Blass
wants to project. As with the other accoutrements of the show, hair is a complement to the
clothes and must never remove audience attention. "This is a fashion show," he says. "Not a
hair show." Garcia insists hairstyles must be
well balanced. In the last show, the clothes were very neat and classic. "That was
the idea so maybe I can do a chignon or French twist and maybe I have to adjust the
hairstyle because some models wear a hat in one part and then not in the next part."

Backstage the morning of the show, Garcia begins with the rest of the show team
at 8:00 A.M. As with everyone, the key is speed. Thirty hairdos in two hours. "I start
right away," he says. "If someone needs a blow dry, they come earlier. Others may
not come till right before the show." In any case he works with whatever cuts the
models already have. But the high-paid cover girl knows what's in style and what's
not. "I can always brush the hair back and use a false braid, false French twist, or
chignon," he continues. Although he rarely does, Garcia can also alter styles in the
two later shows if earlier styles don't work with the line we want to project. And what
if a model doesn't like it? "She brushes it out," Garcia quips. "If she doesn't feel secure
she won't project." And, he adds, "You have to learn fast to take rejection and to deal
with some selfish people—and when you're dealing with it, the glamour goes out.
It's not an easy job."

"I have no idea why I'm successful," says Garcia. "I never thought I'd be a hairdresser. I never thought I'd be here and I never planned anything." Probably so. But

what he did do is position himself, in this case in a Madison Avenue salon, a move that kicked off a series of "lucky" breaks. "If there's something good, I will try it," he insists. Moreover, one can never underestimate the ability and desire to freelance, which Garcia now does. "I hate nine to five," he says. "I don't mind crazy hours. Midnight. Sundays. Early in the morning. I like that but I can't do every week the same thing. I can't even remember what I did the day before." It's only more interesting—and in a way inspiring—that he doesn't think he's talented.

Success tends to breed success. Several more fashion shows, photographic shootings for major fashion publications, and television commercials have followed the Blass show. Garcia's goal: "the movies."

Accessories Designer

How well a show is accessorized is a critical part of a designer's job and of a show's success. There's jewelry, belts, scarves, hosiery, hats, shoes.

As you can imagine, selection for a major fashion show is a big career break for a budding accessory designer. What may surprise you, though, is just how frequently name designers recognize and introduce new accessory design talent. Indeed, it is as a result of being chosen initially, sometimes early in one's career, that an accessory designer shoots into the "name" category.

Tess Sholom is one example. She is more than willing to admit that ever since Oscar de la Renta came across her work after her first year in business and invited her to design jewelry for his show, her jewelry sales took off and so did her career. This included an invitation to do the Bill Blass show in 1978, and for years thereafter.

Tess Sholom designs a collection of bold jewelry which premieres at the Blass show much as do the clothes. "No one sees them until the show," insists Sholom. She works closely with Blass. "We compromise," she says of their relationship. "Sometimes the length will change but we work from what I'm doing." That work begins months in advance with an initial meeting with Blass in December to plan for the Fall show in April.

Sholom was born in Chicago, lived in Vancouver, British Columbia, for two years, grew up in San Francisco, and moved to New Jersey at sixteen. She majored in botany at Barnard College in New York, was a cancer research lab assistant for five years, went back to school for certification as a physical therapist, and worked in that capacity for ten years (see chapter 13). In fact, Sholom is responsible for inaugurating the cardiopulmonary respiratory center of New York's Albert Einstein Medical Center.

Sholom accidentally fell into fashion by virtue of an invitation to a friend's woodsy wedding. Sholom wore the requisite jeans and gauze top and hated the idea, so she spruced things up with a homemade necklace and belt. "They're pretty. Why not sell them? wondered a buddy at the forest feast. In two weeks Sholom accumulated a small inventory of necklaces, went store to store, and bumped into such success that she took a one-month leave from the physical therapy job. A month later she quit. Sholom settled into that initial do-everything-yourself stage noted in chapter 10.

And like Andrew Fezza, Sholom had the smarts to try for press coverage early. Like Fezza she got credits early, namely in *Vogue*. "I went to *Vogue* immediately," she says. Unlike Julian's experience with initial publicity elsewhere, Sholom says of *Vogue*, "They are very approachable. They're always looking for new talent." So apparently was Oscar de la Renta in 1977 when he asked Sholom to do the jewelry for his show.

Sholom agrees aspiring and struggling jewelry designers would give their right arms to be in her shoes. Visibility and contacts are why. "Other designers got to me after that," she says. "I design things Galanos uses, Bill Blass uses, Giorgio St. Angelo uses. I did Lena Horne's jewelry in her Broadway show and, because of Galanos, the first lady wore one of my necklaces the night she had dinner with the queen."

"I'm very scrupulous about my own expression" is Sholom's personal key to success. How many dozens of times did clothing designers in chapter 4 and textile designers in chapter 8 fuss about the importance of concept? Sholom's accessory concept: "Bold, strong, and innovative. Dramatic but quiet drama." That's a pretty decent account of an image name designers aim to project in their fashion shows.

Sholom abides by psychological, not practical, formulas. "Enthusiasm, intelligence, hard work, and being open to suggestion" top her list. "Ask questions," she stresses.

Strategically, "What I do if I'm not familiar with something is ask questions and work with it anyway."

She worked with new materials anyway, new people anyway, with the lack of formal training, with a career change in her thirties. "I'm forty-four," she says. "Age has never been an issue."

CHAPTER 10

STARTING YOUR OWN CLOTHING DESIGN COMPANY

It's mind-boggling the numbers of people who want their own design businesses. Indeed, when a random group of high school students interested in fashion named their dream jobs, more often than not the answer was "to have my own business." In Los Angeles and Dallas, Minneapolis and Philadelphia, young and not so young, the same tune rings out.

Certainly, the very existence of name designers and the possibility of lucrative licensing agreements are a luscious lure. Sadly, some have the ill-conceived impression that it's fun and games, fame and fortune, glamour and glitz. Indeed, one high school senior off to design school planned to gross ten million by age twenty-four. But let this be a warning: You can forget your own business if you are not prepared to pay dues and pay in time, money, effort, and perspiration.

Name designers have done a good turn too. To some extent they've inspired bright, young, talented entrepreneurs like Rebecca Moses and Andrew Fezza, who provide two unusually honest accounts of successful startups. They're typical of a growing group of individualists coast to coast challenged by their own brand of creativity and ideas.

For instance, there's the designer from Shanghai who received a degree in sculpture and was inspired by her artwork to design down coats because of their sculptural shape and perspective. She now has a business partner and has received some national recognition. She maintains her operation away from Seventh Avenue's hustle-bustle and sews in her own workshop, where each person is responsible for a piece of clothing from start to finish.

The idea of making antique lingerie from hand-embroidered handkerchiefs put two women in their thirties, one with a social pyschology doctorate and one a veteran designer, on the fashion map. Indeed, the Metropolitan Museum of Art features two of their originals in its costume collection.

A second two-woman team met on a movie set, where one worked in the art department and the other was an actress. One lived in Los Angeles and one in San Francisco. They now work from a space in the SoHo section of New York and have a wholesale volume of $600,000 after three years in business. Their concept is dresses and separates, recognizable by their easy sophistication, pockets, and antique buttons.

Light breezy dresses in a moderate price range have taken one Minneapolis designer's reputation beyond the Midwest, but haven't budged her. She insists living in the Midwest helps her maintain perspective. (Halston and Blass are proud Midwesterners.) Her company's volume hit the half-million mark by her third year in business, bringing her to the attention of the president of a leading apparel company who bought her company and now handles the business end.

Ford Beckman, a talented Tulsa man in his twenties, comes from a retail background, having opened a sophisticated men's shop in Tulsa (Ralph Lauren, Perry Ellis, and Alexander Julian hail from retail). His stunning and expensive sweaters and vests are earning him recognition, sales, financial backing, and an expanded design range as well as an apartment in New York where he now lives with his wife.

Conversations with apparel design entrepreneurs show powerful similarities in approaches to building a business. Most have a relatively recognizable or salable concept, as is obvious from the previous tidbits. "It's important for new designers to have something to identify with," says Andrew Fezza, who is known for his work with leather and suede. It can be remarkable fabrics, the hallmark of Jhane Barnes. Alexander Julian is known for unique uses of color. A super-feminine look characterizes another. This is your design direction and it surfaces in individuals in individual ways, at individual times.

Most start small, build gradually from a solid foundation, and do everything themselves. As Rebecca Moses says, "It takes a gradual period where you constantly keep
building." The stereotypical young designer might start out making samples with the
help of part-time sewers, friends, or entirely by him or herself at home; cart a few
samples off to a local store; face skeptical buyers; and make an initial sale. Maybe
a nervous trip to New York comes later with sales to prominent department and
specialty stores and meetings with important buyers. If all goes well, orders eventually
exceed home production capability and a typical turning point is upon us. Get serious
or get out. Assuming you're serious, you'll ask around for a suitable factory, for workspace, for money, for a staff (most of whom will turn out to be relatives, friends, and
you doing a lot of everything). Both Moses and Fezza hired their mothers. Initial
employees will inevitably be chosen for their willingness to be all-around-everythings.
The first "real" employee is often a salesperson, followed by others a couple of years
later. The flashy shows and design experiments are years away.

Hurdles, obstacles, mistakes. Most common is the bad business deal, especially
in New York City, with a contractor (factory) or store, and is characterized by not
getting paid—or worse, getting ripped off. "I was so young and I didn't even grow up
in the city. I grew up in the country, and I thought everyone told the truth and was
out there to help you," says Jhane Barnes, the designer. "But for every person that
screwed me there were ten that helped," says Vicky Davis, a tie designer from Oak
Park, Michigan. "I went to the bank and they said, 'You are not in business with a
very honest man.' I was Little Miss Buttercup. I had not found out everything about
him. I learned a lesson. I've grown up." (For Davis details, see chapter 13.) Andrew
Fezza's tale features a doozie. Most say they almost went out of business at least
once; the fashion industry makes it easy. Skip a season and they'll skip you. Mistakes
in a new effort range from ordering too much fabric, as Betsey Johnson did her first
year (she still calls it nightmare pink) to sewing too many garments.

"Getting business background" and "working for someone else first" are the how-
tos of cutting down on mistakes, according to insiders. In addition, retail experience
at any level helps. Your school or major seem irrelevant. "Work and learn and make
mistakes at someone else's cost," stresses Moses. Jhane Barnes, who went into business right out of design school, agrees. "Get a job and learn because if you do,
hopefully you'll spare yourself some mistakes later." "Learn" is the buzzword. To
learn, you *must* do far more than your job requires and you must be infinitely aware,
alert, and curious. Both she and Fezza milked their jobs for all they were worth. Gail
Levenstein became license director of Bill Blass that way (see chapter 13). Fezza has
the final word. "I did far more than the assistant designer job because that's the only
way to learn."

Indeed, business mistakes can cost. Where $5,000, $10,000, $15,000 did the trick
years back, a startup can run $50,000 to $100,000 today. Moreover, naive undertakings

of yesteryear are becoming the sophisticated ventures of today. "I made a lot of mistakes in the beginning because I really didn't know anything about business," says Barnes. "I really wish I had at least taken some business courses. I mean I wouldn't even start a business without courses. The deals, the way we work, the banking business. They came up with different ideas every year."

Starting a business requires sacrifice, much of it personal. Says twenty-four-year-old Rebecca Moses, "You may have to sacrifice going out all the time, social life, maybe getting married for a while. My life revolves around this business. Even when I'm home I'm working or my mind is working. I'd like to have a normal family life too, but right now I have to sacrifice. If going out and partying, having a good job and making a normal amount of money appeal to you, that's what you do. If you want to be the best in a certain area, you have to sit down and say, 'I have to sacrifice.'" "There's never a break," confesses twenty-eight-year-old Andrew Fezza, four years into building his business. "I'm doing too much work others can do. It doesn't allow enough personal time. I'm taking my first vacation and I won't have time again for two years."

Jhane Barnes admits she never thought she'd get married and was as surprised as anyone when, at twenty-eight, she did. As you might expect, husband Howard has joined the business. "He works in the office until nine or ten at night. I start at eight in the morning and don't take a break until he comes home around ten. We eat dinner around eleven or twelve, watch some TV, and if I really have to go to work again, I will." We opened an office in Japan this year (1984). We're there six months a year and when I'm there it's eight in the morning to two A.M. seven days a week. Now when I'm home, working eight to midnight seems like a vacation. People say, 'God! You never get out of it.' But I like it. What's fun is I look my best and feel my best when I'm working."

Highly successful young company presidents seem to be achievers with competitive personalities and a desire to be tops. Some show signs early. Rebecca Moses: "When I was in school, if I got a B on a project, I would do it over till I got an A. Not to prove it to the professor, to prove it to myself." Listen to Jhane Barnes: "I wanted to be an astrophysicist or a musician in a symphony orchestra. I wanted to be better at the French horn than anybody. What really made up my mind not to pursue it was when my music teacher took me aside and told me I'd never really be excellent. But I was the best in designing in high school and my home ec teacher told me that."

Moreover, they're determined, highly motivated, not easily discouraged, and often challenged and strengthened rather than weakened by failure or rejection. Interestingly, you'll notice later in this chapter that being rejected for a head designer's slot prompted Fezza to design clothes himself, just as "inferior" placement-office job interviews prompted him to knock on doors himself. When Rebecca Moses was told she couldn't possibly design sportswear because she had no experience, she set out to do it anyway.

They're risk-takers. "You've got to be able to say, 'My God, I can't pay the rent this month.' There's nothing like not being able to pay rent to make a person take a major career risk," says Jhane Barnes. "You've got to be willing to be scared. You've got to be willing to take a chance. If you work for somebody you've saved five or ten thousand dollars and you say, 'Okay, now's the time.' The thing is you've saved the money and sweated for it and may not be willing to take the risk of losing it all. When I started it wasn't my money. To me that's harder because I had responsibility to another person. That's what made me work so hard." Adds Rebecca Moses on the eve of her second season in business, "My volume is probably a little over half-a-million dollars right now. It's difficult because the stores order late and pay late. It's such a gamble. It's worse than Las Vegas. I have to make commitments when I open up a collection without even getting a piece of paper. I make commitments on piece goods, on everything. So it's a very high-risk business. You really have to love it. I mean you shouldn't be able to imagine doing anything else."

Love is important. Ditto for maturity, people skills, leadership ability, persistence. Talent isn't a bad idea. Neither is intelligence. Our two select up-and-coming designers have these essential ingredients. Rebecca Moses is twenty-four at the time of this interview and Andrew Fezza is twenty-eight. Moses has been in business a little over a year and Fezza about four. If you're not as ambitious as they are, fine. If New York isn't your goal, fine. If your concept isn't set in stone, don't worry.

REBECCA MOSES

Rebecca Moses was born in 1958 in Jersey City, New Jersey, and she is now one of the most promising designers of those in business for themselves. Here's why.

"I love clothes," says Moses. "I love putting clothes together. Maybe it was my Barbie dolls." In high school, Moses's testament to an interest in fashion was painting shirts one summer. One other testament was knocking off high school in three years "because I knew I wanted to study fashion." What she wasn't sure of was the type of college education she wanted. After carefully weighing the pros and cons of a four-year liberal arts degree against a fashion school degree, she opted for the latter. "I was too anxious and I really wanted to get a quick education and start working."

Moses went to New York's Fashion Institute of Technology and "worked real hard for two years."

Upon her graduation, the school's placement office got her a job in a coat and suit house. "Most students at that time didn't want to do coats and suits," she says. "They wanted to do sportswear or dresses. But I felt coats and suits were the way I designed. It was also a great level for me because suits had been out for a while. I felt people needed something new and suits were refreshing and exciting." However unusual for someone of Moses's age, she ended up designing the Pierre Cardin Boutique line. By her own admission, the collection was extremely successful. She subsequently took over two more suit and coat lines and made seasonal trips to Paris for the couture collections. Par for the course with many successful young designers, Moses is humble. "I mean anybody who would have done a coat and suit line at that time would have been successful. Things just flew." And those "things" were expensive and sophisticated.

Moses does admit she spent a lot of on-the-job time learning the business. "It was just like this constant intake of knowledge," she says. She kept a keen eye on the market. She looked for upcoming trends. She listened carefully to people with far more experience in the business. "I mean these people can tell you stories!" she blurts. "Experiences. The stores. They really *are* the industry. It was a very good education."

After three years on the coat and suit line, Moses decided she wanted to do a sportswear collection. Indeed, American sportswear was the tidal wave carrying American fashion into the international forefront. Moreover, she spent three years working for someone else and felt the initial blossoming of a design direction. It was her first inkling of wanting to be her own boss. "The kind of sportswear collection I wanted to do would not be possible to do for a company on Seventh Avenue," she explains. "It was a strong collection, very expensive, and it was my designing, which was on a very high fashion level for that time. I knew the only way I could get it across was if I started my own collection and merchandised the market the way I thought. So I quit my job and tried to figure out how I was going to do this on no money."

Faith in herself and a design focus help but they don't pay the bills. Moses eventually got a small bank loan but not before having her ego batted about. "I went around and talked to several people on the Avenue and they said, 'You should never do sportswear. How can you expect us to put big bucks into something you have no experience in?'" After speaking to a dozen people, Moses says she felt shortchanged. "It just put a bad taste in my mouth."

The bank loan covered expenses for a small sample collection. A factory in Israel was interested in working with her and helped get a major portion of the collection off the ground. The rest she contracted on a freelance basis. "I had a freelance samplehand and a freelance patternmaker. I had a friend at a fabric store who let me use his upstairs loft as a place to hang my hat. I went up there, put a bar up, and hung forty garments that were wool, suede, silk, knit, all coordinated."

Without salespeople, like many design entrepreneurs before her, Moses set out to sell the collection herself. "I picked up *Sheldon's Retail Book* and I learned geography," she says. "Before that I went through magazines like *Harper's Bazaar, Vogue, Town & Country*, and I looked at ads that were cooperative ads with designers with whom I felt I was in the same category, and I contacted the stores." She started "calling and calling." "The most important thing when I started was my phone," she quips. "The bigger stores are much harder to deal with because you have such a bureaucracy," she warns. "You have to talk to the fashion office first, then the fashion director, the merchandise manager, the buyer. Before you find out who the actual buyer is, you could lose the season." She called and called and called. She sold $100,000 her first season.

Then the problem of money to manufacture the collection reared its ugly head. Moses collected money from her retail orders and took out a loan to finance production. "It was hand to mouth constantly," she says. "I packed the boxes myself. I would get in the office at seven in the morning and leave at ten at night because my patterndrafter had a regular job until five and would come in about six and leave at ten. It was wild, I mean really wild."

She credits Bonwit Teller with "getting her going in a major way . . . they were opening up a New York store and they needed new people. It served as a good springboard for me and the collection did really well. Now the majors are looking at us in a very serious way." She smiles. "But it takes a gradual period where you constantly keep building," she reiterates.

The foundation of Rebecca's budding business, or anyone's for that matter, is fused with knowledge of sales, merchandising, marketing, and promotion. Let this be a warning to readers without experience. Moses on merchandising: "I only wanted to sell my clothes as a collection. I wouldn't let a store come in here and say, 'Well, we want this sweater. That's all we want.' There's a minimum on this collection when you buy it. Otherwise it's not represented as a sportswear collection, which it is." On sales and promotion, Moses tries to stick with stores that promote the collection "properly." To Moses, this means advertising and trunk shows to "really introduce an expensive fine line of clothing to the consumer in the proper manner so that it performs for the store and performs for me."

After a year in business, Moses already had two fashion shows, Spring and Fall. One was held in SoHo, the other at the Fashion Institute of Technology, her alma mater. The introduction of her Spring collection in October coincided with her first move to a real workspace. It also coincided to some degree with an expected move to a more sophisticated level businesswise.

Moses was beginning to need full-time help. In hiring, as in designing and merchandising, Moses is focused. Necessarily topping her list of desired qualities at this stage of the game is flexibility, followed by drive and energy. "From packing a box to greeting the president of a store, you have to be up for it all, good and bad," she emphasizes. "We have set jobs but everyone pitches in. If I can pack a box or take a bag over someplace, why can't someone working for me? I don't like prima donnas or princesses. We work late at night, hang-tick garments, do shows, go here and go there."

Moses initially hired four people, beginning with Jackie, a salesperson, who was with Calvin Klein for three years. Moses carefully weighed the virtues and drawbacks of her choice. On one hand, Moses felt the position allowed Jackie to be a big fish in a small pond for a change and offered her greater if chancy future opportunities. On the other, "Jackie was accustomed to picking up the phone and having people take her calls," says Moses. "Here, the initial response was 'Who's Rebecca Moses?'" Next Moses took on her mother, who left a job as a high-level administrative assistant, took a cut in pay, and came aboard to care for administrative duties. Once again, Moses offered opportunity in exchange for sacrifice. "She came here and it was shipping, billing, stores mispaying, not paying. It was a whole new world." Moses's third employee was a patternmaker. Tailors and shippers remained part-time. Six months later,  she took in an assistant designer, a recent graduate of Parsons School of Design in New York. In this case, Moses believes opportunity far outweighs sacrifice. "For some-

"For someone right out of school this is the ideal way to get experience and learn everything, which isn't necessarily possible in a large operation."

On the eve of her second season, after a year or so in business, Moses is already doing a little over half-a-million dollars. Her ultimate career goal, as you might imagine, is to "take this business to as many levels as possible." Moses wants to build it from her initial foundation into "something large on an international scale," which would include lucrative licensing agreements. If all goes well, we may find Rebecca Moses menswear, outerwear, swimwear, sheets, towels, and luggage. "I think American fashion is having great influence throughout the world right now, and I think any American designer who can relate at that level can make money all over the world," says Moses. "But that's a gradual process."

As Rebecca Moses approaches her twenty-sixth birthday things are happening that will lead to further success. Moses has parted ways with a former business partnership and is now part of what she considers an excellent one. Indeed, Moses gives her business partner and company president, Victor Coopersmith, credit for a remarkable 1984 projected sales volume of $10 million. "Victor Coopersmith has been in the industry quite a long time now," says Moses. "He turned this into a business. He knows how to sell merchandise. He said 'Rebecca, the clothes are there, but we have to bring the price points down,' so he took me to Hong Kong and we did the entire line there. We did a collection, the prices came down significantly, and stores recognized us as a business. Our first year [1983] we booked three and a half million dollars!"

Reflecting on her first couple of years, Moses concludes, "I've learned. I've understood the strength of a business and it's educated me as a businesswoman and as a designer. I now know you can't offer everything to everyone. It's hard to be a creative person and a business person all at once. I had gotten so used to struggling, I used to wonder whether the opposite really happens. Well, it happened."

ANDREW FEZZA

Andrew Fezza wanted to be a dentist. Instead he is a rising star on the 1980s design horizon. In 1983 he is twenty-eight years old, but as far back as he can remember he was aware of "the lack of fashion. I always wanted to redesign things." He smiles in a quietly endearing way.

Fezza had no plans to redesign anything, least of all his life, when he entered Boston College, majored in biology and sociology, and graduated in 1976 "with no idea what I wanted to do." Mildly influenced by a friend who had changed careers via design school and by the fact that he was "at a loss," Fezza enrolled in the Fashion Institute of Technology in womenswear design. Fezza knew absolutely nothing about pattern-making, draping, or the language of fashion, and admits to squeaking by. School taught him nothing, he says, of what lay ahead.

Andrew Fezza

Jobhunting. Fezza relied on the placement office approach. "A rude awakening" is how he describes the ensuing job interviews. It seems he hadn't quite expected the likes of companies that make uniforms for fast-food restaurants.

Fezza switched to the knocking-on-doors method, beginning with well-known Seventh Avenue design bastions. One door finally led to an assistant design position with the sportswear division of a "better" apparel manufacturer. That was 1978.

Fezza says his one-and-a-half years as an assistant designer felt like a long time. He sat at a desk in the sample room to which the head designer filtered work. He answered the phone, recorded information about incoming sample fabrics, kept price sheets, and fiddled with swatches for upcoming presentations. He did manage to develop the company's first efficient system of style numbers. He never did any designing. "They wouldn't let me," he says. They also refused him the head designer position when it became vacant. "In smaller companies there's a greater chance of moving up," he laments.

Frustrations like these fuel more than a few flourishing startups. In Fezza's case, he started making clothes on the job. Whether shopping fabric, doing swatches, or choosing threads and trims, Fezza had one roster for them and one for himself. On something of a lark, he took the garments to a tiny men's store known for its fashion-forward clothing. They ordered fifteen pieces.

"Then it all started," he says. He found women who sewed at home. He ran to suppliers for buttons, threads, and fabric on his lunch break. Making the fifteen pieces took two to three weeks. Meanwhile, he picked up more upbeat men's stores for a grand total of six.

Fezza was aware very early of a crucial element: publicity. While the ladies were home sewing and Fezza worked as an assistant designer, he took his first pieces to *Gentlemen's Quarterly* (*GQ*), the well-known men's fashion magazine. "I had to walk in *GQ* three or four times before anyone looked at them," he says. He earned credits in *GQ, Esquire*, and *Menswear*. His employers didn't notice. However, it was time for Fezza to quit.

He set up shop in his studio apartment, took a $15,000 short-term loan from relatives, and a part-time job in a missy skirt factory in Brooklyn. Fifteen thousand bought fabric for his first season, Spring of '79. His first collection included fifteen styles in different fabrics for a total of twenty-five pieces. In order to build press and store contacts, he joined the Designer's Collective, an organization devoted to showing the designs of top menswear designers to press and buyers in major seasonal showings in a New York City hotel. He considered it an honor to be admitted.

Fezza's studio apartment, crammed full of drafting tables and sewing machines, was his showroom. Major New York buyers aren't big on showrooms off Seventh Avenue, least of all in a lowly downtown studio. Surprisingly, some did come. "They'd see the line," he says. "Then they'd realize I lived there." They were turned off.

Out of money, Fezza had reached that critical put-up or shut-up stage. He chose the former, took a lucky $50,000 investment from a friend itching to get involved, and bought a makeshift workspace at $1,300 a month plus the services of three employees. Fezza hired people in sales and promotion, outside production and shipping, and patternmaking, and relied on three samplehands. The $50,000 also bought fabric for his first real season—Fall 1981, normally shown in January of 1981. He settled into his new workspace in late 1980.

His first season wasn't successful. Sales were poor. "The fifty thousand barely got me through. I had three hundred dollars left," he allows. "We were working on top of each other." What's more, Fezza encountered his first bad business deal. A contractor skipped town owing Fezza $7,000.

Poor season aside, Fezza had the significant pieces of the startup puzzle in place. His design direction, focusing on smashing applications of leather and suede, was particularly strong. "I guess I always wanted a pair of leather pants," jokes Fezza, who usually shows up in a pair. Three people do his leather and suede production from their homes. His merchandising and promotion concentrated on early press coverage to entice buyers to write orders. And when the contractor split town with Fezza's $7,000, he had also abandoned his cutting tables, cutting machines, sewing machines, and racks, which Fezza received as a legal settlement. For the first time, Fezza owned equipment. "The business was official then," he says.

Official and broke. Fezza's business partner, the friend who had invested the $50,000, introduced him to a venture capital group who also became investors. If this sounds like the things dreams are made of, remember Fezza's talented track record, timing, charming if humble personality, and hard work. This could just turn out to be one smart investment.

Financing in hand in fall 1981 and working on Spring 1982, Fezza moved from his cramped space to new quarters further uptown yet still off the established Seventh Avenue track. A year and a half later, he has eleven employees. The group includes his initial employees in sales and promotion, shipping and outside production, and patternmaking and samplemaking. In addition, Fezza employs a bookkeeper, who happens to be his mother, four sewers, and one cutter. Ten percent of his company's production is done in the main quarters and the rest is contracted out to factories in the New York area.

In the immediate future looms a lucrative licensing arrangement for womenswear beginning in Spring of 1984. Fezza says he has a five-year plan of action for womenswear. He'll be traveling to Hong Kong to explore less expensive means of production. He projected a sales volume of $650,000 for his Fall 1983 collection, after four years in business, and feels confident he should reach $3 million by 1985.

LICENSING

Licensing is big business. According to *Women's Wear Daily*, Pierre Cardin received $50 million in royalties in one year from his 540 licensing agreements. At Bill Blass, Inc., license director Gail Levenstein says telephone calls from manufacturers wanting to license the Blass name "never let up. It's extraordinary."

In a nutshell, licensing in the fashion business is the sale of a name, often a designer's name, for use on a product. That product can be anything from apparel, sheets, luggage, and shoes to car interiors and chocolates. The scenario goes something like this: A manufacturer of one of these items calls the designer (or more exactly the designer's in-house licensing director or outside licensing agency), the rights to whose name he would like to purchase. In some cases, a designer or his or her agent will seek out manufacturers. Representatives of both companies will confer. On the designer's end, important considerations are maintaining the company's image, usually one of high taste and quality, and possible royalties from sales of the products. The manufacturer seeking the label wants a marketing tool to increase sales. If both agree, a licensing agreement is drawn up promising royalties up to 10 percent of wholesale volume. For any designer, returns can be enormous, relative to workload and overhead.

Easily the most-asked question is whether designers actually "design" licensed products. The answer is that this depends on the designer, although it is fair to say that industry members prefer to talk in terms of "designer input" where licensing is concerned. This input ranges from designers who sketch guidelines and ship them off to the manufacturer, who in turn develops a prototype which is returned for the designer's approval, to designers who give little more than a nod of the head or no input at all.

For consumers, however, the issue is not so much designer input as manufacturer input. The quality of the product, for better or worse, is the manufacturer's quality. So if Halston signs a lucrative licensing agreement with J. C. Penney, as he did in 1982, with the promise of $1 billion in sales over five or six years, Halston may give "input" on the collections but J. C. Penney is manufacturing the clothes.

Anyone interested in the fashion business should know a little about licensing. After all, it does account for about one-third of all products sold and, as Colombe Nicholas, president of the Christian Dior corporate licensing office in New York, says of job applicants, "Most have a misconception as to what our office does." Licensing is not a separate branch of the fashion business. It is part of apparel design and production. But it does seem to attract jobseekers. Levenstein thinks she gets so many letters because "it's hot" and because jobseekers think of it as "a terrific money-making thing."

There isn't a hierarchy of licensing positions nor does every company have a licensing director. There is most often just one person, hired by the apparel company president or owner, who confers with potential licensees and nurtures them once they've signed on. Some may hire assistants. Another option would be to contact licensing agencies that serve as the go-between between designer and manufacturer. Examples in New York include Creative Licensing, and International Management Group.

As license director for Bill Blass, Ltd., Gail Levenstein has two responsibilities. One is selection of potential and new licensees and the other is taking care of them once they're signed on. She spends most of her time on the phone. Levenstein acknowledges that most manufacturers approach her and most are turned down. "The goal is to bring in ones that are money makers," says Levenstein. "Mostly we either have the product already or we don't want it. For instance, I knew we didn't want diet food or

Gail Levenstein, License Director of Bill Blass Ltd.

half-sizes." This instinctive knowledge generates from Levenstein's familiarity with Blass and the Blass image. It is the Blass image which ultimately sells the product.

Once Levenstein and Blass agree, the agreement is written and signed. Levenstein's licensing agreements for Blass usually list the length of time of the agreement (often two or three years) and the monetary arrangement. In this case there is money up front paid against royalties. There may also be a stipulation for advertising.

The best-known decision by Levenstein and Blass was the signing of an agreement with Godiva Chocolatier to produce Bill Blass chocolates. Levenstein admits the decision was questionable but explains that it did have its virtues at the time. For one, the manufacturer, Godiva, is among the best in its field. For another, when Levenstein tossed the idea to retailers, they were for it. Moreover, Bill Blass happens to adore fine chocolate, and did, according to Levenstein, have input. "It was only moderately successful," says Levenstein. "Not everything you do comes out brilliantly." This, by the way, resulted in a popular joke on the fashion circuit: A designer is announcing his upcoming Fall line and says, "This season we're featuring coconut creme with a marzipan center. . . ."

Indeed, a decision to sign a licensing agreement is not always an easy one, and it can be particularly risky if in the attempt to attract new customers you offend and lose old ones. The Halston-J. C. Penney agreement is a stunning case in point. The risk was clearly that Halston's devoted upper-crust clientele and retailers might drop him seriously enough to damage his business. Shortly after the agreement was announced, the chic retailer, Bergdorf Goodman, announced it planned to drop Halston's line. This was especially significant because Halston is a big seller at Bergdorf's and because Halston himself started out in the store's millinery department. Obviously enough, the store firmly believed that every company, manufacturer and retailer alike, must decide on its customer and remain loyal to that customer.

The second aspect of Levenstein's job, that of servicing the licensees, involves "a fair amount of hand holding" of the company's thirty-three licensees. This may mean calling a buyer when a manufacturer is having difficulty getting into a certain prestige store or involving the manufacturer in a catalogue program.

Colombe Nicholas coordinates the efforts of the thirty-odd apparel, jewelry, and accessory manufacturers that make up Christian Dior's licensees and bring in an income in excess of $200 million.

Nicholas's duties fall in four categories. "I supervise the design studio. We're required to give our licensees sketches, prototypes, fabrics, and design input," she says. "I make sure that it is done and that it is done in the Dior image. We are the arbiter of good taste and style," she says. Christian Dior-New York has four designers who maintain close contact with licensees, and who have specific areas of expertise, perhaps leather-goods. They start out looking at sketches for a

Halston at public announcement of J.C. Penney agreement

line, meet again to check fabric, and they see the line again about halfway through its development. On occasion, Nicholas herself will go to see initial concepts for a product. A new swimwear line is one example. "We decided against putting a bra in

And so the Diors sailed off into married life with their faithful best man aboard.

Christian Dior
Activewear for Men and Women

some suits," says Nicholas, "to satisfy the younger customer. That's a heavy marketing decision so I met personally with our own swimsuit designers and with the manufacturers."

National advertising is a second aspect of Nicholas's job. If there is a national advertising campaign, such as the notable one shot by famed photographer Richard Avedon showing the Diors, Nicholas coordinates the efforts of licensees. If the ad calls for swimwear, underwear, luggage, or jewelry, she'll contact the respective licensees.

Store promotions are a third part of Nicholas's job, and call for everything from "Dior weeks" in stores to catalogues and television. There are also retrospectives of Dior clothes. Once again, licensees will be contacted as necessary to give input on products, money or creative notions. In this case, the coordinating is done by the marketing and promotion department.

Fourth for Nicholas is financial and legal management of royalty revenues. Says Nicholas, who is a lawyer, "I actually practice a fair amount of law because all of our licensee arrangements are legal contracts. When they come up for renewal we negotiate a new licensing arrangement, which does require a certain amount of law." And, she adds, referring to a fur operation in which the company is a partner, "We're responsible for the revenue. But I don't go down and say, 'How many coats are you making?'"

To be a crackerjack license director "you need a positive attitude toward people," says Levenstein. "A gut instinct for people. If you're shy, forget it." Nicholas agrees. She says people skills are the key to her success.

Colombe Nicholas with Andrew Flintermann

To pull off a complex juggling act between one's employer, dozens of manufacturers, and stacks of stores demands more than people power. "You must also be able to bridge a gap between the business mind and the creative," says Levenstein. Tack on negotiations skills, whether born of advanced education as with Nicholas or instinctively as with Levenstein. To bridge the business-creative gap as well as that between perspectives of employers, licensees, and stores, Levenstein suggests accumulating some selling skills, some psychology, some legal background, and "a good head for figures."

As a first job, our two licensing experts suggest sales. Indeed, Nicholas draws an analogy between retail and licensing from the licensor's perspective. "It's sort of like working for a department store in that you work with such a broad range of products." And she agrees with Levenstein that expertise should be more akin to retail than, say, apparel production. In fact, she seeks department store experience or fabric house sales experience "unless you begin as a secretary."

Chances are perhaps better that you will encounter licensing from another, often overlooked vantage point—that of licensee. Andrew Flintermann is currently president of Grosse Jewels-New York, Inc., a licensee of Christian Dior. Grosse is one of the thirty-odd licensees under the aegis of Colombe Nicholas at Christian Dior's corporate licensing office. Incidentally, Grosse Jewels is one of Christian Dior's oldest licensees, dating to 1955 (which should dispel rumors that licensing is only a recent rage). Finally, there is no question that Grosse considers the Dior name a crucial marketing tool and a boon to sales.

In day-to-day operations, no significant differences exist between Grosse Jewels-New York and any other jewelry manufacturer—whether or not that manufacturer uses its own labels, buys another label, or lets department stores put on their own labels. Flintermann rose through the sales ranks as administrators typically do. Says Flintermann, "The same principles apply. We manufacture and distribute, do the same kind of planning. We anticipate fashion in the same way."

There are differences, however, and most concern the role played by the Christian Dior parent company in Paris, either directly or through its corporate licensing office. As part of his quasi-design duties, Flintermann regularly visits Grosse's jewelry factory in West Germany to place orders, plan production, and confer with head designer and third generation Grosse, Michael. Michael Grosse himself, however, works with the House of Dior in Paris to finalize designs. Flintermann, too, is occasionally in touch with Paris and its head designer. In addition, he frequently confers with the head of the design studio at the New York corporate licensing office just as he does with Colombe Nicholas.

At the Albert Nipon offices in New York City, Lois Nipon, assistant director of public relations, keeps in touch with Creative Licensing, a father-son team and licensing agency that represents designers much as a theatrical agency represents actors. If the Nipons are interested in getting into shoes, Creative Licensing sets up appointments at appropriate shoe showrooms. Lois Nipon may be in on initial showroom visits and the first one or two meetings to discuss possibilities. Chairman of the board, Albert Nipon, handles all contractual matters once decisions have been made. Design director Pearl Nipon has the final design say. On table linens and scarfs, designs come from the Nipon design room. To licensees in Canada, London, and Australia for two complete clothing lines Pearl Nipon sends patterns, samples, and fabric. Bed linens, manufactured by Burlington Industries, are designed by a Burlington staff. Albert Nipon, Inc., like many manufacturers run by name designers, has a licensing agreement with Vogue patterns for one dress of Vogue's choosing every season. As Albert

Nipon, Inc., acquires more licensees, the day is nearing when a full-time in-house licensing director much like Levenstein at Bill Blass will be a necessity.

But the range of licensing endeavors hardly stops with sheets and towels. In 1983 New York City alone had two licensing shows packed with people willing to sell a logo, designer name, or cartoon character at a price. To put it bluntly, the myriad forms licensing takes are as varied and imaginative as the people out to make a licensing buck. A licensing phenomenon, and one of the most lucrative in history, is the cartoon character Strawberry Shortcake. The movie phenomenon of 1982, *E.T.*, showed up on everything from T-shirts to dolls and videogames. The *Peanuts* characters pop up on glasses in fast-food restaurants. Some apparel companies, often with intermediary agencies, pay sports figures enormous sums to wear their clothing in major tournaments. There are agencies who specialize in this.

As Jane Evans, executive vice-president of the General Mills Fashion Group, stressed at a fashion careers conference, what sells products is "brand identity," and whether that's the name of a living person (such as a designer) or a fabricated label (such as Izod, the popular alligator) is of little consequence. Indeed Evans, who was largely responsible for the enormous success of Izod, favors "inventing" labels and developing brand loyalty, just as Kellogg's has done with corn flakes. In the fashion business, Jordache is a perfect example. Licensing agreements have been forthcoming and no doubt lucrative, yet there is no name designer behind the label. And without question, the *only* reason savvy businessmen will venture into the fashion business is to garner the enormous profits licensing promises once their label catches on. Indeed Norton Simon, a large corporation, wisely purchased Halston years ago and not because they wanted to own a fine womenswear company. What they were buying was the Halston name and the licensing profits it promised down the line.

As Gail Levenstein honestly says of licensing's controversial future: "As long as there's a consumer out there who needs an emotional hang-tag, we'll have licensing."

CHAPTER 12

WOMEN IN MANAGEMENT

There are not enough women in top corporate management in the fashion business. Surprisingly few, in fact, if we talk specifically about corporate managers and not designers. In the early eighties, for instance, if one were to rely on the press, one might think only of Jane Evans, executive vice-president of the $637 million General Mills Fashion Group; Helen Galland, former president of Bonwit Teller; and Colombe Nicholas. Poor Jane Evans was reputedly so hounded by reporters to be a spokesperson for women making it in the fashion business that she cut back on her usual willingness to talk about the subject.

It is silently understood among women in top management that retail was the first to open its doors, followed by apparel manufacturing, with textiles a slow third.

If any field figures as a launching pad for women seeking senior management positions, it's sales. Sales can only be seconded by an executive training program in a well-respected department chainstore and a subsequent rise through the retail ranks, as all three women cited did.

Sales jobs in apparel and textiles are widely considered not only more open to women but are said to allow them an edge on the trip to the top. Such thinking makes sense. For one, sales is a "line" (bottom-line) position and for the most part only line positions are on the track to the top. Indeed, good selling skills are virtually a must for the president of any apparel, textile, or retail operation. (Examples of nonline jobs or what one manager called "the comfort zones" are personnel, design, and public relations.) Furthermore, sales is a field with relatively accessible entry-level jobs—in showroom sales or in a training program. It is a results-oriented job, in which some saleswomen have gone so far as to find being a woman an asset. Finally, sales can be very lucrative.

In addition, some companies, many family owned and operated, are beginning to pass the scepter to the daughter. "If Calvin Klein's daughter has talent and interest in the business, she may take over," said one executive matter-of-factly. The same executive insists it's a myth that women at the top are incapable of maintaining healthy personal, social, and family lives. "The ability to develop and nurture relationships enhances one's life personally and professionally," she says.

Another crucial ingredient is business skills. "You have to have business skills commensurate with running a business. It's difficult for someone who went to FIT (Fashion Institute of Technology) or RISD (Rhode Island School of Design)," says Nicholas. Of designers who have, in effect, ended up in top management by virtue of their own companies, Nicholas stresses that the overwhelming majority have business managers. "It's a rare person who can do both," she continues. "I couldn't draw my way out of a paper bag. Norma Kamali's label is 'OMO' for 'On My Own' because she does everything. She's one of the only ones." (See chapters 4 and 6.)

HELEN GALLAND

From beginning as a Lord & Taylor trainee in 1945 to taking the reins as president of her own consulting firm in 1983, Helen Galland has amassed the kind of experience that easily makes her an important spokeswoman for women interested in pursuing management careers. She is best known for her tenure as president and chief executive officer of Bonwit Teller from 1980 to 1983.

After her initial Lord & Taylor training, Galland took the traditional step to assistant buyer (millinery), then became a buyer at Bonwit's, where she continued to gain responsibility. In 1964, Galland became divisional merchandise manager (DMM) for accessories and cosmetics, then vice-president and associate general merchandise manager in 1970, quickly followed by a promotion to senior vice-president and general merchandise manager (GMM) in charge of five DMMS, thirty-six buyers, seventy-two departments and a $90 million volume. In 1975, she was lured to the home furnishings division of Wamsutta, a leading textile company, where she became the first woman president and chief executive officer. She took over the top Bonwit's post in 1980.

Galland has a son and two daughters, a stepson and stepdaughter, a husband she terms "supportive," and lives in New York City.

When you began your career, did you think at any time about the effect being a woman might have on your progress?

Not at all. I really thought about the job at hand and what I had to do to give a superlative performance.

It seems that many if not most women in top management started in retail. Do you see retail as more open to women than apparel or textiles?

Oh, very definitely. There are many more job opportunities available for women in retail. But we're mixing two things here: job opportunities and acceptance of women. The textile industry, even today, is notorious for being very male chauvinist oriented.

Do you recommend that women pursue management careers, then?

Oh, yes! I recommend it in every way. I think it's a marvelous opportunity for any young woman who is zealous and dedicated. Upward mobility certainly is there. There's reward for a job well done and it's good money once you pass the entrance.

It seems to me that for an industry heavily based on women's attitudes there are few women in senior management positions. Do you agree? Do you see that changing?

I don't see it changing as much as it should. I read a statistic just yesterday that in 1973 there were no female chief executives of any retail stores and there was one GMM and you know who it was? Me. Today, there are seven women presidents and I think maybe twenty GMMs. It's a tremendous advancement, though.

So, what is it that the few women who succeed possess?

They have an excellent sense of psychology, for one thing. It's a given that you're going to know your job and have all the credentials, but above and beyond that you need a certain charm and personality and sensitivity to know how to relate to men in business situations.

Is this innate or learned?

I think it's both. I think you have an innate sense and talent but you can also acquire the nuances of when and how from having seen enough people. A few years ago I joined an all-male board of directors of a very prestigious four-billion-dollar conglomerate. They had never had a woman on their board and none of them came from companies that had women in upper management. I was preconditioned psychologically to know that how I affected them would determine the response I'd have on that board for the rest of my time on it.

Do you feel, as some women do, that you've had to work twice as hard to get where you are?

I always worked harder but I never thought about why. I was driven.

Did you always want to be in upper management?

No. I really didn't. I must tell you quite frankly that I didn't think about it along the way. It evolved.

But you count yourself ambitious now?

I must have always been ambitious, but there are different ambitions. I was very ambitious in my specific job. That's an ambition, too. I was ambitious to be the best buyer when I was a buyer and make the best figures that anyone could ever make in that department or that department's history. So my ambition was contained in a specific area but it was ambition all the same.

And the result of succeeding at those specific ambitions was moving to the next step and the next?

That's right.

Is that true now? You're still trying to do the best you can in this job?

Oh, yes. Even now, in any assignment that I undertake, I might have an opportunity to cut a couple of corners but I can't function that way. I have to give it my all, and my husband would be the first one to tell you that. When you talk about compulsion. . . .

So, whether you're aware of it or not, you may work twice as hard as anyone else?

Absolutely.

But you work twice as hard as anybody else simply by virtue of being you?

That's right. It's standards that people set for themselves, not necessarily to impress somebody else. I have to be happy with me.

Where do you see areas of growth for women interested in corporate management?

As far as jobs are concerned, I must relate my answers to what I know. I know that while the proliferation of branch stores may have slowed, there are still an awful lot of stores out there across the United States, and women have been loathe to move, to relocate, to take store manager jobs. I think that's an area of opportunity that's wide open to women. I also feel that anything involved with computers, especially software, is open. Computers are becoming more and more important to the fashion industry. You're talking about shopping by computer and retailers are dependent on accounts receivable and charges. I have to tell you a funny story. I had occasion to call the chairman of a store the other day and the switchboard operator said, "Oh, does he work here?" I said, "He's the chairman of your company." "Well," she said, "His name's not coming up on the computer screen." I mean, we're that dependent on computers that you can't be the chairman of your company unless the computer says so!

Do you think advanced degrees are a good idea?

Personally, I always feel that any education is wonderful and that you have to have a solid basic education, but as far as moving forward more quickly, on the job experience counts for a lot more.

We've talked about disadvantages, are there any advantages to being a woman?

Many. There is a certain warmth and charm that women can exude that can serve a person in a people situation. Retail, like many other businesses, is a people business. It is more people than merchandise. Also, men still like women and they cotton to the fact, too. Of course, I'm talking strictly business.

You mentioned that you have a supportive husband. Do you see that as necessary?

I see it as very necessary. I don't care what anybody says, your home life does have to reflect itself in your business life. People can't just turn off. If you have to stay out late or you're troubled and upset and you face a very busy schedule in the morning you can't handle it in the same way you would if by and large you have a happy home life.

Finally, would you describe your current business?

I'm an entrepreneur. I do marketing consulting. One of my clients is Grey Advertising; another is Avon; I'm working with a very fine shopping center in Tulsa; I'm guiding a new apparel manufacturing venture. Obviously, I'm undertaking things that relate to my previous experience. That can take the form of being a consultant to the shopping center, so that the mix of stores is exciting and appropriate for today's world and leases are renewed by those who lend something to the center as we move forward. I go from that to working with some of Grey's clients on how to increase their share of market, especially those that deal with retailing.

Do you have employees?

I work with a secretary and freelance people who do marketing surveys, research, and collect data. So when I say Helen Galland Associates, those are the kinds of associates I hire.

An area where women are really branching out is in starting their own businesses.

That's very true. Many women have asked me about going into their own businesses. It sounds wonderful—and it really is—however there are two prerequisites. Either you have to have a broad base of experience in something meaningful to somebody else or you have to be a specialist in a highly technical area so that you supply a service they cannot get easily.

Do you think one of the reasons so many women opt to start their own businesses is that it's easier, in a sense, than climbing the corporate ladder?

I don't know if that's the motivating force. I think it's just the way so many women want to go, especially women who have had experience with the corporate structure and find it not to their liking.

And within the corporate structure they would have gotten excellent background experience.

That's true. As I say, I still feel that until you reach the point where it becomes highly corporate as a structure, the world of retailing has a lot to offer. There's a lot to take advantage of.

REENTERING

Those (they're usually women) who have chosen to enter the work force later in life deserve respect. The fashion business appears to be a big draw for these women, perhaps because there are so many jobs in small companies where on-the-job training and experience easily replace advanced education, and perhaps because family-owned operations proliferate in which friendship, family, or helping the business out take precedence over age and track record. And maybe fashion is something to which many women have related for so long that it's a natural, almost instinctive choice.

Backgrounds vary. Some reenterers have raised a family. Some are in the middle of raising a family. At forty, Nancy Kirby, in charge of out-of-town accounts for Cone Mills, a prominent textile company, is a mother of two. She was married ten years before looking for part-time sales work, but her career gathered steam after her divorce and decision to relocate to New York from North Carolina. (See chapter 8 for Kirby's story.) Tess Sholom, forty-four, Chicago-born, belt and jewelry designer for the Bill Blass show and president of Tess Designs, was a successful physical therapist for ten years. (See chapter 9 for complete details.)

The desire to get a job or start a career for the first, second, or even third time can stem from boredom, from wanting to "do something useful," or from the desire to develop or discover capabilities. Designers Vicky Davis and Tess Sholom stumbled on their new careers by creating accessories for fun that grew into accessories for profit. As we've already read, Nancy Kirby, when asked by her first employer why she wanted a part-time sales job, responded, "to prove women over thirty lead happy, healthy lives." Harriet Winter, fifty-six, a noted womenswear designer, was forty-five and helping her second husband buy antique clothing for a "flea market" he'd opened in a major New York department store when she said to him, "Everybody's coming to buy our samples and they're asking me all kinds of questions about fabric, sleeves, collars, hemlines, shape. I want to become a designer." Her husband's reaction: "He roared. He laughed. He thought it was the funniest thing in his life." However difficult it is for most of us to get a job and stick to a career track, multiply that difficulty ten- if not fifty-fold to gauge the strength, willpower, stamina, and commitment these women possess. In many ways, they are excellent—if ignored—role models.

When asked to advise potential reenterers, most successful reenterers bank on psychological pointers. "Remember to be yourself" is the theme. "Men are not afraid to ask for help and advice," says Kirby. "If women would just remember to be themselves." Sholom credits "being scrupulous about my own expression" for her success. Tips from Winter: "I'm interested in my own tune. If you dance to your tune you're going to do well. You use your own hands and your own head." Vicky Davis echoes group sentiment when she says, "I get frustrated when I see people being pushed down by others. It's the same old insecurity." Concludes Winter, "When people said, 'You can't do that,' I just had to accept it. Now I don't."

On to practical advice. Our group of successful reenterers features three who opted for freelance design work and ended up with flourishing multimillion dollar companies. One started as a part-time salesgirl and worked up to lucrative high-level textile sales for a major company. One took advantage of a weak connection to start out as an all-around assistant for a prominent apparel company and eventually became license director. Women who have done it are encouraging. Those who haven't begun are cautious and fearful.

Most agree that a little planning can go a long way. Look for a part-time job or go back to school in preparation for reentering. On the surface, freelance options (see chapter 15) seem attractive for their flexible hours and the opportunity to circumvent employers who may frown on your age and weak track record. Indeed, designers cite no age barrier when it comes to carting early pieces to stores and magazines. When Sholom showed her jewelry to *Vogue*, she immediately won a credit. "They're always looking for new talent. I'm forty-four. Age has never been an issue." Vicky Davis says, "Here I was, this older woman carrying a bag of ties around. Buyers thought it was quaint. It was borderline charisma." Indeed, the ranks of so-called freelance fashion consultants who assemble wardrobes for private clients or plan escorted shopping trips include quite a few reenterers. Actually starting your own business, as Vicky Davis and Harriet Winter have done, is more complex and hazardous to the reentering psyche, but can be done. In the job market, sales jobs are a good first-experience option, either in retail or in a showroom.

Like many, Vicky Davis, a well-known tie designer who runs a flourishing operation, Vicky Davis, Ltd., felt bored with her life. She was a housewife in Oak Park, Michigan, with a grown son and a fifteen-year-old at home. It was that vague urge to "do something" or "to keep busy"—and a far cry from an urge for a full-blown career. "When I started this in 1969 I didn't think of fashion. I didn't think of anything. All I knew was that I had reached my forties and I had been very active in our small community doing all the things a mother did or does. I led the perfectly typical suburban life. And what happened was I suddenly could see life was over. The boys didn't need me to drive them around anymore or to be room mother at school. I knew I wanted to do something but I didn't decide I'd be a fashion leader twelve years later."

Vicky Davis

The feeling and attitude may be typical of the majority of reenterers. Take Gail Levenstein, the enormously successful license director for Bill Blass Ltd. "I had a B.A. in English literature with zero plans to do anything with it," she says. "I got married and had children. Then one magic day, my littlest was in nursery school and I no longer felt needed and I panicked."

So Levenstein made a joke to her husband. She nonchalantly joked that if Bill Blass, with whom her husband maintained a slight business acquaintance, happened to need someone, to let her know. "If she's serious, let her call me herself," was Blass's response.

"I had nothing to offer," says Levenstein of her initial phone call to Blass. "But on some level—probably energy—he liked me. So I started out as a sort of assistant doing trunk shows for a couple of years. I just watched and listened and learned. I made it my business to be alert. I also had no interest in design and selling. I didn't like either.

"Boom! I fell into it," is all she says of her appointment as license director after two years as an assistant. "Licensing was there before, but it took off since I've been on the job," says Levenstein. "I can get fifty calls in a six-month period and it doesn't let up. If we wanted, Blass could be like Pierre Cardin with five hundred licensees. I don't have an assistant but it's getting to be a bit much."

Levenstein's least favorite part of the job is "when I'm right and I can't get anywhere." This usually happens when she feels hampered because she'd like to go into a product and Blass says no. What she likes best is never being bored. "It changes all the time. One day it's down coats. Another it's shoes. There are also close friendships."

When asked her ultimate career goal, Gail Levenstein answers, "I don't know. I have no desire to have my name on the door."

Vicky Davis's foray into fashion dates from the time she and husband, Larry, planned to take a cruise out of New York City. Disgusted with tie selections in hometown stores and hellbent on making the ultimate impression in the big city, Davis made her own. "I was a PTA president and all my chairwomen were very creative ladies so I asked one of them if she would sew the ties if I bought some fabric. She said she'd try."

Davis infuses her story with pride. "I went to a little fabric shop, we made the ties, and we went on the cruise. Everybody on the cruise kept asking where Larry got them. One person said, 'Oh, did you get that at Bloomingdale's?' and I said to Larry, 'God! I hope that's a nice store'!" But Davis knew enough to say, "Golly, maybe I can sell these ties." So, on a lark more reminiscent of a newfound hobby than serious career, Davis and her PTA chairwomen made twelve ties. "I put them in a paper bag and I went to our finest little specialty store. If the buyer had said no, I wouldn't be sitting here because I would have taken the no. I've learned not to take nos anymore. In the meantime, he said yes.

"Before long, I took the ties to somebody else and he bought some and pretty soon I had a bunch of my PTA girls working down in the basement. They were all my age. The one who sewed for me became my partner. The two of us chipped in—are you ready for this?—twenty dollars for fabric and three dollars to register the name. We actually started the business on twenty-three dollars. But we didn't care at that point if we made money. It was just something to do. And so it went. And the ties started to sell and I started to enjoy it. I just fell in love. To this day, I feel like this business is my child."

But all wasn't well in the Davis basement. Davis and her partner were putting in forty-hour weeks. The eight PTA women were tired of sewing ties. The lark was up. When Davis told her partner their lark had become serious business and it was high time to invest money, she said goodbye. Davis had asked for $200. "I crashed," she says. "I was so upset. I thought, Oh my God, how am I going to do this alone? I can't even sew!" The next step was a frustrating attempt to search Detroit for sewers or a manufacturer willing to help out.

"The only place I could find anybody was New York," Davis explains. "I didn't come to find fame or fortune. I needed somebody to sew my ties. And I had never flown alone. My husband had to give me a little pill because my heart was beating so fast. And I came to New York knowing nobody. I can't believe I did it.

"So I came to New York, found myself a contractor, and started to lead an insane life because I had two cities and two worlds. My boys were still in their teens and I had never left them before, but before I knew it I was commuting seven hundred miles every week. I'd pick up a cheesecake, be on that plane to Detroit Friday, Larry would pick me up at the airport, drop me off at the supermarket, and I'd cook. That night I'd always have a big dinner and my friends would come over because they always wanted to know what happened to me. Saturday and Sunday I'd be doing the laundry and getting ready for the next week. Monday morning I'd be on that plane again.

"My family reacted with mixed emotions. I'd be at home in Michigan and I'd get a call from my contractor or I'd be in New York and my son would call. 'I have a hundred and two fever. What do I do?'" I think it helped them to grow up because I was a very overprotective mother. My husband was not happy with it and I was not happy because I wasn't making my family completely happy. Yet I loved what I was doing. I was a very torn lady.

"At that time I went into business with someone because I didn't think I could handle it alone," Davis continues. "This is my lowest story, but when I lecture to kids from around the country I tell them because you've got to learn to go through all these things. This man did everything I didn't want him to do with the business. He was taking money from our little business and filtering it into his. I was a wreck. I went to the bank and they told me I wasn't in business with a very honest man. I was Little Miss Buttercup. I hadn't really found out everything about him at all.

"I borrowed money from everyone to sue him and I dropped my business completely," says Davis. "At the end of the whole lawsuit I got five thousand dollars. I was the one who pushed the bow tie rage then. There were thirty thousand bow ties, so the court said fifteen thousand for him and fifteen thousand for you. I went back to that factory and counted bows for one week and I thought, I'm going to do something with these bows. I don't know what I'm going to do, but I'm going to do something.

"I shipped the bows to Michigan and went to a New York apartment I had rented. I had two dollars left on me. Now imagine, I have a beautiful little home, a husband who loves me—upset with me but loves me—kids, and here I am struggling. I had a bottle of wine that night, a bunch of bow ties on my back, a folding bed, and an antique table. And I was happy." Davis credits a department store buyer with turning her around. He told her to get started again, gave her the biggest order she had ever had, and insisted she never use any name on the ties other than her own. "I didn't know it was important to have a name in the market," says Davis. "And that's how I got rolling all over again."

Vicky Davis Ltd., now distributes in the finest stores nationwide. She has a showroom in the women's accessory building on lower Fifth Avenue, an apartment on Park Avenue, a place for production, and a combination design studio, office, shipping department, and cutting room elsewhere in the city. Husband Larry is now vice-president of the company, and son Rob, a graduate of Parsons School of Design, designs with his mother. Youngest son Ken goes in and out of the business as he sees fit. All three now live in New York City. Davis won a prestigious Coty Award for her ties in 1976.

Does Davis encourage reentering? "If I did it anyone can. It's pure guts and push. But I wouldn't trade the years with my kids for anything. I gave it my all-out. But what's wrong with another all-out?"

And a final word from Harriet Winter, the womenswear designer: "I think everybody's time span and time frame is different. We're not allowed to think that way. You have to accomplish immediately. Some people just have to take their time."

CHAPTER 14

PROMOTION, PUBLICITY, PUBLIC RELATIONS, SPECIAL EVENTS

The purpose of jobs in these areas is to generate publicity and thus sell merchandise. Tools of the trade are creativity, organizational ability, a sense of priority, press releases, press kits, fairly good writing, and a personable manner. The fields have an appealing element of show biz. They can also sometimes offer only low pay and long hours.

Promotion, publicity, public relations, and special events directors exist in apparel manufacturers, textile companies, department and specialty stores, at fashion magazines, as separate companies in and of themselves, as interesting niches in an organization or an apparel mart, or purely of one's own creation.

A department store is likely to have a rather formal setup—a vice-president and director of sales promotion at the helm, a publicity director, and a director of special events. Each may or may not have an assistant. An apparel manufacturer is less likely to have such an elaborate structure, perhaps instead with a single director of promotion or a publicity director and an assistant director, aided by fashion directors, stylists, and their assistants on fashion and trunk shows.

Aspiring promotion and publicity people might do well to consider a combination of merchandising and public relations experience with a solid liberal arts background. Peggy Kaufman, the veteran Lord & Taylor vice-president and director of fashion promotion we'll meet shortly, went through a liberal arts college, Macy's executive training program, and then worked for a leading public relations firm. Carol Edwards, who, at twenty-seven, is news/information director at Hartmarx, formerly Hart Schaffner & Marx, one of the most respected menswear manufacturers and retailers, took a similar route. She got a joint degree in journalism and clothing and textiles, went through Marshall Field's executive training program, and then landed an entry-level public relations job at Hartmarx. She's been promoted once. Kaufman, after her stint at the public relations firm, ran fashion promotion, publicity, and public relations at Bonwit Teller for eight years.

And, as Kaufman says, "Someone who works in our area generally stays on the creative side of the business. They might leave us and go to a publication. At this moment the head of merchandising at *Harper's Bazaar* came from this area. Another woman who left us went to set up a publicity department at Concorde Watches. A promotion department in a leading department store is a very good training ground because we do diverse things and because people in this area deal with the public and with other companies and with the publications." Indeed, as a former public relations director of the California Mart admits, there are "lots of opportunities to get job offers."

Promotion tends to be the highest rank of the three, tends to involve the development of comprehensive concepts for the likes of storewide promotions, and tends to be filled by someone with much experience and with immediate access to the president (who delegates details rather than doing them him or herself). If Bloomingdale's opts for a storewide "America the Beautiful" promotion or to spend $20 million on a French theme, the promotion person is in on it from the ground up.

Publicity and public relations are closely related. The name of the game here is contacts, decent writing, novel ideas, and in some way being able to sell them. Publicists and their assistants write press releases, maintain contacts with key editors at newspapers and magazines, contact TV producers, and generally keep the company's name, current activities, and promotions in the public eye. If Levi Strauss is manufacturing clothing for the Olympics, the company's elaborate public relations network will interest magazine editors and freelance writers in doing stories or at least incorporating the idea in another piece. It's not unusual for "P.R." people to find themselves organizing a photo shoot for editorial pieces requested by magazines or newspapers.

One of the tools of the publicity trade is wining and dining editors and writers. In New York, at least, the more powerful the publication the more powerful the publicity person who does the entertaining. Similarly, publicists or P.R. people at department stores or manufacturers offer "exclusives" to more powerful and influential publications. So, if a hot new boutique is being introduced, a leading writer on a leading publication may be given the scoop.

Publicists are infinitely aware of tailoring ideas to specific publications and lead-time requirements at magazines and newspapers. In July, Lord & Taylor held a special Christmas press preview for which they made private appointments with members of the press, who were then escorted to a room beautifully decorated with clothing and gift items resembling displays to appear four months hence. Present at the private showings (complete with elegant service of tea and biscuits) were the store's fashion director (see chapter 7) and its head of publicity. The vice-president and director of fashion promotion and public relations, Peggy Kaufman, was in her office nearby.

Department stores are most likely to have a separate director of special events, although manufacturers and fashion magazines certainly sponsor events from press showings of the latest fashions to luncheons or dinners probably arranged by the public relations staff. To some extent, special events people (with great overlap with publicity and public relations) must know the detailed and often elaborate rules of entertaining for hundreds. They're the ones biting their fingernails wondering whether the chef will slip up or no one will show.

In every major city in this country, Fall is heralded by a series of gala events in finer department stores, from I. Magnin in San Francisco to Neiman-Marcus in Dallas, Marshall Field in Chicago to Bloomingdale's, Saks Fifth Avenue, Bergdorf Goodman, and Lord & Taylor in New York City. Often, these are gala black-tie affairs sprinkled with the rich, famous, and well-born as well as the press.

In every case, events are tied in with an overall storewide promotion spearheaded by a team including the promotion director and president, in turn tied into advertising and window displays. Of course, every store maintains its own image and clientele, and its promotions (including events and ads) are developed accordingly.

Several years back, every major store in Manhattan focused on the overall promotional theme of American fashion, but that's where similarities stopped. Lord & Taylor, in keeping with its classic clean-cut image, called its promotion "The American Look" and chose a genteel rooftop black-tie soiree of society guests. Bloomingdale's chose "America the Beautiful" and was as only Bloomies can be—dazzling, loud, glittering, out for splash and attention. As usual they got it with a $150-a-head evening benefiting a museum and featuring awards for "America's Top Ten All-Stars." The lineup included Bill Blass, Perry Ellis, Norma Kamali, Oscar de la Renta, and Halston. Saks Fifth Avenue held a "SFA USA" sit-down-dinner charity bash for about 600 supported by minifashion shows by Blass, de la Renta, McFadden, Beene, and Adolfo.

If you can fathom dinner for 600, invitations for 600, presentation boards laying out the run-of-show for the designers, table settings, caterers, and seating arrangements, you already have an idea of the work involved.

To get a better idea of how promotion, publicity, public relations, and special events work hand in hand we'll go behind the scenes at Lord & Taylor's flagship store in New York City. Peggy

Marvin Traub (second from r.) at Bloomingdale's "America the Beautiful" bash

Kaufman, vice-president and director of fashion promotion and public relations, spearheads concepts for storewide promotions and has nine people in her department. Her one assistant handles merchandising and personal appearances for major storewide promotions. For the ninth floor promotion Kaufman talks about on page 183, she makes sure all the manufacturers and vendors are coming, that they have everything they need, that the advertising department spells their names correctly in related ads, that they are going to arrive on such and such a day at such and such a time. A divisional vice-president is in charge of all special events. One person with two assistants takes care of promotional follow-through to the branch stores, of which there are forty. Two people work on "special promotions," which can be anything from a morning breakfast for employees to working with the in-house television studio on tapes describing upcoming promotions for branch store employees. The one person spearheading the publicity part of the department works directly with newspaper and magazine editors and has an assistant who helps with such things as pulling merchandise for an upcoming special section of the *Houston Chronicle*. Finally, the department has a secretary who makes sure all scheduling is done, press releases sent out, memos printed. She'll likely work her way up as others have before her.

Finally, publicists and public relations people start their own agencies as well, and for aspiring publicists, working as an assistant for one of these is an excellent way to learn the business. An independent agency is likely to be very small, maybe one, two, three to a dozen people at best, and will handle many accounts which pay on retainer (a monthly fee). There are agencies well-known for handling fashion accounts, others for fragrance accounts, others for menswear, others for European designers.

Those who start their own agencies have usually worked for advertising agencies, or as a publicity director for an established company, so that when they leave there's a decent chance of lining up accounts. That means contacts. Once an account is in tow, this hard-working publicist and small staff may be responsible for the whole shebang—special events, the ideas which generate them, press releases, all press contacts, even advertising.

THE DEPARTMENT STORE

PEGGY KAUFMAN

VICE-PRESIDENT, DIRECTOR OF FASHION PROMOTION AND PUBLIC RELATIONS

LORD & TAYLOR

"You know, I often say our area of the store is very much like show business. You create a stage, you put together a production, it comes on, it has its run, it closes, and you go on to your next thing.

"Now we are doing a promotion on the ninth floor starting the thirteenth of September. It's the renovation of the floor and we are going to do events every single solitary day, six events a day for two weeks.

"Now, one day you might be asking one of society's hostesses to come in and do an entertainment-book signing. You might call a pillow manufacturer and ask him to come in and tell people why down is different from goose feather. Or I might pick up the phone and call Bill Blass and ask him to come in and talk about his sheets or do a demonstration.

"Let's say all three say yes. Is the society hostess going to sit behind a great big desk? Is she going to sit behind a parsons table? Is she going to have lunch with the chairman of the board afterwards? Do I meet her at the door? Do you send a car to pick her up? Does she get treated like a celebrity or a vendor?

"The person who is doing your feather demonstration—does he need a huge lucite cube to demonstrate feathers in? Does he need a fan? Is there an outlet on the floor? Does his merchandise have to get here the day before? What does he look like? Is it a gentleman who might want to borrow a sports jacket because he normally works in a factory uniform? What do we do with everything when he leaves the floor? Does he take it with him? Is it sent back to him? Do you send him a thank-you note? Do you ask him to stay for lunch?

"If it's Bill Blass, who designs not only ready-to-wear for us but menswear and home furnishings, maybe you give him a little lunch afterwards and invite the merchandise managers of all the divisions or the president of the store. Do you send him a little note to thank him or do you send him a gift? What are you doing about his visuals? Who goes over to Seventh Avenue and gets them and discusses them and sets them up? How does he get here?

"Then we are about to open our newly renovated soup bar. It's happening the exact same day our ninth floor promotion is happening, so turn off the ninth floor promotion and turn on the soup bar opening. Have all the invitations gone out to the food press and the fashion press? What are we serving that evening? How will the press get into the building after store hours? Are we playing music? What is the press leaving with? Do we hand out a press kit beforehand or will they leave with a menu that tells what we are going to be serving? Who are they going to interview once they get here? Who from the store is going to be on hand that evening? Does everybody in the store know this is happening?"

THE APPAREL MANUFACTURER

CAROL EDWARDS

NEWS INFORMATION MANAGER

HARTMARX

Carol Edwards is news information manager for Hartmarx, formerly Hart Schaffner & Marx, one of the largest menswear manufacturers and retailers in the country and certainly one of the best known and most respected. The Chicago-based company produces thirty-five brands including the prestigious Hart Schaffner & Marx and Hickey Freeman lines. She is right hand to the corporate director of public relations/vice-president of Hartmarx Marketing Services Group—Robert Connors—who happens to be a leading promotion and publicity maven in the industry.

Edwards was born in Saint Louis, Missouri, and went to the University of Missouri for a joint degree in clothing and textiles plus journalism in order "to tap the best of both degree programs. I initially thought I'd go into retail special events or shopping mall promotion," she adds. Edwards's first job was at Marshall Field's flagship store in Chicago as part of the executive training program (see chapter 7). In 1978, while in college, she was savvy enough to push for a summer internship program at Marshall Field's "doing everything from inventory to customer relations, display and stock work." Although Edwards says Marshall Field's was "good to her," she left six months into the two-year buying program to pursue promotion. She had, however, already worked as a department manager responsible for a sales staff, stock, and merchandising in menswear. Edwards scanned the classifieds and ended up as corporate communications manager at Hartmarx in 1980.

Edwards's job involved both external and internal communications. She began with the internal, an employee publication and management newsletter. "It was a one-woman operation," says Edwards. "I did all the writing, editing, photography and layout." Along with the employee publication, Edwards was encouraged to develop press contacts by assisting in the writing of an industry newsletter published by her company that is devoted to covering the goings-on in the lives of those who write about, or work in, the menswear industry.

As communications manager, she also helped produce press kits, the splashy newsy folders of releases and photos that regularly go to reporters announcing new collections. Edwards attends the Men's Fashion Association seasonal national previews of the latest men's collections and chats with the leading fashion editors who fly in for the show. She watches the company's fashion shows. If she's in Dallas for a press preview, for example, she'll also zip off to a Hartmarx retail outlet and do a feature story on an employee for the employee publication.

Two years ago, Edwards became news information manager and the public relations director's right hand, and is now completely involved in public relations (external) work. Media contact work comes first. "I work as hard as I can to promote the company name, its thirty-five brands, and the retail stores," says Edwards. "I'll arrange for a television crew to visit a factory, for an executive of the company to be interviewed by a media person, for Luciano Franzoni, our fashion relations director, to make an appearance. I'll pull garments for the Chicago *Tribune*, travel to New York and show a line to the consumer press, have photos taken so we can offer them to writers and plan shows and seminars for the press."

"I still feel I have a lot to learn," she says, "I can look over the week and see new requests and crises to tackle all the time. My loves were always journalism and clothing and textiles, and I'm fortunate to be using them all."

Recently, the University of Missouri flew Edwards back as a guest speaker during Home Economics Week to give an overview of her job. "Students are not exposed as much as they could be to career paths other than merchandising," she says. "When informed, they're interested in styling, photography, public relations, but a lot aren't willing to strike out and leave their hometowns, although there is a trend toward going to Texas."

Edwards wants to say something else. "I love being a woman in the menswear business," she confides. "I'm viewing how clothing looks on someone else for a change."

CHAPTER 15

A SELECT GLOSSARY OF CREATIVE CAREERS

If you were to picture fashion as the hub of a giant wheel, its spokes would be the dozens of related fields without which the fashion business would be sadly diminished if not altogether crippled. These related fields contain very special careers, terribly talented people, and rare opportunities.

Advertising/Art Director

Many art directors in fashion work from department or specialty stores; Don Florence was one of them before starting his own small advertising agency with partner Karin Smatt, a firm called Smatt/Florence, Inc. that specializes in fashion and beauty. He has capitalized beautifully on his creativity and drive.

Florence grew up in California and "like most art directors I didn't start out to do this." While at the California Institute of Fine Arts in Los Angeles he, through a friend, finagled a "low-paying, very entry-level" job at I. Magnin doing layouts for ads. At Magnin's, Florence discovered he liked both fashion and advertising. Upon graduation, he continued at I. Magnin doing paste-ups and layouts, became assistant art director "working fifty to sixty hours a week," and, in three years, art director. Meanwhile, Florence managed night school in advertising design.

"The art director is sort of a producer," he explains. "By the time I left, I supervised the newspaper advertising, hired photographers and stylists, directed illustrators and layout artists. I did catalogues, chose the concept, hired models, photographers, and was involved with budgets." In larger stores, he goes on to explain, responsibilities are more segmented. One art director will do fashion ads for newspapers, one will do direct mail, and another national ads.

Florence wanted the big time, came to New York, and was offered the art director slot at Filene's in Boston. He stayed six months when Bonwit Teller lured him away. "After I. Magnin, my goal was to be art director for a Fifth Avenue store," says Florence happily. "So I took the Bonwit's job." That was 1976 and Florence was twenty-seven years old.

"Then I was in New York!" he says. "I went to the collections and was involved in merchandising. 'That dress photographs better than that one.'" As executive art director, Florence ran the show. "Because Bonwit's art department was relatively small, I was involved in long-range planning, concepts for new departments, names for new departments, working with merchants, reviewing what the store looked like, what ads looked like." Moreover, the sales promotion director and the store president listened. "I'd say, 'I think we should do a whole campaign in red,' and they'd listen." After four years, the stunning Fifth Avenue bastion where Florence worked was sold.

Fifth Avenue Bonwit Teller was torn down and Florence moved up, this time to creative director of Marshall Field's in Chicago, a store that does "five hundred million a year relative to Bonwit's sixty to eighty million," says Florence. "Field's is second in the country to Macy's. I was responsible not only for design and look but for copy and a staff of thirty including two art directors, a copy chief, copywriters, layout artists, staff artists, paste-up artists, clerical people." He stayed one year.

"The job was more administrative and not as much fun as New York," says Florence freely. "I couldn't go on shoots and I missed New York. There I'd know in days who the new hot model was or I'd have something to do with making those girls big. Most models who'd be a *Vogue* cover girl or a photographer with potential left Chicago. There was no scene."

Scared is what Florence was when he left his high-paying job in Chicago to go freelance in New York. Busy as hell is what he was after calling everyone he knew. Within two weeks he was working every day. Florence did national ads for *Vogue*, *Harper's Bazaar*, and *Town & Country*, and for a small high-fashion store in California. "Advertising campaigns for small stores like this differ from advertising campaigns for department stores because you can't use the same slogan or ad again and again," says Florence. "You do a separate one for each magazine." Florence was busiest during the collections. "Blass only makes one sample of a particular style, so we'd borrow the dress at five after the show, set up props, lighting, book models; the photographer would do the lighting, and there'd be one to four assistants. And the ad would be due at the magazine in two days."

Another type of freelance account Florence sought was catalogues for department and specialty stores. He succeeded in luring some of the top accounts in the country, including catalogues for Bullock's in Los Angeles, Filene's in Boston, Garfinckel's in Washington, and Marshall Field's in Chicago.

At one point, Florence's schedule was "L.A. one day, Chicago next, Florida, Washington, and Boston like a maniac! I worked 'round the clock."

So, Florence and Smatt, a former creative director for Estée Lauder, formed "a very small, very specialized advertising agency specializing in fashion and beauty" in late 1983. Already his credits include Macy's direct mail and Garfinckel's fall catalogue and advertising, Estee Lauder's Prescriptives, Alexander Julian, Kasper, and New York's Leo Castelli Gallery.

But Florence is particularly proud of landing Filene's entire Christmas program. "It's something no one else is doing," he says. "It's a total concept of advertising from catalogue to television, wrapping paper, shopping bags, and daily ads. It's usually hard to have one look unless it's in-house."

Why are the honchos using Florence instead of the big advertising agencies? "Few have the fashion background," he says. "They don't know photographers and models. The big agencies just aren't interested. There's one fashion agency that's made it and they do Blass and Blackglama. Advertising's either done by small specialized agencies, in-house, or freelance."

Store Design/Display Person

How merchandise is presented is crucial to everyone in apparel, textiles, and retail. It's not the easiest field to get into, but one fairly typical route includes first-hand experience in a store, a design degree, and an entry-level job in the display department of a department store.

A major department store, a plum spot for an ambitious display person, is likely to have a display director in charge of windows, another for interior design, and a staff of assistants. In New York City, department store windows are considered something of an art—drawing tourists, natives, and, at times, much media attention. Tiffany's Christmas windows, by Gene Moore, are legendary. The Norma Kamali store on Fifty-sixth Street is a must for display nuts.

Shan DiNapoli is director of store design at Bloomingdale's. She reports to Barbara D'Arcy, vice president of visual merchandising and a legend in her field. DiNapoli has been in the department ten-plus years, first as a junior designer, then senior designer. DiNapoli is in charge of all design in the New York store and some big new branch stores. Her duties include the interior plan, design concept, architecture, decorating, and fixtures. "If you can detail, have a color sense, the sensitivity to design, and an ability to create an environment, you can design anything," says DiNapoli, who supervises a design staff of ten, some of whom began as store designers and others who started as secretaries.

DiNapoli has a degree in interior design and fine arts from The Pratt Institute in New York City. Her first job after college was for a firm that specialized in residential interiors; her second for an architectural firm concentrating on Wall Street interiors. Because "stores always interested me and I happen to like shopping," when a job came up at B. Altman, DiNapoli took it. She stayed just one year before going to Bloomingdale's.

Of her job, DiNapoli says, "I know every vendor in ready-to-wear, food, and home furnishings because I do every part of the store. Rather than being restricted to residential units or law firms, I get to design offices, restaurants, a beauty shop, a living room, a bathroom, a hallway, a corridor, ready-to-wear departments, food shops, everything." Bloomingdale's, like other major stores, uses outside store design firms too.

Fashion Editor or Writer

Even though publishing is a separate business, we'll give it a go with some short, to-the-point guidelines. At the helm of any fashion magazine is an editor-in-chief who oversees the editors. Before sending off résumés to major magazines, study the magazine well and read the masthead, the roster of employees usually found in the first few pages, that lists publisher and editor-in-chief at the top, then editors by areas of expertise, contributing editors (freelance writers), and finally merchandising, advertising, and production people.

On major fashion magazines, "editor" is tossed about in a rather cavalier manner. There are so many different kinds of editors that those dying to be fashion editors or writers have good reason for alarm when they find themselves handling chores they never dreamed of. There is the editor, for instance, who spends the bulk of her time sampling and selecting merchandise and/or covering the collections. Other editors spend more time in the office editing copy, writing headlines, and following copy through to production. A features or articles editor assigns stories, some to freelance writers who might be listed as contributing editors. In the merchandising department of a fashion magazine, editors spend their time on the phone with stores making sure deliveries are made and store credits are correct. Still others focus on styling. Entry-level jobs are available for assistant editors or editorial assistants.

Not surprisingly, the most frequently mentioned journalism dream job among fashion school students is that of "fashion writer." Jobs for fashion writers, meaning those who literally *write* articles of some length on the subject of fashion, are few and far between. If you study the fashion magazines, you'll discover that most fashion coverage is photographs with the bulk of the writing in the form of captions. Feature-length stories are often not directly fashion related and are written by freelance writers. So, is it writing you want or are you more interested in being an editor? Or maybe you'll eventually establish your own novel niche.

A fashion writer for a major newspaper is one of the few who does write lengthy stories on fashion on a regular basis. She majored in journalism in college and has a master's degree in English. She says she was always interested in writing in and of itself. The fashion part happened by accident.

First, during school this fashion writer worked on a special six-week public relations project writing press releases and holding lights for photographers. After college, she lasted one miserable day on the city desk of a newspaper. "I brought 7-Ups to the editors," the writer says; she was then getting her master's at New York University at night. After scanning papers for six months, she finally heard from a weekly newspaper called *Fashion Trades*, "which was supposed to be to *Women's Wear Daily* what *Time* magazine was to *The New York Times*," she says. What got her the job was mentioning a brief stint listed in the help wanteds as "millinery research" and that she had taken less than seriously and had quit for exams. At *Fashion Trades* she was hired as a hat and shoe editor. From there she went to *Women's Wear Daily*, as a result of a phone call to someone who just happened to know of an opening.

"I think of myself as a writer," she says again. "I always thought I'd teach English and write." As chief fashion writer of a major daily, she explains she "does the same thing whether in London, Paris, Milan, Japan" or at her video display terminal at the paper. "If the collections are on, I do something every day. I'll go to two, three, four in a day, write it up, pick pictures, do the captions, and go home," she says nonchalantly. "In Europe I telex or go to the Bureau office." she also writes a page once a week. "Last week I did something on what people are wearing on the street. I go with the photographer, we choose people, and then I choose the pictures." She insists on writing her own captions.

For beginners, she suggests a four-year liberal arts degree and doesn't think it's necessary to major in anything special. "You could come in as a copy gal. One kind of job you can always get is salesperson. I did it. Move into merchandising and then into something else. *Women's Wear Daily* always hired assistant buyers from Macy's. There are modeling jobs," she offers. "I've only discovered one writer from résumés and she's now chief fashion writer for a major newspaper. Good writing you can spot immediately."

As with all creative careers, fashion journalism has its share of those who strike out after a new idea. Leona Bowman is a well-known example. Her business is *The Fashion Newsletter*, a newsletter devoted to predicting industry trends and giving important information. Like Morris, she wrote for *Women's Wear Daily*, became an account executive for a fashion ad agency, and then executive vice-president.

"One of the accounts I had was a shoe company and I had to write a fashion report for them," explains Bowman. "I suddenly started to write it in a much more flip way than straight fashion writing. I thought then that nobody has really ever done a newsletter for the fashion industry. I had lunch with the then publisher of *Harper's Bazaar* and within two days they had me signed up." Bowman's newsletter is twenty years old. She has owned the publication for the last fourteen. (She recently sold *The Fashion Newsletter* to Newsletter Services, Inc.)

Of her interest in fashion, Bowman says she's always had a "sixth sense" about what was going to happen next. "So beyond writing fashion, I could forecast where the industry should go. I think you're born with a feeling about fashion or color. It's something you just feel or have a talent for," she says.

Bowman prefers the freedom of her own publication to writing for a magazine or newspaper. "When I owned it myself I started going to Europe, and since then I've covered all the collections. Two or three times a year I go to resorts that are very much in. I think we were one of the first to go into Sardinia, and, well, Capri and St. Tropez when it was smart to go there. The purpose of all this is to predict and inform the fashion industry in cases where clothing might be an influence six months later in the resort collections."

"It's a letter of predictions," Bowman goes on. "We cover anything we feel has any influence on fashion. It can be a book, a new play, a fashionable new resort, theater, a craze, a fad, anything. It fascinates me to see how art and world events and current events influence fashion. One of my claims to fame was predicting the influence the film *Chariots of Fire* would have on clothes, which, as you know, it had. I think, for instance, Indira Gandhi coming to the Metropolitan Museum will focus a lot of interest on Indian clothes a year from now."

Bowman correctly predicted a sharp increase in the costume jewelry business based on the rash of gold-chain robberies on New York streets several years back. "I think the same applies to furs," adds Bowman. "Women who bounce around New York in sable coats can be looking for trouble. That's one reason I think reversible coats became so important."

As for her coverage of the major collections, Bowman explains, "We never work with a press release. It's all inside information or an analysis of things that are developing that we try to put in focus. I would not go to a Saint Laurent show and report that Saint Laurent did peasant skirts. I would try to analyze it in the framework of the general feeling in the whole *prêt-à-porter* showings and the directions that will likely evolve from there. I will predict for six months ahead that gabardine is going to be the next incoming fabric, but I won't talk about it once it arrives, like a newspaper or magazine."

Indeed, the newsletter's subscribers list, like its focus, is far-reaching. The newsletter goes to the menswear, womenswear, home furnishings, textiles, shoe, cosmetics, and retail businesses. "Subscribers would be from the president all the way down to advertising director, stylist, general merchandise manager. Many stores take as many as ten or twelve subscriptions. We're in Japan and Italy, schools, newspapers, modeling agencies."

Bowman employs one assistant full-time and American journalists in Paris and London part-time who filter information to her. Her assistant covers some shows, makes appointments, types the letter every month, and does research.

Bowman and her staff write the newsletter roughly, doing three drafts and two revisions once it's in type. "But it's not something you just turn on and off," insists Bowman. "Something will hit you in the morning paper or on TV."

Of the possibilities of starting from scratch and developing a tiny little business that has "a certain importance," Bowman says, "I really think anyone who has a good valid idea can sell it. I think there has to be a good reason for its being and a place for it. But in a business like fashion, people are eager for information. And any little spark of an idea will start their creative juices flowing. I really believe that."

Fashion Photographer

The trick to making a mark in fashion photography is a portfolio with a recognizable, personal style. Individual style put Avedon and Penn on the map. It put newcomer Steven Meisel there, too. And Bruce Weber's striking and stark ads for Calvin Klein menswear helped raise men's fashion photography to a level previously reserved for women's.

For beginners, a job assisting an established photographer is the standard route. From there, you can open your own studio or get a staff job with a publication or ad agency. Your style, the impressiveness of your portfolio, your area of specialization (men, women, stills, ads, editorial) is up to you. Or, as some insist, it's up to the work that happens to come your way.

Chuck Baker grew up in Illinois, worked in a camera store in high school, for the *Dallas Time's Herald* summers, majored in fine arts at Ohio University, and says he's always been interested in photography. Typical of successful photographers, he moved to New York right after college and looked for an assistant's job. He landed one with a commercial photographer who concentrated on corporate ads. "He was a great guy to work for because I could learn the business of photography. I was a bag handler, built sets, set up lights, ran his darkroom, kept the studio clean and neat, helped with casting, took polaroids of models he was considering, and scouted locations," Baker recalls. Nights, he shot models for his own growing portfolio. He stayed two years.

Deciding to freelance after two years, Baker admits may have been a mistake. "I spent more time tending bar than doing magazine jobs," he says. His break came when he was offered a job at Neiman-Marcus in Dallas through family friends in that city. Even though it was as a still not a fashion photographer, Baker stayed two years, made lots of money, met a fair number of people, further developed his portfolio, and like many ambitious photographers at this stage, grew anxious to do fashion photography and to be in New York.

In 1974, Baker moved to Manhattan, opened a studio, continued to work on his portfolio, and supported himself with what came his way—still photography jobs. Baker echoes the sentiments of others when he complains of the field's strict type-casting. "The Catch-22 of the business is you can't tell people you want to take pictures on an island and show pictures of a studio. This is an exact business. It's like a heart transplant. You don't go to a general practitioner. You don't spend $30,000 sending someone to Hawaii who hasn't shot islands before." It took Baker years, he says, to get out of the still business and into the fashion business. "I just kept plugging away on my portfolio and working on jobs for small magazines," he says. "In my own personal estimation, I'm where I want to be right now, I only want to do more of it. I now have the right things in my portfolio."

For a typical editorial project, Bakers says "first the phone rings and I get the job." Next, he forms an idea for or focus of the shoot. He's so far done just that for *Italian Bazaar, French Bazaar, Italian Cosmo, Self, Mademoiselle*, and *The New York Times* magazine. "For the 'Men's Fashions of the Times,' Martha [stylist and wife, Martha Baker] and I came up with the idea of shooting in Hawaii because it was right for the clothes. We were talking about black clothes so the idea of black beaches, black lava, and black mountains made sense."

Second, Baker is involved in picking models. The extent of his involvement depends on the job. In general, a photographer has more freedom, pending agreement of editors and stylists, in editorial work. "Advertising clients often have a specific idea of which models they want," says Baker. In preparing for the *Times* swimwear spread, Baker admits he was "nervous" about his idea of using athletic props so he "ran  it by the fashion director." He's also part of the team that agrees on hair stylists and makeup artists.

Third, a photographer visualizes his shots so he can plan for everything he'll need once on location. "I decide what kind of lenses and film I need and get an assistant who's right for the job," says Baker. "In some cases, I find hotels and make travel arrangements. I also figure how we're going to get around. Do I need a van? How will we eat in the middle of nowhere? How will we get coffee at six in the morning?"

On location, "The first thing you do is run around and look at the place, especially if you've never been there before. You pick a spot to shoot. Because I don't have a great sense of direction, I use a compass and figure out where the sun's going to be and set up a schedule. You shoot some things in the morning and when the light's gone, you shoot something else. Then you just do it."

Chuck Baker talks about credibility for beginners. "Working for the *Times* gives you instant credibility," he says. "Two years ago I did my first men's fashion section and I was an instant men's photographer, but I'm not a chic photographer in the social sense like Avedon or Penn. I'd like to work for *Vogue* in the end." Baker also emphasizes the importance of a portfolio with a point of view. His point of view, which he says took years to fine-tune, is "simple, natural. I try to make models look like real people."

Stylist

A stylist's job is much like a producer's. He or she is adept at organizing details for a photographic shoot, from renting or borrowing clothes and accessories to hiring models and selecting locations. Whether a stylist works for an advertising agency or a fashion magazine, is freelance or in-house, he or she is involved in arranging deliveries of jewelry, watches, shoes, props of any kind, and depending on the job, may be involved in the selection of those items. If the Olympics is a theme, the stylist shops for a shot put or discus.

Pay is by the day or by the project for freelancers and straight salary for staff stylists. Top-notch, self-employed stylists make very good money, although, as Martha Baker, our stylist, notes, if a stylist manages to make as much as $750 a day, that compares poorly in terms of workload, responsibility and aggravation with the high wages of a shoots' makeup artist or hair stylist. "My assistant and I sometimes joke," says Baker, "that in another life we'll come back carrying our little bags as a hair stylist and make-up person."

On a January morning, Martha Baker is harried. She is also tall, thin, very attractive, and, not surprisingly, a former model.

After growing up in Grosse Point, Michigan, and Connecticut, Baker studied art history at the University of Michigan. Her original dream of a career in architecture never quite materialized. On her first attempt at architecture school, she met a fellow student, married, left school, and moved to New York, where she became a housewife and mother. Separated from her husband, she began modeling, met Chuck Baker (who would become her second husband), and then began styling for him. Having left a second degree program in architecture, she accompanied Chuck to Paris for a year. On their return, she was waiting for her third program to begin when she was offered a job as a fashion associate at *Self* magazine. She stayed for nearly a year. After *Self*, Baker accepted a styling position at *Harper's Bazaar*, where she stayed for seven months before leaving to have her second child. In 1980, Baker went freelance as a stylist.

To Martha Baker and other top stylists, it is magazine experience that a novice should seek out in order to break in as a well-paid freelancer. Because *Self* was just getting off the ground, Baker says, she did a little of everything and really learned the ropes. At *Harper's Bazaar*, as at any major fashion magazine, however, Baker was "pigeon-holed." There she worked as a so-called "sittings editor," organizing details for shoots.

On her decision to freelance, Baker remarks, "It is just like being back at *Self*. It's much more creative not to be pigeon-holed." Baker's responsibilities vary with the jobs she takes on. On an advertising job, she says, "sometimes you just get accessories." At the *New York Times Magazine*, she coordinates clothing, accessories, models, locations, hairstylists, and makeup artists. "Everyone goes about the business differently," she says. "The idea is not to have the responsibility overwhelm you. But if you're not overprepared, you're the one they'll dump on. You have to be very organized. I used not to be super particular in my life, but through this job, I am. At times I'm like a psychologist. You have to make everyone happy. For instance, advertising clients may like what you picked out but they don't like that *you* picked it, so you have to present it as though it's not your idea."

According to Baker, the Hawaii swimwear shoot for January's *New York Times Magazine* as well as the one she did for the "Men's Fashions of the Times" supplement were "pretty involved." Typically, Baker starts out having meetings with an ad agency's or a publication's art director, fashion director or editor, and fashion photographer to discuss the point of view they want to project. In the *Times'* case, Baker chose models next. "I wanted to get new and exciting models that hadn't been editorialized to death but were within the publication's range," explains Baker. "When we shot men, we found fantastic men trying out for rowing teams in Philadelphia and hired them as models. They're huge guys way beyond sample size.

"It was a nightmare with the women's bathing suits. The *Times* wanted a Christie Brinkley type but I can't use her because she's old news. We finally ended up with seven girls. After I make a choice, the fashion director has to approve it, then the models have to be available for a ten-day trip and they have to fit the clothes. It's agonizing. Next, we decide where to shoot. But before I suggest to a publication to go to Hawaii, I find out the cheapest flight or else why not shoot in Florida? Then there are plane tickets. You can't book flights all at once because you don't know yet which models are available. Then you meet again to edit down the clothes and make the final choice."

As for the men's supplement, Baker recalls shooting models in summer suits on Wall Street in the dead of winter in the freezing cold. "I got shirts, ties, socks, watches, tie pins, brief cases, lots of stuff. At the same time, I'm running around, messengering for last-minute items, editing out, preparing for Hawaii and for two more shoots taking place right when I get back."

On a shoot with her husband, Baker stands behind him and tries to visualize the shot. "I try to play art director to his photographer because we think so much alike," she adds.

Baker says the key to breaking in is credibility through solid magazine experience "so when you call people up to borrow clothes they know your name." Stylists without credibility, she says, give the job a bad name. "Some say they want Perry Ellis clothes and the clothes don't come back or they're used for some low-life ad." As for key skills for styling success, "People think if they have good taste and a fashion sense they can style. Styling is really having stick-to-it-iveness, rolling with the punches and being able to spread yourself thin."

Fashion Illustrator

For this career, you go to art school, do a portfolio, and make the rounds. "Anybody who's going to buy artwork is fair game," said one noted illustrator of just where you make those rounds. "You may even find a corporate president who's crazy enough to like you." You call the art director, introduce yourself, make an appointment, and barrel in with your portfolio. You'll probably eventually work for yourself from your home and sell your work yourself or through an agent. But agents don't generally beat down your door till you've made something of yourself first.

Illustration by Richard Ely

The truth about fashion illustration, however, is dismaying at best. Indeed, fashion illustration has been on the downswing as fashion photography has been on the upswing. Moreover, retail is fast becoming the only market left for fashion art. "There's basically no more fashion illustration," fifty-five-year-old Richard Ely, a veteran fashion illustrator with credits ranging from Bloomingdale's to Saks Fifth Avenue, *Vogue* and *Harper's Bazaar*, says nostalgically. "Be a regular illustrator. Never mind specializing in fashion."

Jim Howard, fifty-three, a top illustrator with ads to his name for Franklin Simon, Saks, Bloomingdale's and Bullock's, among others, basically agreed. "Fashion illustration is a dying craft," he said. "We're the last of an era in many ways. It's very limited. There are only three major New York stores using art on a regular basis. The bulk of my work is out of town because they still use illustrations. I would encourage someone only if he or she really wanted it bad enough and had something special. But you've got to compete with photographers. The jobs are less and less as newspaper reproductions get better and better." Howard, however, acknowledges harboring hope of a fashion illustration revival.

When Richard Ely started full force in the early fifties, fashion illustration was in its heyday. Indeed, Ely, who has drawn all his life, remembers 1947 for the "Dior New Look." Moreover, in high school, Ely took editorial pages photographed for *Vogue*, made drawings inspired by these photographs, and brought them to the attention of an executive at a local store who wondered immediately if Ely had ever considered being a fashion artist and subsequently introduced him to the art director. "Wow!" is what Ely says of his first half-page ad for the store. "I was never singleminded," adds Ely. "I just grew up with a pencil in my hand. If a drawing isn't fun, forget it."

After six months at college, Ely quit and landed a job at a local women's specialty shop. He began illustrating, but his roster of duties increased. Ely's job eventually included planning ads, going to ad meetings, picking clothing for the ads, working with copywriters and production people. In five months, Ely was named art director; in his new job he worked with a stable of three illustrators, two copywriters, the advertising director, and the production man.

Like many fashion illustrators before him, Ely put together a portfolio of his ads, answered a blind ad in *The New York Times* and was summoned to an interview that resulted in a staff job in a 57th Street women's specialty shop for $100 a week doing the illustrating for the store's ads. "Here I was in New York, a kid, sending money to my folks and looking out on the RCA building at night," says Ely. "What more could I want?"

A similar stint at a larger store, Abraham & Straus, followed, and in 1950 Ely joined the ranks of most illustrators and went freelance. There's more money in freelance than in staff work. Admits Howard, freelance since the late fifties, "I like clothing and I like the industry but the money part was a complete surprise. I was prepared to starve." Says Ely, "I live a middle-class existence. I sent my daughter to college and all that, only I did it as a fashion illustrator."

First thing after going freelance, Ely found an agent, or actually an agent fell in his lap. Jim Howard says he had a good agent "off the bat" too. Today, Ely reps his own work, as some choose to do. "A lot today use mailers," says Ely. "But it used to be a lot easier. There's a certain amount of gambling but people do want to see work."

Jim Howard, who has an agent repping only him, suggests the best way to get an agent or rep is to read newspapers and magazines carefully, make a note of stores using art in their ads, call the art director, and ask if they use agents and if so, who they are. Then call them and make appointments to show your portfolio. Howard warns newcomers that their portfolios must be immediately salable. "Agents aren't interested in training, and portfolios out of school are often not complete."

Among numerous places where he sells his work, Ely enjoys editorial work for magazines like *Vogue, Harper's Bazaar*, and *L'Officiel*. "I would be sent to a Seventh Avenue manufacturer and they would ask me to draw a woman wearing a suit or a hat," says Ely. "I'd draw it any way I wanted and give it to them. Occasionally a designer would want me to draw it on a particular model." Ely landed the prestigious *Harper's Bazaar* work via a local class taught by the magazine's art director.

For his work with department stores like Lord & Taylor and Saks Fifth Avenue: "Clothes would be sent to me, I'd book a model, get the layout for the ad, she'd put on the clothes, and I'd draw her," says Ely of his daily ad routine.

Howard follows a similar routine, although he has an agent and emphasizes that he uses his own special group of local girls rather than paying enormous sums for photo models. Moreover, the work can be very last-minute, maybe due within days of an assignment.

But, as Ely said earlier, anyone's fair play in the illustration-selling game. Expanding beyond fashion might be a good idea. Corporations use illustrations in ads and annual reports. Movie companies use poster art. "For movie campaigns, they'll look at portfolios and hire five or six people to do finished artwork," explains Ely. "The film *Raiders of the Lost Ark* had fifteen different campaigns. There are a thousand ways to sell a movie."

However, Howard disagrees somewhat. "People who do book covers and corporate rarely can do fashion. They don't get into draping and proportion. It takes such a long time to know how seams go, to know buttons."

For Ely, the virtue of a career in fashion illustration is earning a living doing what he loves to do. "It always goes back to that," he says.

"I think fashion is exciting and interesting because it always involves how people see themselves. You can always put how things are seen in perspective," says Ely. "It's the body and it's display and it's show."

The keys to success, according to Ely, include believing in yourself, knowing which skills are salable, as well as having selling skills and getting a traditional art background.

Similarly, Jim Howard extols the virtue of a broad art background. Of the key to his success, he says, "Other than learning to draw, staying on top of trends, not getting stale, and watching people who buy clothes and not just the industry, I don't know."

Video

Department stores have in-house television facilities that produce tapes explaining upcoming promotions for use by branch stores. Major textile companies have in-house studios to create promotional video tapes for their products and their customers' products, as a manager of the video department at Cone Mills will explain. Moreover, cable television is increasingly including fashion segments and hiring on-air style reporters. We'll meet one of the top reporters. Local networks are inaugurating shows devoted to fashion as well. The field is exploding.

The Textile Company

For Rob Smolanoff, manager of the video department at Cone Mills, one of the country's major textile firms, the key ingredient for success in video is contacts. "You have to be persistent. Most important is impressing people with what you do," he says. "Unfortunately, not always do people with talent get the job." Smolanoff made a mental note about contacts while majoring in television broadcasting and minoring in journalism in college. "We were told a very small percentage of us would work in areas we dreamed about," he says. His last semester at college, Smolanoff lined up an internship at the ABC affiliate in Rochester, New York. (He also worked in a seafood restaurant.)

Smolanoff knew the first rule of contacts—speak up. "There was a cameraman hired from New York who was a big shot," says Smolanoff. "I thought maybe he'd have advice." He did and Smolanoff was introduced to a company called Broadcast News Service, where he was hired as a camera operator/director. "I was stuck because it wasn't an affiliate or network news so I was actively looking to get out of there for six months." It was in that job, however, that Smolanoff did a project for Cone Mills, made contacts, and was offered his current job.

Smolanoff describes his job as "promoting our products and our customers' products and turning this into a profit center by offering a full-service production facility." By full service, Smolanoff means he'll both write a script and shoot the show.

Full production facilities like Smolanoff's are a rarity in the fashion business. "No one has a facility like ours in textiles," says Smolanoff. "There's great opportunity, particularly in fashion. Producing a videotape is getting less expensive. Just go into Macy's or Bloomingdale's and look at the TVs in the window displays. More and more companies are getting into the act, but we're unique in our production capability."

At twenty-five, Smolanoff has extraordinarily perceptive five-pronged advice for aspiring video experts. First, when going to school, "always work so you never lose your ability to deal with people." Second, don't get discouraged and abandon the field. "It's possible for anyone to get a job in their field." Third, an internship during school for credits is great, always remembering that "school can only imitate real life." Fourth, make contacts. "Always get letters of recommendation wherever you are," he says. Fifth, if you get a job anywhere near your field, take it. "I began on TV news and now I'm at a textile company. Rather than wait for your dream job in this industry, you'll have many jobs."

Indeed, Smolanoff's original goal of doing documentaries has changed somewhat. For the first time he sees potential in staying put, although he'd still like to be an independent producer with his own company.

Cable TV

Elsa Klensch is style editor of Cable News Network (CNN). She is one of the foremost fashion reporters in the country, and well-known to subscribers of Cable News Network, the twenty-four-hour-a-day all-news brainchild of wealthy maverick entrepreneur Ted Turner.

"The fact that we've done it—producing fashion, beauty and design as daily and weekly newsfeatures—has made the networks realize there are stories out there that are interesting. I hear a lot of other fashion things are coming up in television," says Klensch.

Klensch began as a general newswriter for a newspaper in her native Sydney, Australia. Next, while a journalist in Hong Kong, Klensch met her husband and moved to the United States. "Being a woman journalist, I had often been pushed onto women's stories, but I wasn't interested in fashion. I became a fashion specialist after I came to America." Klensch found fashion at *Women's Wear Daily*. "I did hosiery, sportswear, knitwear, ready-to-wear, and fur, so I really got a background in fashion," says Klensch. "Anyone interested in a career in fashion who gets a job offer at *Women's Wear*—grab it!" From *WWD*, Klensch went to *Vogue* for three years, *Harper's Bazaar* for two, and finally the *New York Post* as fashion and beauty editor.

Her main entree into television was the odd result of a New York newspaper strike. "I did a fashion presentation on local CBS news every night," says Klensch. "I also did some work for Channel 11. I used to do a weekly story for them. I wanted to do fashion for television, but television news directors do not regard fashion and beauty as newsworthy. It happened, however, after a newspaper colleague of mine mentioned to the president of CNN that I had done quite a lot for television, and he asked me to join the team launching CNN in June 1980."

For beginners, Klensch thinks journalism "is the best training in the world, because you learn to get to the root of the problem and develop a story." You should learn electronics. Then you have to be interested in fashion. Read *Women's Wear Daily* and visit innovative stores. "I think if you are a woman you are still going to be pushed into women's interest areas anyway. I mean the men are going to grab all the Washington spots unless you are terribly assertive. I never thought I would be satisfied working in fashion. I always thought it was what we used to call in Australia 'social reporter' stuff. But now I think nothing is quite as boring as one fire after another or covering a state or national legislature—it all gets boring after a while. The beauty of design is that it is fun to see some of the handsomest houses in the world and talk with the most innovative designers. I am perfectly satisfied."

ELSA KLENSCH

A WEEK AT CNN

"I do a piece a day, which runs about three minutes and forty-five seconds Monday to Friday. That's three fashion pieces, one decorating, and one beauty (which can include health or accessories that I sometimes throw in). The decorating piece may cover anything from a house to an antique show to an exhibition at the Metropolitan Museum.

"During the New York collection showings, I run the best three fashion shows that week. At other times I might take three great sportswear designers—one from Milan, one from Paris, one from New York—or I might do three great American women designers. It just depends.

"Well, then I pass the idea on to my assistant producer, who sets it up, then I go out with the crew and interview the people.

"After taping the interviews we systematically photograph everything referred to in the interview. When they talk about the living room, for instance, we show the living room. When they talk about the chair their grandmother gave them, we show the chair. Then we go back to the studio and log everything. I go through the interview, cut it, and write the script.

"I write all my own material. You don't write about the story, you write about the pictures. If you have shots on Fifth Avenue you start with that. You have to train your mind to think of the pictures. Some newspaper writers just can't make that transition.

"Then I go in and do a voice-over, and explain to the editor what I want. Sometimes I stay and work with the tape editor, but most of the time I'm off on another shoot and they put it together and send it off to Atlanta headquarters.

"At the end of the week, on Thursday morning, I write my standups, which is the copy that holds together the five pieces for the week. Then at nine o'clock Thursday morning I go upstairs with the crew and I am on camera and I do the standups, bring it down to the editor who puts the show together for the week. Then it is sent to Atlanta where they do all the technical things. I also write promos and odds and ends like that. I do a promo a week for the various shows. That's it."

Select People

DIANA VREELAND

On occasion, a rare individual surfaces whose point of view and influence on an industry is larger than any single career. In the fashion business, Diana Vreeland is a legend.

With Yves St. Laurent at opening of Yves St. Laurent Show

As Special Consultant to the Metropolitan Museum of Art's Costume Institute since 1972, Vreeland has mounted twelve annual exhibits, as famous for their opening-night festivities as for their inherent quality. As Editor-in-Chief of *Vogue* from 1962–1972, Vreeland made her mark by injecting the magazine's pages with exoticism and fantasy. As Fashion Editor of *Harper's Bazaar* beginning in 1937, she wrote a column that proved both popular and a testament to the lush life Diana Vreeland both imagines and lives.

After moving to New York with banker husband T. Reed Vreeland in 1937, she continued the kind of life she had led in Paris (where she was born), London, and Lausanne, a life that counts Yves Saint Laurent, Givenchy, and other luminaries as close personal friends and that casts Vreeland as a superstar of European and American society. Her passion for luxurious clothes, impeccable manners, outrageous stories, and an apartment draped with as much eccentricity and high-living humor as Vreeland herself, became the stuff of chic cocktail party chatter and magazine articles.

Vreeland says the key to her popularity and enormous success is "a sense of pleasure, beauty, and charm in life." This is also the philosophy Vreeland offers to the hundreds of job-seekers who write her for advice. "I tell them to be born in Paris and have lots and *lots* of pleasure in life," says Vreeland. As usual, she isn't talking down. She's enjoying herself. "A sense of pleasure is innate but it also can be reborn and renourished and reconstructed because you're having such a wonderful, *wonderful* life."

So how does one go about having a wonderful life? "History, language, literature," Vreeland responds. "I think literature's *wonderful*. It has enormous power in it." Moreover, Vreeland recommends going about this pleasure business deliberately. "I think you'd like to know a great deal about English, French, Italian and European society and I think you'd have to know about the Japanese and Chinese." Not surprisingly, Vreeland's brand of learning isn't the classroom variety. "No, no, not *just school*!" she cries. "School just gives you *school*. It doesn't give you *environment*."

In her enthusiastic seventies (she doesn't say exactly how old she is), environment is something with which Vreeland's days are packed. In 1975, for instance, for the Costume Institute's "The Glory of Russian Costume" exhibit, Vreeland and Thomas Hoving, then director of the Metropolitan Museum, flew to Moscow. There she convinced reluctant Russian officials to lend the institute costumes from the Kremlin and the Hermitage never before seen outside Russia.

For the 1982 exhibit, Vreeland chose "La Belle Epoque." She accumulated 141 garments from 1890–1914 because she felt the period ultimately bridged the gap between the staid nineteenth century and the twentieth century as we know it today.

In December of 1983, Diana Vreeland launched her much-publicized Yves Saint Laurent exhibit. Of her controversial choice of a living designer, Vreeland simply says "I felt it coming towards me based on what's gone on in the last twenty-five years." She insists she considered no other living designers.

For the December YSL show, Vreeland went to work in January of that year. "Like all preparations," she notes, "it's details." Vreeland first contacted Saint Laurent, arranged to meet him in Paris, and selected clothes with him. She ordered mannequins from a favorite Zurich artisan. Then she "collected many, *many* more clothes from individuals. *Many* people wrote to tell me what they had and I made *many* long-distance calls. The showroom and workroom came later. And, of course, the painting and the decorating and the music. . . . Accoutrements!"

Right up to the final two or three days before the opening, Vreeland's throng of loyal assistants and volunteers is working until midnight or 1 A.M. By December 5, over 243 mannequins sport; among other garments, YSL's wool-jersey "Mondrian" dresses from his Fall/Winter 1965–66 collection, his famous moiré "Picasso" evening dress from his Fall/Winter 1979–80 collection, and his extraordinary brocade "Shakespeare" wedding dress from 1980–81.

At 7 P.M., the crush of photographers to snap dinner guests as they arrive is thicker than that at a presidential press conference. Bill Blass accompanies Mrs. Vreeland, as usual. Nancy and Henry Kissinger show up; Pat and Bill Buckley; Mariel Hemingway on the arm of Perry Ellis; a tidal wave of papparazzi charge after Catherine Deneuve and Brooke Shields. At $500-a-plate, the dinner is long sold-out. So is the $100-a-ticket black-tie cocktail party for which the museum reopens its doors to another 2,000 less-famous at 10 P.M. By midnight, black-tie fashion afficionados are still being refused at the door, a twenty-piece orchestra is playing in the museum's spectacular Temple of Dendur, and dinner guests quietly escape to waiting limosines. The night is pure Diana Vreeland.

"Fortunately, what I do has become a job because so many people want to give so many things away," explains Vreeland. "I believe we have 45,000 items in the Costume Institute. Little veils, little shoe buckles. Our collection of shoes [a personal Vreeland passion] is extraordinary! We can't take everything, of course, but I mean, people are *clearing house*."

And when Vreeland isn't receiving mail on how to break into fashion, she's hearing from young people who want to join her horde of low-paid helpers. As with everything she does, Vreeland makes no bones of her intentions. She has two requirements: "hard work and no hours." Naturally, she isn't interested in educational credentials. "I never ask them. If they can get cracking, they can do anything."

In response to those who want to follow in her stylish footsteps, Vreeland brings us down to earth again. "You see, it takes quite a long career. A lot of background. You can't just do it unless you're European and you have a sense of history. I'm not talking about society. I'm talking about social history . . . how people were *then*. I was born in Paris, I've had a very full life, but I don't expect everyone to be like me."

CHAPTER *16*

HUSTLING A JOB

Some jobhustlers pick up the phone and say, "Hello. May I please speak with Ralph Lauren?" They drop the president of Bloomingdale's a note, requesting a few minutes of his precious time. They scrape up the money and nerve to fly to New York, settle into a Manhattan hole in the wall, show up at Macy's New York and ask to meet the placement director.

They follow the rule that one twenty-five-year-old super-successful jobhunter offered, "If they're important, treat them with respect. If they're not, make them feel important." They make appointments with vice-presidents of large textile firms, take them to lunch, and ask for inside tips on the industry and advice on breaking in. Moreover, they meet with considerable success. Here's why.

BASIC BUILDING BLOCKS

Below are the most frequent responses of successful people in textiles, apparel, and retail to the question "What do you look for in someone you hire?"

Work Experience

Don't hold your breath, MBA or not, if you have no work experience. Time and time again—retail, textile, apparel, at every level and in every department—the same advice rings out. "If you can't find a job, then get one helping out in a local store at Christmas." At all cost, volunteer somewhere, anywhere. Take it from the top.

By working, you've demonstrated interest. You've shown a realistic attitude. Chances are you're more confident. Most of all, you've shown you can *work*.

Education

Times have changed. And so have credentials required for most jobs. Everyone's upped the ante. "I didn't go to college because I desperately wanted to be on a fashion magazine," says Catherine di Montezemolo, vice-president and fashion director of Lord & Taylor. "I graduated high school in 1943 and back then there weren't all these marvelous fashion schools. Designers as names didn't exist. Lots of young people today think, Oh, I'd love to work for Bill Blass or Oscar de la Renta. Back then it was easy to get some kind of apprenticeship in a fashion house, to work doing errands and all sorts of things, to just work in the place. Now, the pace here is so fast we really don't have the same amount of time to teach anyone. So, I suggest the best way is to go to fashion school. I know that in New York or any other big city with an apparel market, a good student probably has a job by the time he or she leaves school. Most of the time, I get my assistants right out of school. I think a fashion school like Parsons or FIT is a wonderful background even for retail. A training program is fabulous. I wish I had done it.

Maximize education, whether that means attending a liberal arts, fashion, or textile college, and/or going on to graduate school. The need for business majors or "those taking business courses" is large, and of course training in your own field of interest is a good idea. Combine this with merchandising or sales experience and you're on your way. Education is also one of the easiest ways for career changers and reentrants to accumulate credentials. (See the appendix for a list of top fashion schools.)

People Skills

"Being pleasant" is such an important career skill that the President of Christian Dior-New York called it *the* "key to success."

As one top executive said, "It's how you get along with people that determines your advancement."

Everyone agrees fashion is a "people business." Indeed, "people business" is one of the most frequently used descriptive phrases for the fashion industry.

Moreover, there appear to be direct links between pleasantness and solid working relationships with a wide range of people and success itself. With few exceptions, those at the top live by the above advice. And people skills don't always come naturally. More frequently, they must be cultivated. In fact, for many industry leaders, "pleasantness" is the result of conscious, controlled efforts "to be pleasant" that require constant forethought, patience, and hard work. In any event, for them at least, it pays off.

A Taste Level

Although some refer to "appearance," others prefer "taste" or "taste level." For buying jobs the term is usually "flair." Naturally, dress codes are relative to the job in question and geographical location. Los Angeles's dress codes are more casual than New York's. For corporate jobs, many sales and marketing jobs, and lots of jobs in New York, traditional business gear reigns: navy blue or grey three-piece business suits for men; straightforward suits or dresses (mainly knits and silks), perhaps with a strand of pearls, for women.

Some employers, like noted menswear designer Alan Flusser, have strong opinions. "I don't care what a person has to say. I want to see how they're dressed. There is a definite relationship between the way you dress and the image you project. You should know about that relationship. That's the only kind of person I'm going to hire. Someone who loves clothes, is knowledgeable enough about them to know how I would want them to dress, and, therefore, knowledgeable enough to dress someone else." Continues Flusser, "When I was in the process of hiring a designer, one girl dressed as if she wanted to be seduced. Another came in leather pants. If you want a job with me or Brooks Brothers, dress the way you think we would like you to look. You only get one chance."

To other employers, the way you dress may be a clue to the "good eye" or "good instincts" or "sensibility" they're looking for, particularly in assistant buyers and assistant designers. Geraldine Stutz, of Henri Bendel, looks for those whose heart and soul are akin to hers—and that undoubtedly calls for a combination of style and imagination.

Like employers, career counselors take dress seriously. Sharon Bermon describes one client. "She had a lot of flair. She just put different things together and looked great. I felt strongly just looking at her that she should find a place where that would be an asset. If you don't have flair and imagination, maybe you shouldn't look for a job in an industry which demands flair." Berman also feels strongly that jobseekers shouldn't "wear costumes. . . . Do a self-assessment, figure out what you like to wear, and then find a place that will take *you*," she advises.

So, *what is* taste or flair? Flusser says that's "like asking Ray Charles about soul." Helen Galland, the former president of Bonwit Teller, is somewhat more encouraging, though not much. "Taste is definitely acquired. As a child I leaned toward the refined. You must be exposed to quality."

How do you acquire taste? To some degree careful observation of your environment helps. Walk around top stores. Check out people in companies, restaurants, on the street. Read books. Libraries and bookstores offer infinite numbers of guides on how to dress, particularly "for success." Even Flusser has a book out on buying and wearing men's clothes. You'd do well to read it if you've garnered an interview with him.

Who cares anyway? Not a lot of people, maybe. But if you want to stack the deck in your favor, it can't hurt to pay attention.

Versatility and Flexibility

The fashion business respects versatility and flexibility. Unlike other industries, it doesn't count heavily on individuals with education-related "specialties," save perhaps in technical and manufacturing jobs. This is an industry awash with "mom and pop" companies and burgeoning entrepreneurial efforts where those who "do a little bit of everything" reign supreme and exact job titles are few and far between. Although the fashion industry is becoming more sophisticated, thus requiring special expertise, if the truth be told, the more you know and can do the better off you will be.

You'll never lose taking sales experience onto a technical or design job, or having production experience in retail or textiles. Says one executive "You are at a tremendous disadvantage later on if you don't move around." In retrospect, successful people report having been better off with added knowledge gained in jobs not necessarily their ultimate desires.

Guts

As top career counselors agree, the formula for success is guts and goals.

"I didn't know I had guts," notes Michael Arceneaux, the fashion show producer and director. "But other people say it about me all the time." It took guts for Arceneaux to approach his first job, for a prominent designer for whom he was dying to work. "I begged him," Arceneaux admits. "I told him, 'I want to do this. I'm good. I want to be here. I've won awards and worked in the business six months.' I was twenty-four and thought I knew everything. I wanted it and knew it. I couldn't hear no." He didn't. It also took guts to leave Louisiana for New York. It took guts for designer

Alexander Julian to open his own store, to relocate to New York from North Carolina, to approach a staid old company with innovative new ideas, to stay in business, to win over impossible fashion editors. It took guts for Vicky Davis, the tie designer and former housewife, to leave the comfort of her Michigan home for the big city, to approach strange manufacturers. No wonder she still recalls her initial terror. All successful people are gutsy from the first job to the last.

Additional Pluses

Other pluses industry leaders cited include intelligence, common sense, articulateness, willingness to work, enthusiasm, ambition, drive, wanting the job, a high energy level, and "knowing what's going on." Some emphasize "being well-rounded" in the sense of cultural interests, sports activities, reading, and travel. Other attributes include "being quick or sharp," and possessing an "eye," or a "sensibility." The latter most easily means an ability to take in the world around you, and translate your perceptions and observations into concrete, practical acts. Tack on self-confidence, poise, self-esteem.

JOB-FINDING SKILLS OR HOW THE INSIDERS DO IT

Selling yourself is the basis of jobhunting success. All careers are based on it. All top-notch positions require practical evidence of sales skills. Wherever you are, whether a conference, placement office, talking to a relative or the guy next to you on a plane, an employment agency representative, or answering an advertisement, do as career counselors advocate and "shape your credentials" into a success story. Make that summer sales job a stunning accumulation of management skills and evidence of a love of retail. Sell yourself with your appearance by being well-groomed. Sell with your résumé by keeping it brief, neat, and accurate. Sell by the way you talk. Sell with pleasantness, humility, and interest in the person you're talking to. Most successful people could sell you the Brooklyn Bridge, never mind themselves. Here's how to begin.

Rigorous Research

Admittedly, "research" is a nasty word bringing term papers, more than good jobs, to mind. But as one enormously successful jobseeker lamented, "one of the most important things we'll ever do in our lives is look for jobs, yet hardly anyone knows how to do it. If you're prepared, you feel good. Working hard is nothing. Working smart is everything. Knowledge is power."

Steep yourself in industry lore so that, in time, you become a card-carrying member. Read *Women's Wear Daily*, fashion magazines like *Vogue* and *Harper's Bazaar*, style sections of local newspapers, and trade publications pertinent to your area of interest like *Textile World*. If you need a list, visit a school library or call a trade organization. Talk to anyone in the industry and ask questions. Call and ask for advice. If you're persuasive, polite, and keep the questions short, he or she could be an important contact later.

Keep a running list of names, titles, addresses, and phone numbers of everyone in the business you meet, however, casually. Names in *WWD*, a newspaper, or magazine are fair game. Use the library to read up on the fashion industry. Use the *Occupational Outlook Handbook* for the most basic job descriptions and supplement with calls or inquiring notes to people you've listed. Then there are workshops, lectures, conferences, professional organizations, trade associations, unions, government agencies, and employment agencies. Chances are newcomers can't join professional organizations, but you can call and get permission to attend a meeting or two. Such meetings often have a cocktail hour when you can circulate, introduce yourself, and research what people do and how they got where they are (see Contacts). You can send for catalogues of local schools and noncredit evening classes. Keep an eye out for advertisements and buried "mentions" in *WWD* and local papers of important conferences. A fabulous conference on "Challenges for Women in the Fashion and Beauty Industries" is sponsored every November in New York by the American Women's Economic Development Corporation (AWED), and it's advertised in *WWD* extensively. Each year it attracts over 2,000 experts and novices. The real researchers make it their business to fly in. Experience is the best form of research.

Finally, if you're in school, go to your placement office, make sure they know you, and keep in touch on job openings. Try to line up an in-school internship. If your school doesn't offer one, why not create one yourself? Choose a local company that excites you and write a note proposing yourself.

Research the companies that excite you (see Getting In and the Company Match). Send for an annual report; in retail send for information on executive training. Call the personnel office and request background information. Keep a list.

People are crucial sources of information and jobs. Rob Smolanoff, video manager of Cone Mills, has always asked for a letter of recommendation, starting with high school jobs. He always asks people for advice as well as background info on their jobs and their companies. As a rule, people love to talk about themselves. Also as a rule, they don't want to hear you go on about yourself, your school, your boyfriends, or your uncle in the business.

Making Contacts

I'd bet 80 percent of all jobs are the result of word of mouth. Contacts, who-you-know-not-what-you-know, and networking are frequently used terms. "Contacts," however, are frequently misunderstood. They are not, as many believe, important business relationships reserved for the well-born, properly placed, and powerful. They don't come with the job. They come before. Contacts, rather, can be and are friends, relatives, friends of friends, an ex-boyfriend, friends of relatives, someone you hung out with at the beach, a salesgirl at a local store. We've all got them. It's what you do with them that counts.

Moreover, contacts don't necessarily wear a recognizable label reading "I'm a Great Contact." If you're snotty to a secretary and gush with warmth when the boss shows up, you're treading on touchy turf. Not only do you have no idea where that secretary may turn up in the future but you have no idea what anyone will be doing. You have no idea who they know. Moreover, you have no idea how to treat people. Experience proves that vital connections show up in the least likely circumstances.

As Phyllis Brodsky, chairman of the patternmaking department at the Fashion Institute of Technology in New York City, wisely commented, "I stress to my students that networking begins now, at whatever age or place you are. The people sitting next to you in class can be your best contacts for the future." Experience proves that the absolute least likely souls turn up with a friend or friend of a friend out of the blue.

Contacts can be easily manipulated by placing yourself where potential employers hang out. This can be done as part of your rigorous research. Attend conferences, trade organization meetings, go to restaurants fashion pros frequent, take a class a bigshot teaches.

Tricks of the contacts trade include thank-you notes and dropping notes after you've met anyone, even in passing. Trickier still, should you catch an announcement of someone's promotion in the newspaper, drop the honcho a note of congratulations. Then make a follow-up call and give your two-minute success story spiel.

Contacts must be nurtured in order to bear fruit. Keep a contact file or notebook with the name, title, address, and telephone number of everyone you meet personally and where and when you met them; of names you spot in publications like *Women's Wear Daily*; of people whose names are dropped in conversation. The conversation goes like this: "Oh, I think you'd really like my cousin Ted"—and you know cousin Ted is a menswear designer or a merchandise manager. You call cousin Ted and say, "So and so said we might enjoy meeting each other." Drop contacts a line when you accomplish something of importance like a promotion, award, new office, or having your scarves in an upcoming movie. Drop a note if you think you can do that person a favor. Invite him or her to a gathering. Remember special occasions like birthdays, weddings, births.

Finally, the key to contacts is the human touch. Well-connected people are friendly, pleasant, and gregarious even when they'd rather not be. They join organizations and strike up conversations, including ones with the chap next to them on the bus. The strongest contact is a friend and the best way to make friends in or out of business is by being alert and interested.

Recognizing and Creating Opportunity

What sets successful people apart is a well-developed ability to recognize opportunity. It is an expanded version of two top executives' upcoming definitions of aggressiveness. Recognizing opportunity requires openness to your surroundings at all times. That means listening carefully in your daily rounds whether in local shops, museums, school, conversations with friends or relatives, on the street, or in a hallway. Recognizing opportunity can also be more deliberate in the case of purposely attending conferences or joining organizations in order to introduce yourself to crucial industry members, then getting up the guts to pick up the phone.

We are all surrounded by opportunity every minute of the day. Do we define our parameters as the tips of our noses or do we take in more? How do we negotiate our world? Do we *act* on it?

There is as much in your environment as there was in Alexander Julian's or Colombe Nicholas's or in someone's with an MBA or in a company president's. What successful people do well is harness opportunity—they spy it and fly with it—fueled with guts. In other words, one huge difference between luck and you is action.

All successful sorts create opportunity. Michael Arceneaux, the fashion show director, honestly admitted: "I hate discussions of career strategies . . . *just do it* . . . there's no magic." At the height of his career, Arceneaux relocated to Los Angeles, and when he returned, he felt the fear all over again. He picked up the phone, pounded the pavements, knocked on doors, had doors slammed in his face, and set out again. On her first job for a movie magazine, Geraldine Stutz of Henri Bendel called Samuel Goldwyn and landed one of the movie tycoon's only interviews. Jeffrey Aronoff, after weaving scarves, called and said, "Hello, may I speak to Ralph Lauren?" He did, ended up doing extraordinary skirts for Lauren's collection and some show-stopper shawls for Faye Dunaway in *Eyes of Laura Mars*. Says one executive, based on her encounters with bright industry lights, "I'm convinced there are no special people—just very determined people. Jane Schauffhausen of Belle Fleur says she doesn't believe in luck. "We *just did it* and it's not easy."

Being in the right place at the right time is frequently mistaken for recognizing opportunity. If you read *Women's Wear Daily*, see an ad for a conference on challenges and opportunities in the fashion and beauty business, have the wherewithal to clip it out, go snag an important panelist, introduce yourself, promote yourself briefly and mention your desire to contact him or her sometime soon, follow through on your promise and make an appointment, and he or she just happens to have an opening and think of you, your friends may shrug it off to your being in the right place at the right time. You may just consider it 90 percent perspiration and 10 percent luck.

Overcoming Fear of Competition

If you've read career guides, you've no doubt found scary statistics. A good rule to follow is that if the job to which you aspire is at all perceived as "glamorous," competition is stiff, hours long, and pay relatively low at the entry level. It doesn't mean you should be paralyzed and fearful of failure when approaching sought-after jobs. Successful people report never considering the competition in tackling their first or second jobs. If they did consider it, it became a device to fuel their drive and ambition. It also spurred them to take advantage of every opportunity, develop a keen eye to timing, research prospective employers that much more carefully, enter interviews fully if not overprepared, and work hard at initial jobs.

Aggressiveness

Aggressiveness is fashionable. After all, isn't every successful businesswoman aggressive? It came as something of a surprise, then, to hear one executive, a veteran of thousands of interviews with jobseekers, define aggression very carefully. "We define aggression as an environmental word. We define it as someone who successfully defines the parameters of his or her environment. People usually tell us they're assertive. Most truly aggressive people are excellent at interpretive skills and, as far as personal qualities go, they're charming."

Aggressiveness for its own sake can be obnoxious. Aggressiveness, as a single "method" of job acquisition, is no cure-all.

Ellen Sills-Levy is a partner in a market research firm and teaches a popular class at New York's New School for Social Research called "Entrepreneurism: What It Takes." Guests include leaders in the fashion industry like Jane Schaffhausen, founder and president of Belle Fleur, and Richard Conrad, founder of Diane von Furstenberg and Castleberry Knits. "What it takes" is what she hears most and knows best.

On aggression, she isn't far off our mark. "Aggression can be a harsh term. There are those who think it means hostility. If you look at the guests in my class, you'll see lots of introverted people and lots of humility. I'd rather hear the words determination, listening, and hearing what's around you—listening to your environment."

TOOLS OF THE TRADE
The Résumé

In a résumé, pay serious attention to simplicity, neatness, accuracy, and brevity. One page is fine. The standard section headings can be your "Objective" or "Purpose," "Education," and "Work Experience." Your name, address, and phone number are at the top. Which of the two headings comes first after your job objective depends on your age and on which heading includes the more impressive material. If your education isn't impressive and/or you've been out of school a while, you can remove the reader's attention by putting it at the bottom.

Gimmicks are the number one reason industry leaders reject résumés. Frills are a hazard of the business and a risk to be carefully weighed. Whether you typeset or type neatly isn't earthshaking. It's far more important that you spell every word correctly and keep the listings short and to the point. Fussing over the quality and color of paper isn't crucial either. If you're debating, go with white bond and forget it. Too often, such nonsense replaces far more important jobhunting activities like research and breaking down doors.

Although some career counselors say the more creative the job the artier your résumé can be, when artiness goes awry you lose. A résumé is a written exercise. If your talents run to the visual, you're better off facing the fact and showing your résumé to those you think excel in written organization, spelling, and tight writing. Career counselors and résumé services abound if you don't have a friend to ask.

As for tips on organizing your résumé, be forewarned it can't be done well if you don't know what you want and the company or types of companies you seek. If all you know is that you "want something in fashion," research first, pin it down, and then compile an appropriate résumé or résumés. And, if you're unemployed for a long period, you're better off showing evidence of *work*, even if, as we mentioned earlier, it's "slinging hash."

A résumé is organized to emphasize either functions/skills or companies, whichever is more prestigious. Just as you would do when selling yourself to future contacts or in an interview, the idea is to shape your credentials to tell a success story. If you've worked for name companies, you're probably better off organizing your résumé by company. For example, after your name, address, phone number, and job "objective," you'd put "Work Experience" and then list company name, title, dates, and a sentence or two about your duties. If, on the other hand, the company is a small and relatively unknown store but you managed to pick up skills beyond your calling, emphasize function. In this case, you can list titles first followed by company name, date, and a glowing rendition of your experience. Emphasize the wide range of skills you picked up such as visual merchandising, buying, taking inventory, working with customers. Did sales increase while you were there? Did you implement anything? Did you work long hours? Were you promoted in any way?

In sum, your résumé is a selling tool and you put your most salable foot forward. Moreover, it's a relatively minor selling tool. The crucial selling tool is you.

The Portfolio

In portfolios, "nothing fancy" seems to be the rule too. Let your college placement office and design professors show you the ropes. When Oscar de la Renta was asked where he thinks aspiring designers go wrong most frequently, he replied, "When you are showing your book, you don't have to talk a lot because you are showing what you can do. Kids usually show me their school portfolio and I don't want to see the school portfolio because they did that with their teachers and it's not their point of view. I don't want to see a tremendous number of sketches. It doesn't matter that they are beautifully color illustrated. I will just say, 'If you were to work for me on my next collection, show me how you would do it.' That's what I would like."

Moreover, de la Renta and other designers don't expect design portfolios to predict next spring's look. On fabrics, de la Renta says, "I want to see maybe a few to get an idea of your color sense but mostly I want to see black and white sketches. I think it is much more important to see a point of view of how they would put a collection together, even if it is a group of just twenty dresses. I want to see if there is follow-through and identity from one sketch to another. Sometimes, you know, an aspiring assistant will look at the market and have a hundred points of view. They will kind of copy one of this and one of that from many different designers. It is much better to do twenty and do your own stuff."

For illustration portfolios, Jim Howard, the veteran fashion illustrator of chapter 15, says many fashion illustration portfolios err most in not being immediately salable. No decent agent or art director, he says, is interested in an incomplete portfolio. Scan newspapers and magazines for stores using illustrations, call and ask what they look for. See if veterans whose names adjoin illustrations you particularly like are willing to give you a minute. Snag anyone you can. Howard says the key to his success is an ability to illustrate a variety of styles well, and ventures that newcomers go wrong in becoming adept at one trendy look. Showing versatility in your portfolio may help.

For a first-time photographic portfolio, you want to demonstrate technique, composition, organization, and detail. The idea here, as experts point out, is to show a certain eagerness to assist the photographer who will be the one doing the artistic work. You'll be an assistant. The freelance photographer, on the other hand, conveys personal style, concepts, creativity, and identity.

As de la Renta notes, a portfolio has about twenty items. Those items are usually organized into groups by color, fabric, or an overall design theme or shape. This is how collections are presented in the major fashion shows and in showrooms. Try to put your best work forward, don't fuss about reproduction techniques, and keep it up to date.

GETTING IN AND THE COMPANY MATCH

Your job options are the results of contacts you've developed, help-wanted ads, placement office referrals, and companies that happen to interest you. Lists of major retail stores, textile companies, and apparel manufacturers are available at local fashion schools, libraries, or by calling appropriate trade organizations (see chapter 17).

Send your résumé to a vice-president in your field of interest if there is one—call to get his or her name. Also include a note requesting a few minutes of time at his or her convenience. If you get in the president's office, he or she will be impressed.

Keying into specific companies far surpasses plastering the country or your area with résumés, 99 percent of which will be ill-tailored to the company and the job. Indeed, you should do just the opposite: Make a company feel special. Companies have identities just as we do and somewhere out there is a likely match for you. Your sense of identity with the company should motivate you. Just pick companies that excite you.

For budding fashion designers, it's a cinch. So much is written about designers and apparel manufacturers, from *Women's Wear Daily* to *Vogue* and local papers, that you should have little trouble selecting those whose work you particularly like. Do you want a large or small company? As a textile stylist, for example, do you prefer small decorative firms or an enormous company specializing in mass-produced synthetics with a formal heirarchy, a prestigious name for your résumé, and specialized routines? Would you like to do a little bit of everything for a small operation because you dream of starting your own company? Naturally, you can't key into companies if you haven't done your research.

However, after all is said and done, as one employer said, "The best way to get a job is to be there. If you have to live on peanut butter, do it, but get there." As we said, your résumé is a weak selling tool. Guts and enthusiasm are a smarter package. So walk into the personnel department if not the president's outer office and wait for a two-minute interview. You may very well get it, particularly if you've traveled. Or call a vice-president in your field and ask for a brief appointment at his or her convenience. And always show respect for someone's time with a line like "I appreciate your time and effort" at the end of the thank-you note you'll undoubtedly send.

THE PERSONAL MATCH

Fashion is a business to which many become addicted (see chapter 2). Career counselor Sharon Bermon, who sees many fashion clients, says the fashion business is like few others in that we become devotees of our industry rather than of specialized, transferable skills like writing, marketing, or sales. Unfortunately, most clients seek Bermon because they want to get out of the business. They find fashion "too crazy, too emotional," she says. In retail, for instance, clients detested the long hours and working weekends. "If you don't want ups and downs and adrenaline charges, you don't want this industry," she reiterates. "Basically, it's the lifestyle they don't like."

Match your skills to your lifestyle. Are you comfortable traveling? Can you picture yourself doing business in Hong Kong, perhaps alone, for a department store or apparel manufacturer? Can you rent a car?

Match your skills to your temperament. Competitive high-strung Type A personalities fit buying jobs beautifully. How do you react to stress? To working under pressure? To aggravation? To constant change? Do you prefer working in a close-knit team or would you prefer the isolation of a textile researcher's job? Do you have the patience of a textile artist to do repeat patterns yard after yard?

If anything can be said of the fashion industry, it's that you have to love it to survive.

INTERVIEW TIPS AND TURN-OFFS
Tips

Rehearse the interview in advance, so when the interviewer asks a typical question like "So, why should I hire you?" you're not stuck. Instead, you tick off a few ways you're an asset to the company, telling the interviewer that your experience, energy level, motivation, and contacts are a plus. Moreover, you're a self-starter.

Come in with a clear idea of what you want and of your skills. Come in with a clear idea of the company. One superstar jobhunter researches a firm in Standard and Poors, Dun & Bradstreet, Standard Rate and Data; specialized trade publications; and sends for an annual report before walking into an interview. Moreover, he checks on special programs the company may be initiating. "It's the kind of thing that gives you the job over anyone else," he says. "My boss said, 'You knew our circulation program and that's why I gave you the job.' But I only called and talked to a secretary."

Go for the human touch again. One successful interviewee swears by his method of "making the interviewer his buddy." Our superstar jobhunter actually finds out who his interviewer will be and looks him up in *Who's Who*, not only as part of general preparation for the interview but to determine if he has anything in common with his interviewer—from college to hobbies to outside interests. If the interviewer then says, "So, what do you do to relax?" guess what our star answers if he can? "Getting a job isn't qualifications," he stresses. "It's being a human being with someone." He says it again. "If you understand people you can land any job without qualifications." Our star also says if you have a friend at the company, you should call and ask for the interviewer's likes and dislikes, for clues into his personality. Finally, be sure to pick up on any personal subjects, whether the birth of a new child or a weekly baseball game, if the interviewer drops it casually during your chat. Send a note afterwards.

Turn-Offs

Misunderstanding the company is in first place. Colombe Nicholas of Christian Dior-New York says jobseekers go wrong in thinking her corporate licensing office is a manufacturer of apparel and come in flaunting inappropriate experience, say, in a boutique. The personnel director of Cone Mills, a large producer of denim and corduroy, says it's not unusual for jobseekers to think the company makes jeans, rather than manufactures denim, because their ads show jeans. Catherine di Montezemolo, corporate fashion director and vice-president of Lord & Taylor, says jobhunters don't understand the function of a fashion office and think it has something to do with being a buyer.

Not knowing what you want is in second place. "I want something in fashion," is something experts hear often in interviews when they ask, "So, where do you see yourself fitting in our organization." They also say it turns them off pronto. Di Montezemolo insists she wants to hear people say: "I want to work in a fashion office of a major department store." At a textile company, you might do well to say you'd like to be a salesman in a specific division. A department store executive wants you to say you'd like to join the store's executive training program with the goal of becoming a buyer.

Lacking humility is the third interview turn-off. One popular form of humility-lessness is asking for a gigantic salary when you have a teeny-weeny bit of expertise. "Kids today just walk in and ask for thirty-five thousand dollars," said one bitter employer, echoing the sentiments of many others. "I don't know where they get it from." Moreover, a know-it-all attitude, particularly if you've just completed school is a loser. Employers know your learning is just beginning.

Dressing for failure is a fourth. Just be well-groomed and simply dressed. Colombe Nicholas hated having to mention chipped nail polish, sandals, dirty hair, too much makeup. Alan Flusser, the menswear designer, mentioned leather pants and seductive clothing. Don't over or underdo it. A business suit for a man or woman with a clean cotton or silk shirt is a safe bet if you're unsure.

Being too honest is last. Telling a success story means molding your experience and activities and lifestyle to sound absolutely positive. Don't be caught off-guard and respond as you would to a close friend who casually remarks, "So, what do you do to relax?"

RESOURCES

FASHION SCHOOLS

APPAREL, TEXTILES, AND/OR RETAIL PROGRAMS

Fashion Institute of Design and Merchandising
Office of Admissions
818 West Seventh Street
Los Angeles, California 90017

A.A. and Certificate Programs: Merchandising, Fashion Design, Retail Administration, Manufacturing Management
Certificate Program Only: Textile Design

The largest school of its kind on the West Coast, in an area where the fashion market has reportedly grown 120 percent in seven years. It offers a research and resource center, European and New York City tours, fashion shows, visits by designers like Oscar de la Renta and Bob Mackie, leaders in merchandising, and local and national recruiters come graduation.

The Fashion Institute of Technology
Office of Admissions
227 West 27th Street
New York, New York 10001

A.A.S. (2-year): Advertising Design, Display and Exhibit Design, Fashion Design, Illustration, Jewelry Design, Textile Design, Photography, Leather Accessories Design and Production, Fine Arts, Interior Design, Menswear Design and Marketing, Pattern-making Technology
A.A.S. (1-year): Advertising and Communications, Advertising and Design, Fashion Design, Fashion Buying and Merchandising, Textile Design, Apparel Production Management, Textile Technology
B.S.: Marketing: Fashion and Related Industries, Production Management: Apparel, Production Management: Textiles
B.F.A.: Advertising Design, Package Design, Product Design: Apparel and Accessories or Textiles, Illustration, Fur Design and Marketing, Interior Design

FIT is a public institution in the heart of the fashion capital. Extensive and up-to-date facilities include sketchbook and costume collections. The school says most grads (from all over the country and the world) are placed in New York and many start their own businesses. Special programs include continuing education, night classes, a weekend college, winterim program, Saturday courses for high school students and work/study programs. Calvin Klein and Norma Kamali went to FIT.

Laboratory Institute of Merchandising
Office of Admissions
12 East 53rd Street
New York, New York 10022

A.O.S./B.P.S./A.A.S.: Fashion Merchandising

Training in the business of fashion. Management is the top career choice of grads, followed by Buying and then Manufacturing, says the school. The program includes work study, internships in non-retailing fashion industries and a London program.

Placement in 1981 was 88.5 percent immediately and 11.5 percent within three months of graduation.

L.A. Trade Technical College
Office of Admissions
400 West Washington Boulevard
Los Angeles, California 90015

A.A.: Merchandise Display, Fashion Design, Marketing
Certificates of Completion, Fashion Design, Industrial Sewing, Tailoring, Marketing, Visual Merchandising and Display

Pratt Institute
Office of Admissions
200 Willoughby Avenue
Brooklyn, New York 11205

A.O.S.: Graphic Design, Illustration
B.F.A.: Fashion Design, Fashion Merchandising

Pratt says it's geared to "the whole artist" or designer. The four year B.F.A. or B.P.S. program in Merchandising and Fashion Management at Pratt combines both business and creative approaches. The Fashion Design Program incorporates field trips, museum trips, and consultation with designers. All faculty are working professionals; seniors intern one semester in the industry. Continuing education available.

Tobe-Coburn School for Fashion Careers
Office of Admissions
686 Broadway
New York, New York 10012

A.O.S.: Fashion Merchandising, Marketing, and Management

9-month program for students with 30 credits from an accredited post-secondary school; 12-month program for those with 15 credits; 16-month for students directly from high school or with brief college experience.

Tobe-Coburn has a practical emphasis including nine weeks of cooperative work experience. Quite a few grads land public relations/promotions positions.

DESIGN/ART PROGRAMS (APPAREL AND/OR TEXTILES)

California College of Arts and Crafts (CCAC)
Office of Admissions
5212 Broadway at College Avenue
Oakland, California 94618

B.F.A./M.F.A. (22 programs total) Drawing, Printmaking, Sculpture, Photography, Film/ TV, General Fine Arts, Metal Arts, Textiles, General Crafts, Environmental Design, Graphic Design and Illustration, General Design

Like any art school, CCAC emphasizes the purely creative, and as such their grads often find their way into more artistic jobs: textile design, art director, etc. The Textile Program offers a wide range of courses in its five areas: weaving, printing, hand-construction, costume, and history. Class work includes critiques and field trips. There is an annual senior textile show and three galleries for the display of students and visiting artists' work.

Cooper Union
Cooper Square
New York, New York 10003

B.F.A.: Fine Arts, Graphic Arts

Moore College of Art
Admissions Office
20th and The Parkway
Philadelphia, Pennsylvania 19103

B.F.A.: Fashion Design, Fashion Illustration, Textile Design

Moore College of Art is the only college in the country devoted to women artists. The College is small (about 500 students); graduates from the Design Studies and Graphic Studies programs include leaders in fashion and textile design. According to the school, many students find jobs in Pennsylvania and New Jersey. There is an annual fashion show, visits by leading artists, and a Co-Op Program that includes participation by Bergdorf Goodman, Halston, and Neiman-Marcus. Continuing education programs are available.

Parsons School of Design
Office of Admissions
66 Fifth Avenue
New York, New York 10011

Otis Art Institute of Parsons School of Design (Otis/Parsons)
Office of Admissions
3401 Wilshire Boulevard
Los Angeles, California 90057

B.F.A.: Fashion Design, Fashion Illustration, General Illustration, Fine Arts, Photography, Environmental Design, Interior Design, Communications Design, Art Education Clay, Fiber, Metal Design
A.A.S.: Illustration, Fashion Design, Interior Design, Photography, Clay, Fiber, Metal Design

(Programs slightly different in L.A.)

Parsons is one of the most respected, if not *the* most respected, and rigorous fashion design schools in the country. The school's top grads regularly land jobs with name designers. Perry Ellis hired from both the 1982 and 1983 graduating classes. Moreover, students are critiqued by top designers such as Calvin Klein. The entire third year is devoted to studio design; you may study at Parsons Los Angeles or in Paris. Evening, Saturday, and summer programs available.

Rhode Island School of Design ("RISDY")
Office of Admissions
2 College Street
Providence, Rhode Island 02903

B.F.A.: Textile Design, Apparel Design, Graphic Design, Film, Illustration, Photography (11 degrees total)
M.F.A.: Jewelry and Light Metals, Graphic Design, Photograhy (9 degrees total)

RISD is among the top design schools in the country. No retailing or marketing courses are offered, but the Apparel and Textile Design programs maintain fully equipped workshops and studios. Graduating design students enter many fields, from opening local boutiques in their home towns to designing for large New York firms. According to the school, graduates are frequently placed outside the New York area. Winter session and summer internships are offered and there are critiques by name designers like Mary McFadden.

School of the Art Institute of Chicago
Admissions Office
Columbus Drive and Jackson Boulevard
Chicago, Illinois 60603

B.F.A.: Fashion Design, Textile Design (in Fiber Dept.)

The program includes costume history, visits to the Chicago Historical Society, fashion shows, critiques by outside designers, senior apprenticeships with American and European designers. There is an extensive fashion library.

School of Visual Arts
209 East 23 Street
New York, New York 10010

B.F.A.: Video, Media Arts, Photography, Film, Fine Arts, Art Education, Journalism (print, broadcast, public relations)
M.F.A.: Fine Arts, Illustration

TEXTILE PROGRAMS

Clemson University
Office of Admissions
College of Industrial Management and Textile Science
101 Sikes Hall
Clemson, South Carolina 29631

B.S./M.S./Ph.D.: Textile Chemistry, Textile Science, Textile Technology

One of the foremost textile programs in the country.

Georgia Tech
Office of Admissions
School of Textile Engineering
Atlanta, Georgia 30332

B.S./M.S./Ph.D.: Textile Engineering, Textile Chemistry, Textiles

Georgia Tech is particularly interested in encouraging women to opt for their engineering program. The program is one of the few with an apparel manufacturing option within the textile degree. Tex Tech Enterprises is an interesting business venture in which students design, develop, manufacture, and market their own textile products.

Institute of Textile Technology
P.O. Box 391
Charlottesville, Virginia 22902

M.S./Ph.D: Textile Technology (10 students a year)

North Carolina State University
Office of Admissions
Raleigh, North Carolina 27650

School of Textiles
B.S.: Textiles, Textile Management, Textile Science, Textile Chemistry
M.S.: Textile Science
Ph.D.: Textile Technology, Fiber & Polymer Science

School of Design
B.S.: Textile Design Concentration

With 700 graduates from all over the world, NCSU has the largest textile school in the world. About 100 recruiters visit the school each year; placement officers secure positions in this geographical center of the textile industry. Robert Coleman, a grad of NCSU, is president of the Textile Manufacturers Institute. The school's Burlington Textiles Library is one of the country's most complete textile libraries.

Philadelphia College of Textiles and Sciences
Office of Admissions
School House Lane and Henry Avenue
Philadelphia, Pennsylvania 19144

B.S.: Apparel Management, Fashion Merchandising, Marketing, Retail Management, Textile Chemistry, Textile Design, Textile Engineering, Textile Management and Marketing, Textile Technology
M.B.A.

PCTS is among the most respected textile schools in the country, with a strong emphasis on learning a field from start to finish. It is possible to blend business and textile courses in the above programs. The career office places over 80 percent of its grads and offers lifetime services. The Goldie Paley Design Center houses more than 200,000 fabric samples (some from the 4th century) and there is a design museum. There is also an annual student design competition and six shows a year.

Texas Tech University
Office of Undergraduate Admissions
P.O. Box 4350
Lubbock, Texas 79409

College of Engineering
B.S.: Textile Technology and Management, Textile Engineering

College of Home Economics (Clothing and Textiles Program)
B.S./M.S.: Specializations in Fashion Design, Merchandising, Textile Science

This is the only university west of the Mississippi offering a B.S. in Textile Technology and Management. In this program students are trained to be managers and executives in the industry. In 1981 all Texas Tech grads obtained positions in the industry before graduation, according to the school. The Textile Research Center has one of the better research labs. Summer employment, recruitment and internships.

SOME COLLEGES AND UNIVERSITIES WITH FASHION PROGRAMS

Drexel University
Office of Admissions
32nd and Chestnut Street
Philadelphia, Pennsylvania 19104

B.S.: Design and Merchandising, Fashion Design
M.S.: Fashion Design

Iowa State University
Textiles and Clothing Department

140 LeBaron Hall
College of Home Economics
Ames, Iowa 50011

B.S.: Majors in Fashion Merchandising, Apparel Design and Patternmaking, Textile and Clothing Related Science
M.S.: Textiles and Clothing

Kent State University
Office of Admissions
145 Rockwell Hall
Kent, Ohio 44242

College of Fine and Professional Arts
B.A.: Fashion Design
B.S.: Fashion Merchandising

Purdue University
Admissions Office
West Lafayette, Indiana 47907

Department of Consumer Sciences and Retailing
B.S.: Apparel Technology, Retailing, Textile Science

Stephens College
Office of Admissions
Columbia, Missouri 65215

B.A.: Fashion, Fashion Merchandising (with Business Administration Department)
B.F.A.: Fashion

Syracuse University
Admissions Office
Syracuse, New York 13210

College of Visual Arts
B.F.A.: Fashion Design, Fashion Illustration, Fiber Structure and Interlocking

College for Human Development
B.S.: Management: Retailing/Marketing, Retailing, Textile and Clothing Studies.

University of Arizona
Admissions Office
Division of Clothing, Textiles, and Interior Design
Tucson, Arizona 85721

School of Home Economics
B.S.: Clothing and Textiles, Merchandising and Fashion Promotion

University of Maryland
Admissions Office
Department of Textiles and Consumer Economics
College Park, Maryland 20742

College of Human Ecology
B.S./M.S./Ph.D.: Textile Science, Consumer Textiles, Textile Marketing/Fashion Merchandising, Apparel Design

University of Massachusetts
Admissions Office
Amherst, Massachusetts 01003

Division of Home Economics
B.S.: Fashion Marketing

University of Missouri
Admissions Office
Columbia, Missouri 74328

College of Home Economics
B.S./M.S./Ph.D.: Textiles and Clothing

University of Tennessee
Admissions Office
Knoxville, Tennessee 37996

College of Home Economics
B.S.: Textiles and Apparel with Options in Merchandising, Textile Science, Apparel
and Textiles

University of Wisconsin—Madison
Undergraduate Admissions
140 Peterson Building
750 University Avenue
Madison, Wisconsin 53706

Graduate Admissions
1300 Linden Drive
Madison, Wisconsin 53706

School of Family Resources and Consumer Sciences (Environment, Textiles and De-
sign program area)
B.S.: Apparel Design, Retailing, Textiles and Clothing, Textile Science
M.S.: Concentrations in Textile Science, Social/Psychological Aspects of Dress, Ap-
parel Design, Textile Design
Ph.D.: Individual programs in Textiles and Design

Washington University
Campus Box 1089
St. Louis, Missouri 63130

School of Fine Arts
B.F.A.: Fashion Design

PUBLICATIONS

Like any large industry, fashion offers a wide range of trade and professional publications appealing to individuals working in every area, including fur, hosiery, shoes, jewelry, textiles, public relations, display, advertising, and many more. Many are produced by trade and professional organizations. The most important publication(s) for those breaking in (and staying in) however, is *Women's Wear Daily* followed by "W" and *The Daily News Record* or "DNR" (menswear). All of these can be ordered by writing to *Fairchild Publications, 7 East 12th Street, New York, New York 10003*. The same company is the source of an excellent catalogue titled "Fairchild Books and Visuals" from which you can easily send for a variety of books on industry subjects.

ORGANIZATIONS

This listing is useful mainly in acquainting you with the language of the industry and with the names of trade and professional groups that pop up again and again in conversation and in *Women's Wear Daily*. Once you become a card-carrying member of the business, you will probably belong to one or another of these groups. If you are particularly ambitious, of course, there is nothing to stop you from calling your local or national representatives and asking permission to attend an upcoming meeting, trade show, conference, or seminar, or to visit an in-house library. It's not a bad way to make contacts and learn something of the industry.

Apparel

Associated Fur Manufacturers, Inc.
101 West 30th Street
New York, New York 10001
*High school groups are brought on tours of plants, auction houses and manufacturers.

American Apparel Manufacturers Association
1611 North Kent Street Suite 8000
Arlington, Virginia 22209
*AAMA Education Committee provides career brochures, a publications directory and other materials to encourage students in apparel careers and recruit them for college programs. AAMA helps member apparel companies offer scholarships, co-op programs, and recommend training programs in apparel management and production technology.

Clothing Manufacturers Association
135 West 50th Street
New York, New York

Designer's Collective
c/o Elyse Kroll
E.N.K. Productions
3 East 54th Street
New York, New York 10022

Federation of Apparel Manufacturers
450 Seventh Avenue
New York, New York

International Association of Clothing Designers
7 East Lancaster Avenue
Ardmore, Pennsylvania 19003

Men's Fashion Association of America
1290 Avenue of the Americas
New York, New York 10104
*Will supply educational material to schools and provides lectures.

Men's Fashion Guild
47 West 34th Street
New York, New York 10001

National Association of Men's Sportswear Buyers
535 Fifth Avenue
New York, New York 10017

National Outerwear and Sportswear Association
1 Penn Plaza Room 2414
New York, New York 10119

New York Fashion Council, Inc.
185 East 85th Street
New York, New York 10028

Textiles

American Association of Textile Chemists and Colorists
Research Triangle Park, North Carolina
*Student chapters

American Textile Manufacturers Institute
400 South Tryon Street
Charlotte, North Carolina 28285
*Career pamphlet available. Also books, fabric samples, posters.

Knitted Textile Association
51 Madison Avenue
New York, New York 10010

Man-Made Fiber Producers Association
1150 17th Street N.W.
Washington, D.C. 20036
*Educational publications and filmstrips are available to students and the public and information on training programs in large textile companies is supplied. Letters and inquiries from textile grads are referred to the group's corporate members.

Northern Textile Association
211 Congress Street
Boston, Massachusetts 02116
*NTA library in Boston is open to the public by appointment. The group maintains contact with educational organizations, gives lectures at local schools, and gives student honor medals each year to outstanding grads of certain U.S. colleges.

Textile Economics Bureau
101 Eisenhower Parkway
Roseland, New Jersey 07068
*The group for background statistics on the textile industry.

Textile Distributors Association
1040 Avenue of the Americas
New York, New York 10018

Textile Designers Guild
30 East 20th Street
New York, New York 10003

Retail

Menswear Retailers of America
2011 "Eye" Street, N.W.
Washington, D.C. 20006
*Booklet available on retail careers.

National Retail Merchants Association
100 West 31st Street
New York, New York 10001
*Excellent careers bibliography titled "Sources for Careers in Retailing & Fashion" (it's free) and brochure "Your Opportunities in Retailing."

National Shoe Retailers Association
200 Madison Avenue
New York, New York 10016
*Career information requests are forwarded to the Board of Directors which is made up of department store executives.

Industry-wide

Association of Women in Apparel Resources (AWARE)
350 Fifth Avenue, Suite 2718
New York, New York 10118
*New group for women in the apparel industry to exchange information and ideas. Started in 1983.

The Fashion Group, Inc.
9 Rockefeller Plaza
New York, New York 10020
*Group has over 5,000 women in its membership and 34 regional groups. The group provides scholarships, educational programs, and career-related books.

Unions

Amalgamated Clothing and Textile Workers Union
15 Union Square West
New York, New York 10002

The International Ladies Garment Workers Union
1710 Broadway
New York, New York, 10019

United Garment Workers of America
200 Park Avenue South
New York, New York 10003

United Textile Workers of America
420 Common Street
P.O. Box 325
Lawrence, Massachusetts 01842

Councils/Bureaus

American Printed Fabrics Council, Inc.
1040 Avenue of the Americas
New York, New York 10018

Cotton, Inc.
1370 Avenue of the Americas
New York, New York 10019

Fur Information and Fashion Council
101 West 30th Street
New York, New York 10001

Jewelry Industry Council
608 Fifth Avenue
New York, New York 10020

Wool Bureau
360 Lexington Avenue
New York, New York 10017

Miscellaneous

American Society of Magazine Photographers
205 Lexington Avenue
New York, New York 10016

American Woman's Economic Development Corporation (AWED)
60 East 42nd Street, Room 405
New York, New York 10165
*Devoted to women entrepreneurs. Excellent annual career conference open to the public on "Women in the Fashion and Beauty Business."

Art Director's Club, Inc.
488 Madison Avenue
New York, New York 10022
*Art education promoted via portfolio review, scholarships, advice to schools and students. The club's members and staff answer hundreds of inquiries annually. The interests of members, however, come first.

Educational Foundation for the Fashion Industries
227 West 27th Street
New York, New York 10001
*Off-shoot of FIT that raises money for the school. It's worth noting that some of their seminars are open to the public.

National Association for Display Industries
120 East 23rd Street
New York, New York 10010

National and International Federation of Business
  and Professional Women's Clubs, Inc.
Carl Byoir & Associates
1899 L Street, N.W.
Washington, D.C. 20036
*Call for local chapters

Public Relations Society of America
845 Third Avenue
New York, New York 10022
*P.R. Student Society nation-wide

Society of Illustrators
128 East 63rd Street
New York, New York 10021
*Education Committee conducts seminars and portfolio review sessions at local art institutions and offers a scholarship to attend evening art classes at Society headquarters. "Career Guidance in Illustration and Graphic Art" is $2 from the Society.

Women Business Owners of New York
322 8th Avenue, 12th floor
New York, New York 10001
*Annual Women in Business Conference

Women In Communications
P.O. Box 9561
Austin, Texas 78766
*Booklet available titled "Careers in Communications." There is an Associate membership as well for those with less than two years professional experience.

Career Assistance

Catalyst
14 East 60th Street
New York, New York 10022
*Devoted to career guidance for women with publications available on careers in "Retailing and Fashion" in their Career Opportunities Series by mail order. There's a national network of resource centers and bibliography of publications.

ILLUSTRATION CREDITS

p. 2, photo by Dustin Pittman; pp. 3, 5, photo by John Ford; p. 8, photo by Harlan Kayden; p. 11, photo © 1983 John Pilgreen; p. 19, photo by Bob Stern; p. 22, Jhane Barnes photographed by Jim Saulton; p. 25, photo by Dan Lecca; p. 32 photographed by Robert M. Klein; p. 35, photo by Dustin Pittman; p. 38, Dustin Pittman/*WWD*; p. 41, photo by Dustin Pittman; p. 43, © Roxanne Lowit; p. 44, sketch by Betsey Johnson; p. 44, 1983 Bob Murray; p. 46, photo by Julia Gittes; p. 47, sketches by Carol Elliott; p. 50, photo by Don Banks; p. 62, photo by Larry Lapidus; p. 72, © Evan Broadman; pp. 76, 77, photo by Pierre Scherman; pp. 78, 82, 83 Reproduced by permission of Catalyst, 14 E. 60th St., New York, N.Y. 10022. Catalyst is the not-for-profit organization that works to promote the full participation of women in business and the professions © Catalyst 1976; p. 85, J. C. Penney Company, Inc.; pp. 94, 95, photos © 1983 John Pilgreen; p. 103, photo © Jill Krementz; p. 116, photo by E. J. Camp; pp. 130, 131, 132, 133, 135, 138, 140, 141, 142, 143, 145, photographs by Robert M. Klein; p. 146, photo by Michael Chan; pp. 153, 155, photo by Richard Warren; p. 157, photo by Gerard Gentil; p. 159, photo by David Gordon; p. 162, photo by Gideon Lewin; pp. 163, 164, Dustin Pittman/*WWD*; p. 175, photo by Michael O'Brien; p. 182, photo by Pierre Scherman; p. 188, photo by Gordon Munro; p. 195, photo by Chuck Baker; p. 198, Richard Ely/Elymedia 1984; p. 202, copyright Cable News Network; p. 204, photo by Dustin Pittman.

ABOUT THE AUTHOR

Melissa Sones has written on a broad range of subjects, from science and health to relationships, fashion, and food. Her articles have appeared in the *New York Times*, *Glamour*, and *Cuisine*, among others. She lives and works in New York City.